THE ARCHDRUID REPORT
The Twilight of Progress
Collected Essays, Volume IX, 2015

THE ARCHDRUID REPORT

The Twilight of Progress
Collected Essays, Volume IX, 2015

JOHN MICHAEL GREER

FOUNDERS HOUSE PUBLISHING

The Archdruid Report: The Twilight of Progress
Collected Essays, Volume IX, 2015
Copyright © 2018 John Michael Greer
Published by Founders House Publishing, LLC
Cover art copyright © Grandfailure/Dreamstime
Cover and interior design © 2018 Founders House Publishing, LLC

Paperback Edition: March 2018
ISBN-13: 978-1-945810-19-0
ISBN-10: 1-945810-19-X

The contents of this book appeared in a slightly different form on the blog www.thearchdruidreport.blogspot.com during its eleven-year run.

For more information please visit www.foundershousepublishing.com

Published in the United States of America

CONTENTS

THE ARCHDRUID REPORT
The Twilight of Progress
Collected Essays, Volume IX, 2015

INTRODUCTION

By 2015 my weekly *Archdruid Report* essays had already covered most of the factors driving the accelerating decline of modern industrial civilization and explored most of the narrowing range of options for dealing with the resulting mess, and I had reached the stage of filling in details. Certain of those details involved excursions into the most intellectually challenging territory the blog covered—I'm thinking here especially of "The Externality Trap, or, How Progress Commits Suicide," on the one hand, and the three-part post "The Cimmerian Hypothesis" on the other—and others, a good many of them, pointed in directions that would eventually lead me beyond *The Archdruid Report* entirely.

At the same time, other factors forced me to begin putting more attention into the political dimension of the predicament of our time than I'd done before. It became clear to me early on that the populist revolt that eventually took Britain out of the European Union and put Donald Trump in the White House was far more important than the dismissive analyses of the mainstream media thought it was; it became just as clear that the kneejerk responses to that revolt so common among sustainability activists were far more often motivated by an ugly stew of privilege and class bigotry than by the ideals those activists so loudly touted. The result was a series of increasingly edgy posts on the failure of the political Left that fielded me hate mail and notoriety in equal measure.

The core theme of 2015's posts, though, was the failure of the myth of progress and the unsuspected possibilities open to those who were willing to ignore the central taboo of our time—the insistence that individuals aren't allowed to pick and choose among technologies, but must accept the latest gimmickry no matter how poorly it meets their needs, and must abandon older technologies no matter how much better they work. That theme yielded a flurry of lively and fiercely debated posts, and it also resulted in a fictional narrative, *Retrotopia*, which accounted for close to a third of 2015's posts and has since been published in book form. (The posts in that series are therefore not included in this anthology.) All in all, it was a lively year, and one that featured some of the best prose and fiercest debates in *The Archdruid Report's* eleven-year run.

—John Michael Greer

397: A CAMP AMID THE RUINS

(Originally published 7 January 2015)

Well, the Fates were apparently listening. As I write this, stock markets around the world are lurching through what might just be the opening moves of the Crash of 2015, whipsawed by further plunges in the price of oil and a range of other bad economic news; amid a flurry of layoffs and dropping rig counts, the first bankruptcy in the fracking industry has been announced, with more on their way; gunfire in Paris serves up a brutal reminder that the rising spiral of political violence I traced in last week's post is by no means limited to North American soil. The cheerleaders of business as usual in the media are still insisting at the top of their lungs that America's new era of energy independence is still on its way; those of my readers who recall the final days of the housing bubble that burst in 2008, or the tech-stock bubble that popped in 2000, will recognize a familiar tone in the bluster.

It's entirely possible, to be sure, that central banks and governments will be able to jerry-rig another round of temporary supports for the fraying architecture of the global economy, and postpone a crash — or at least drag out the agony a bit longer. It's equally possible that other dimensions of the crisis of our age can be forestalled or postponed by drastic actions here and now. That said, whether the process is fast or slow, whether the crunch hits now or a bit further down the road, the form of technic society I've termed abundance industrialism is on its way out through history's exit turnstile, and an entire world of institutions and activities familiar to all of us is going with it.

It doesn't require any particular genius or prescience to grasp this, merely the willingness to recognize that if something is unsustainable, sooner or later it won't be sustained. Of course that's the sticking point, because what can't be sustained at this point is the collection of wildly extravagant energy- and resource-intensive habits that used to pass for a normal lifestyle in the world's industrial nations, and has recently become just a little less normal than it used to be. Those lifestyles, and most of what goes with them, only existed in the first place because a handful of the world's nations burned through half a billion years of fossil sunlight in a few short centuries, and stripped the planet of most of its other concentrated resource stocks into the bargain.

That's the unpalatable reality of the industrial era. Despite the rhetoric of universal betterment that was brandished about so enthusiastically by the propagandists of the industrial order, there were never enough of any of the necessary resources to make that possible for more than a small fraction of the world's population, or for more than a handful of generations. Nearly all the members of our species who lived outside the industrial nations, and a tolerably large number who resided within them, were expected to carry most of the costs of reckless resource extraction and ecosystem disruption while receiving few if any of the benefits. They'll have plenty of company shortly: abundance industrialism is winding down, but its consequences are not, and people around the world for centuries and millennia to come will have to deal with the depleted and damaged planet our actions have left them.

That's a bitter pill to swallow, and the likely aftermath of the industrial age won't do anything to improve the taste. Over the last six months or so, I've drawn on the downside trajectories of other failed civilizations to sketch out how that aftermath will probably play out here in North America: the disintegration of familiar political and economic structures, the rise of warband culture, the collapse of public order, and the failure of cultural continuity, all against a backdrop of rapid and unpredictable climate change, rising seas, and the appearance of chemical and radiological dead zones created by some of industrial civilization's more clueless habits. It's an ugly picture, and the only excuse I have for that unwelcome fact is that falling civilizations look like that.

The question that remains, though, is what we're going to do about it all.

I should say up front that by "we" I don't mean some suitably photogenic collection of Hollywood heroes and heroines who just happen to have limitless resources and a bag of improbable inventions at their disposal. I don't mean a US government that has somehow shaken off the senility that affects all great powers in their last days and is prepared to fling everything it has into the quest for a sustainable future. Nor do I mean a coterie of gray-skinned aliens from Zeta Reticuli, square-jawed rapists out of Ayn Rand novels, or some other source of allegedly superior beings who can be counted upon to come swaggering onto the scene to bail us out of the consequences of our own stupidity. They aren't part of this conversation; the only people who are, just now, are the writer and the readers of this blog.

Within those limits, the question I've posed may seem preposterous. I grant that for a phenomenon that practically defines the far edges of the internet—a venue for lengthy and ornately written essays about wildly unpopular subjects by a clergyman from a small and distinctly eccentric fringe religion—*The Archdruid Report* has a preposterously large readership, and one that somehow manages to find room for a remarkably diverse and talented range of people, bridging some of the ideological and social barriers that divide industrial society into so many armed and uncommunicative camps. Even so, the regular readership of this blog could probably all sit down at once in a football stadium and still leave room for the hot dog vendors. Am I seriously suggesting that this modest and disorganized a group can somehow rise up and take meaningful action in the face of so vast a process as the fall of a civilization?

One of the things that gives that question an ironic flavor is that quite a few people are making what amounts to the same claim in even more grandiose terms than mine. I'm thinking here of the various proposals for a Great Transition of one kind or another being hawked at various points along the social and political spectrum these days. I suspect we're going to be hearing a lot more from those in the months and years immediately ahead, as the collapse of the fracking bubble forces people to find some other excuse for insisting that they can have their planet and eat it too.

Part of the motivation behind the grand plans just mentioned is straightforwardly financial. One part of what drove the fracking bubble along the classic trajectory—up with the rocket, down with the stick—was a panicked conviction on the part of a great many people that some way had to be found to keep industrial society's fuel tanks somewhere on the near side of that unwelcome letter E. Another part of it, though, was the recognition on the part of a somewhat smaller but more pragmatic group of people tht the panicked conviction in question could be turned into a sales pitch. Fracking wasn't the only thing that got put to work in the time-honored process of proving Ben Franklin's proverb about a fool and his money; fuel ethanol, biodiesel, and large-scale wind power also had their promoters, and sucked up their share of government subsidies and private investment.

Now that fracking is falling by the wayside, there'll likely be a wild scramble to replace it in the public eye as the wave of the energy future. The nuclear industry will doubtless be in there — nuclear power is one of the most durable subsidy dumpsters in modern economic life, and the nuclear industry has had to become highly skilled at slurping from the government teat, since nuclear power isn't economically viable otherwise — it's worth recalling that no nation on earth has been able to create or maintain a nuclear power program without massive ongoing government subsidies. No doubt we'll get plenty of cheerleading for fusion, satellite-based solar power, and other bits of high-end vaporware, too.

Still, I suspect the next big energy bubble is probably going to come from the green end of things. Over the last few years, there's been no shortage of claims that renewable resources can pick right up where fossil fuels leave off and keep the lifestyles of today's privileged middle classes intact. Those claims tend to be long on enthusiasm and cooked numbers and short on meaningful assessment, but then that same habit didn't slow the fracking boom any; we can expect to see a renewed flurry of claims that solar power must be sustainable because the sticker price has gone down, and similar logical non sequiturs. (By the same logic, the internet must be sustainable if you can pay your monthly ISP bill by selling cute kitten photos on eBay. In both cases, the sprawling and almost entirely fossil-fueled infrastructure of mines, factories, supply chains, power grids, and the like, has been left out of the equation, as though those don't have to be accounted for: typical of the blindness to whole systems that pervades so much of contemporary culture.)

It's not enough for an energy technology to be green, in other words; it also has to work. It's probably safe to assume that that point is going to be finessed over and over again, in a galaxy of inventive ways, as the fracking bubble goes whereved popped financial bubbles go when they die. The point that next to nobody wants to confront is the one made toward the beginning of this week's post: if something is unsustainable, sooner or later it won't be sustained — and what's unsustainable in this case isn't simply fossil fuel production and consumption, it's the lifestyles that were made possible by the immensely abundant and highly concentrated energy supply we got from fossil fuels.

You can't be part of the solution if your lifestyle is part of the problem. I know that those words are guaranteed to make the environmental equivalent of limousine liberals gasp and clutch their pearls or their Gucci ties, take your pick, but there it is; it really is as simple as that. There are at least two reasons why that maxim needs to be taken seriously. On the one hand, if you're clinging to an unsustainable lifestyle in the teeth of increasingly strong economic and environmental headwinds, you're not likely to be able to spare the money, the free time, or any of the other resources you would need to contribute to a solution; on the other, if you're emotionally and financially invested in keeping an unsustainable lifestyle, you're likely to put preserving that lifestyle ahead of things that arguably matter more, like leaving a livable planet for future generations.

Is the act of letting go of unsustainable lifestyles the only thing that needs to be done? Of course not, and in the posts immediately ahead I plan on talking at length about some of the other options. I'd like to suggest, though, that it's the touchstone or, if you will, the boundary that divides those choices that might actually do some good from those that are pretty much guaranteed to do no good at all. That's useful when considering the choices before us as individuals; it's at least as useful, if not more so, when considering the collective options we'll be facing in the months and years ahead, among them the flurry of campaigns, movements, and organizations that are already gearing up to exploit the crisis of our time in one way or another — and with one agenda or another.

An acronym I introduced a while back in these posts might well be worth revisiting here: LESS, which stands for "Less Energy, Stuff, and Stimulation." That's a convenient summary of the changes that have to be made to move from today's unsustainable lifestyles to ways of living that will be viable when today's habits of absurd extravagance are fading memories. It's worth taking a moment to unpack the acronym a little further, and see what it implies.

"Less energy" might seem self-evident, but there's more involved here than just turning off unneeded lights and weatherstripping your windows and doors—though those are admittedly good places to start. A huge fraction of the energy consumed by a modern industrial society gets used indirectly to produce, supply, and transport goods and services; an allegedly "green" technological device that's made from petroleum-based plastics and exotic metals taken from an open-pit mine in a Third World country, then shipped halfway around the planet to the air-conditioned shopping mall where you bought it, can easily have a carbon footprint substantially bigger than some simpler item that does the same thing in a less immediately efficient way. The blindness to whole systems mentioned earlier has to be overcome in order to make any kind of meaningful sense of energy issues: a point I'll be discussing further in an upcoming post here.

"Less stuff" is equally straightforward on the surface, equally subtle in its ramifications. Now of course it's hardly irrelevant that ours is the first civilization in the history of the planet to have to create an entire industry of storage facilities to store the personal possessions that won't fit into history's biggest homes. That said, "stuff" includes a great deal more than the contents of your closets and storage lockers. It also includes infrastructure—the almost unimaginably vast assortment of technological systems on which the privileged classes of the industrial world rely for most of the activities of their daily lives. That infrastructure was only made possible by the deluge of cheap abundant energy our species briefly accessed from fossil fuels; as what's left of the world's fossil fuel supply moves deeper into depletion, the infrastructure that it created has been caught in an accelerating spiral of deferred maintenance and malign neglect; the less dependent you are on what remains, the less vulnerable you are to further systems degradation, and the more of what's left can go to those who actually need it.

"Less stimulation" may seem like the least important part of the acronym, but in many ways it's the most crucial point of all.

These days most people in the industrial world flood their nervous systems with a torrent of electronic noise. Much of this is quite openly intended to manipulate their thoughts and feelings by economic and political interests; a great deal more has that effect, if only by drowning out any channel of communication that doesn't conform to the increasingly narrow intellectual tunnel vision of late industrial society. If you've ever noticed how much of what passes for thinking these days amounts to the mindless regurgitation of sound bites from the media, dear reader, that's why. What comes through the media — any media — is inevitably prechewed and predigested according to someone else's agenda; those who are interested in thinking their own thoughts and making their own decisions, rather than bleating in perfect unison with the rest of the herd, might want to keep this in mind.

It probably needs to be said that very few of us are in a position to go whole hog with LESS — though it's also relevant that some of us, and quite possibly a great many of us, will end up doing so willy-nilly if the economic contraction at the end of the fracking bubble turns out to be as serious as some current figures suggest. Outside of that grim possibility, "less" doesn't have to mean "none at all" — certainly not at first; for those who aren't caught in the crash, at least, there may yet be time to make a gradual transition toward a future of scarce energy and scarce resources. Still, I'd like to suggest that any proposed response to the crisis of our time that doesn't start with LESS simply isn't serious.

As already noted, I expect to see a great many nonserious proposals in the months and years ahead. Those who put maintaining their comfortable lifestyles ahead of other goals will doubtless have no trouble coming up with enthusiastic rhetoric and canned numbers to support their case; certainly the promoters and cheerleaders of the soon-to-be-late fracking bubble had no difficulty at all on that score. Not too far in the future, something or other will have been anointed as the shiny new technological wonder that will save us all, or more precisely, that will give the privileged classes of the industrial world a new set of excuses for clinging to some semblance of their current lifestyles for a little while longer. Mention the growing list of things that have previously occupied that hallowed but inevitably temporary status, and you can count on either busy silence or a flustered explanation why it really is different this time.

There may not be that many of us who get past the nonserious proposals, ask the necessary but unwelcome questions about the technosavior du jour, and embrace LESS while there's still time to do so a step at a time. I'm convinced, though, that those who manage these things are going to be the ones who make a difference in the shape the future will have on the far side of the crisis years ahead. Let go of the futile struggle to sustain the unsustainable, take the time and money and other resources that might be wasted in that cause and do something less foredoomed with them, and there's a lot that can still be done, even in the confused and calamitous time that's breaking over us right now. In the posts immediately ahead, as already mentioned, I'll discuss some of the options; no doubt many of my readers will be able to think of options of their own, for that matter.

I've noted before more than once that the collapse of industrial society isn't something located off in the nearer or further future; it's something that got under way a good many years ago, has been accelerating around us for decades, and is simply hitting one of the rougher patches of the normal process of decline and fall just now. Most of the nonserious proposals just referred to start from the insistence that that can't happen. Comforting in the short term, that insistence is a rich source of disaster and misery from any longer perspective, and the sooner each of us gets over it and starts to survey the wreckage around us, the better. Then we can make camp in the ruins, light a fire, get some soup heating in a salvaged iron pot, and begin to talk about where we can go from here.

398: MARCH OF THE SQUIRRELS

(Originally published 14 January 2015)

Prediction is a difficult business at the best of times, but the difficulties seem to change from one era to another. Just now, at least for me, the biggest challenge is staying in front of the headlines. So far, the crash of 2015 is running precisely to spec. Smaller companies in the energy sector are being hammered by the plunging price of oil, while the banking industry insists that it's not in trouble—those of my readers who recall identical expressions of misplaced confidence on the part of bankers in news stories just before the 2008 real estate crash will know just how seriously to take such claims.

The shiny new distractions disguised as energy breakthroughs I mentioned here two weeks ago have also started to show up. A glossy puff piece touting oceanic thermal energy conversion (OTEC), a white-elephant technology which was tested back in the 1970s and shown to be hopelessly uneconomical, shared space in the cornucopian end of the blogosphere over the last week with an equally disingenuous puff piece touting yet another rehash of nuclear fission as the answer to our energy woes. (Like every fission technology, of course, this one will be safe, clean, and affordable until someone actually tries to build it.)

No doubt there will shortly be other promoters scrambling for whatever government subsidies and private investment funds might be available for whatever revolutionary new energy breakthrough (ahem) will take the place of hydrofractured shales as America's favorite reason to do nothing. I admit to a certain feeling of disappointment, though, in the sheer lack of imagination displayed so far in that competition. OTEC and molten-salt fission reactors were already being lauded as America's energy salvation back when I was in high school: my junior year, I think it was, energy was the topic du jour for the local high school debate league, and we discussed those technologies at length. So did plenty of more qualified people, which is why both of them — and quite a few other superficially plausible technologies — never made it off the drawing board.

Something else came in for discussion that same year, and it's a story with more than a little relevance to the current situation. A team from another school in the south Seattle suburbs had a brainstorm, did some frantic research right before a big debate tournament, and showed up with data claiming to prove that legions of squirrels running in squirrel cages, powering little generators, could produce America's electricity. Since no one else happened to have thought of that gimmick, none of the other teams had evidence to refute them, and they swept the tournament. By the next tournament, of course, everyone else had crunched the numbers and proceeded to stomp the squirrel promoters, but for years thereafter the phrase "squirrel case" saw use in local debate circles as the standard term for a crackpot proposal backed with seemingly plausible data.

The OTEC plants and molten-salt reactors currently being hawked via the media are squirrel cases in exactly the same sense; they sound plausible as long as you don't actually crunch the numbers and see whether they're economically and thermodynamically viable. The same thing was true of the fracking bubble that's messily imploding around us right now, not to mention the ethanol and biodiesel projects, the hydrogen economy, and the various other glittery excuses that have occupied so much useless space in the collective conversation of our time. So, it has to be said, do the more enthusiastic claims being made for renewable energy just now.

Don't get me wrong, I'm a great fan of renewable energy. When extracting fossil carbon from the earth stops being economically viable — a point that may arrive a good deal sooner than many people expect — renewables are what we'll have left, and the modest but real energy inputs that can be gotten from renewable sources when they don't receive energy subsidies from fossil fuels could make things significantly better for our descendants. The fact remains that in the absence of subsidies from fossil fuels, renewables won't support the absurdly extravagant energy consumption that props up what passes for an ordinary middle class lifestyle in the industrial world these days.

That's the pterodactyl in the ointment, the awkward detail that most people even in the greenest of green circles don't want to discuss. Force the issue into a conversation, and one of the more common responses you'll get is the exasperated outburst "But there has to be *something*." Now of course this simply isn't true; no law of nature, no special providence, no parade of marching squirrels assures us that we can go ahead and use as much energy as we want in the serene assurance that more will always be waiting for us. It's hard to think of a more absurd delusion, and the fact that a great many people making such claims insist on their superior rationality and pragmatism just adds icing to the cake.

Let's go ahead and say it in so many words: there doesn't have to be a replacement for fossil fuels. In point of fact, there's good reason to think that no such replacement exists anywhere in the small corner of the universe accessible to us, and once fossil fuels are gone, the rest of human history will be spent in a world that doesn't have the kind of lavish energy resources we're used to having. Concentrations of energy, like all other natural resources, follow what's known as the power law, the rule—applicable across an astonishingly broad spectrum of phenomena—that whatever's ten times as concentrated is approximately ten times as rare. At the dawn of the industrial age, the reserves of fossil fuel in the Earth's crust were the richest trove of stored energy on the planet, and of course fossil fuel extraction focused on the richest and most easily accessible prizes first, just as quickly as they could be found.

Those are gone now. Since 2005, when conventional petroleum production peaked worldwide, the industrial world has been engaged in what amounts to a frantic game of make-believe, pretending that scraping the bottom of the oil barrel proves that the barrel is still full. Every half-baked scheme for producing liquid fuels got flooded with as much cheap credit as its promoters could squander. Some of those—biodiesel and cellulosic ethanol come to mind—turned out to be money pits so abysmal that even a tide of freshly printed money couldn't do much more than gurgle on the way down; others—above all, shale fracking and tar sand mining—were able to maintain a pretense of profitability for a while, with government subsidies, junk bonds, loans from clueless banks, and round after round of economic stimulus from central banks over much of the world serving to prop up industries that, in the final analysis, were never economically viable in the first place.

The collapse in the price of oil that began this June put paid to that era of make-believe. The causes of the oil crash are complex, but back of them all, I suggest, is a straightforward bit of economics that almost everyone's been trying to avoid for a decade now. To maintain economic production at any given level, the global economy has to produce enough real wealth—not, please note, enough money, but enough actual goods and services—to cover resource extraction, the manufacture and replacement of the whole stock of nonfinancial capital goods, and whatever level of economic waste is considered socially and politically necessary. If the amount of real wealth needed to keep extracting resources at a given rate goes up steeply, the rest of the economy won't escape the consequences: somewhere or other, something has to give.

The economic history of the last decade is precisely the story of what gave in what order, or to put it another way, how the industrial world threw everything in sight under the bus to keep liquid fuel production around its 2005 peak. Infrastructure was abandoned to malign neglect, the last of the industrial world's factory jobs got offshored to Third World sweatshops, standards of living for most people dropped steadily—well, you can fill in the blanks as well as I can. Consumption remained relatively high only because central banks flooded the global economy with limitless cheap credit, while the US government filled the gap between soaring government expenditures and flat or shrinking tax receipts by the simple equivalent of having the Fed print enough money each month to cover the federal deficit. All these things were justified by the presupposition that the global economy was just going through a temporary rough patch, and normal growth would return any day now.

But normal growth has not returned. It's not going to return, either, because it was only "normal" in an era when cheap abundant fossil fuels greased the wheels of every kind of economic activity. As I noted in a blog post here back in 2007, the inevitable consequence of soaring oil prices is what economists call demand destruction: less formally, the process by which people who can't afford oil stop using it, bringing the price back down. Since what's driving the price of oil up isn't merely market factors, but the hard geological realities of depletion, not everyone who got forced out of the market when the price was high can get back into it when the price is low — gas at $2 a gallon doesn't matter if your job scavenging abandoned houses doesn't pay enough for you to cover the costs of a car, and let's not even talk about how much longer the local government can afford to maintain streets in driveable condition.

Demand destruction sounds very abstract. In practice, though, it's all too brutally concrete: a rising tide of job losses, business failures, slumping standards of living, cutbacks to every kind of government service at every level, and so on down the litany of decline that's become part of everyday life in the industrial world over the last decade — leaving aside, that is, the privileged few who have been sheltered from those changes so far. Unless I miss my guess, we're going to see those same changes shift into overdrive in the months and years ahead. The attempt to boost the world out of its deepening slump by flooding the planet with cheap credit has failed; the global economy is choking on a supersized meal of unpayable IOUs and failed investments; stock markets and other venues for the exchange of paper wealth are so thoroughly gimmicked that they've become completely detached from the real economy of goods and services, and the real economy is headed south in a hurry.

Those unwelcome realities are going to constrain any attempt by the readers of this blog to follow up on the proposal I made in last week's post, and take constructive action in the face of the crisis that's now upon us. The energy situation here in the US could have been helped substantially if conservation measures and homescale renewables had received any kind of significant support from the oh-so-allegedly-green Democratic party, back when it still had enough clout in Congress to matter; the economic situation would be nowhere near as dire if governments and central banks had bitten the bullet and dealt with the crisis of our time in 2008 or thereafter, rather than papering things over with economic policies that assumed that enough money could negate the laws of physics and geology. At this point, it's much too late for any sort of collective action on either of those fronts — and of course the political will needed to do anything meaningful about either one went missing in action at the end of the 1970s and hasn't been seen since.

Thus all of us will have to cope with a world in which the cost of energy suffers from drastic and economically devastating swings, and the sort of localized infrastructure that could cushion the impact of those swings wasn't built in time. All of us will also have to cope with a global economy in disarray, in which bank failures, currency crises, credit shortages, and crisis measures imposed by government fiat will take the place of the familiar workings of a market economy. Those are baked into the cake at this point, and what individuals, families, and community groups will be able to do in the years ahead will be constrained by the limits those transformations impose.

Those of my readers who still have a steady income and a home they expect to be able to keep would still be well advised to doublecheck their insulation and weatherstripping, install solar water heating and other homescale renewable energy technologies, and turn the back lawn into a vegetable garden with room for a chicken coop, if by any chance they haven't taken these sensible steps already. A great many of my readers don't have such options, and at this point, it may be a long time before such options are readily available again. This is crunch time, folks; unless I'm very much mistaken, we're on the brink of a historical inflection point like the ones in 1789 and 1914, one of the watersheds of time after which nothing will ever be the same again.

There's still much that can be done in other spheres, and I'll be discussing some of those things in upcoming posts. In terms of energy and the economy, though, I suspect that for a lot of us, the preparations we're going to be able to make are the ones we've already made, and a great many people whose plans depend on having a stable income and its associated perks and privileges may find themselves scrambling for options when the unraveling of the economy leaves them without one. Those of my readers who have been putting off the big changes that might make them more secure in hard times may be facing the hard decision of making those changes now, in a hurry, or facing the crisis of our age in the location and situation they're in right now. Those who've gone ahead and made the changes—well, you know as well as I do that it's time to review your plans, doublecheck the details, batten down the hatches and get ready to weather the storm.

One of the entertainments to be expected as the year draws on and the crisis bears down on us all, though, is a profusion of squirrel cases of the sort discussed toward the beginning of this essay. It's an interesting regularity of history that the closer to disaster a society in decline becomes, the more grandiose, triumphalist, and detached from the grubby realities its fantasies generally get. I'm thinking here of the essay on military affairs from the last years of the Roman world that's crammed full of hopelessly unworkable war machines, and of the final, gargantuan round of Mayan pyramids built on the eve of the lowland classic collapse. The habit of doubling down in the face of self-induced catastrophe seems to be deeply engrained in the human psyche, and I don't doubt for a moment that we'll see some world-class examples of the phenomenon in the years immediately ahead.

That said, the squirrel cases mentioned earlier—the OTEC and molten-salt fission proposals—suffer from a disappointing lack of imagination. If our society is going to indulge in delusional daydreams as it topples over the edge of crisis, couldn't we at least see some proposals that haven't been rehashed since I was in high school? I can only think of one such daydream that has the hallucinatory quality our current circumstances deserve; yes, that would be the proposal, being made quite seriously in the future-oriented media just now, that we can solve all our energy problems by mining helium-3 on the Moon and ship it to Earth to fuel fusion power plants we have absolutely no idea how to build yet. As faith-based cheerleading for vaporware, which is of course what those claims are, they set a very high standard—but it's a standard that will doubtless be reached and exceeded in due time.

That said, I think the media may need some help launching the march of the squirrels just mentioned, and the readers of this blog proved a good long time ago that they have more than enough imagination to meet that pressing need.

Therefore I'm delighted to announce a new contest here on *The Archdruid Report*, the Great Squirrel Case Challenge of 2015. The goal is to come up with the most absurd new energy technology you can think of, and write either the giddily dishonest corporate press release or the absurdly sycophantic media article announcing it to the world. If you or a friend can Photoshop an image or two of your proposed nonsolution to the world's energy needs, that's all the better. Post your press release or media article on your blog if you have one; if you don't, you can get one for free from Blogspot or Wordpress. Post a link to your piece in the comments section of this blog.

Entries must be posted here by February 28, 2012. Two winners — one picked by me, the other by vote of the registered members of the Green Wizards forum — will receive signed complimentary copies of my forthcoming book *After Progress*. I can't speak for the forum, which will doubtless have its own criteria, but I'll be looking for a winsome combination of sheer absurdity with the sort of glossy corporate presentation that frames so many absurd statements these days. (Hint: it's not against the rules to imitate real press releases and media articles.)

As for the wonderful new energy breakthrough you'll be lauding so uncritically, why, that's up to you. Biodiesel plants using investment bankers as their primary feedstock? A vast crank hooked to the Moon, running a global system of belts and pulleys? An undertaking of great energy profit, to misquite the famous ad from the South Sea Bubble, but no one to know what it is? Let your imagination run wild; no matter how giddy you get, as the failure of the fracking bubble becomes impossible to ignore, the mass media and a great many of our fellow hominids are go much further along the track of the marching squirrels than you will.

399: THE MARINER'S RULE

(Originally published 21 January 2015)

One of the things my readers ask me most often, in response to this blog's exploration of the ongoing decline and impending fall of modern industrial civilization, is what I suggest people ought to do about it all. It's a valid question, and it deserves a serious answer.

Now of course not everyone who asks the question is interested in the answers I have to offer. A great many people, for example, are only interested in answers that will allow them to keep on enjoying the absurd extravagance that passed, not too long ago, for an ordinary lifestyle among the industrial world's privileged classes, and is becoming just a little bit less ordinary with every year that slips by. To such people I have nothing to say. Those lifestyles were only possible because the world's industrial nations burnt through half a billion years of stored sunlight in a few short centuries, and gave most of the benefits of that orgy of consumption to a relatively small fraction of their population; now that easily accessible reserves of fossil fuels are running short, the party's over.

Yes, I'm quite aware that that's a controversial statement. I field heated denunciations on a regular basis insisting that it just ain't so, that solar energy or fission or perpetual motion or *something* will allow the industrial world's privileged classes to have their planet and eat it too. Printer's ink being unfashionable these days, a great many electrons have been inconvenienced on the internet to proclaim that this or that technology must surely allow the comfortable to remain comfortable, no matter what the laws of physics, geology, or economics have to say. Now of course the only alternative energy sources that have been able to stay in business even in a time of sky-high oil prices are those that can count on gargantuan government subsidies to pay their operating expenses; equally, the alternatives receive an even more gigantic "energy subsidy" from fossil fuels, which make them look much more economical than they otherwise would. Such reflections carry no weight with those whose sense of entitlement makes living with less unthinkable.

I'm glad to say that there are fair number of people who've gotten past that unproductive attitude, who have grasped the severity of the crisis of our time and are ready to accept unwelcome change in order to secure a livable future for our descendants. They want to know how we can pull modern civilization out of its current power dive and perpetuate it into the centuries ahead. I have no answers for them, either, because that's not an option at this stage of the game; we're long past the point at which decline and fall can be avoided, or even ameliorated on any large scale.

A decade ago, a team headed by Robert Hirsch and funded by the Department of Energy released a study outlining what would have to be done in order to transition away from fossil fuels before they transitioned away from us. What they found, to sketch out too briefly the findings of a long and carefully worded study, is that in order to avoid massive disruption, the transition would have to begin twenty years before conventional petroleum production reached its peak and began to decline. There's a certain irony in the fact that 2005, the year this study was published, was also the year when conventional petroleum production peaked; the transition would thus have had to begin in 1985—right about the time, that is, that the Reagan administration in the US and its clones overseas were scrapping the promising steps toward just such a transition.

A transition that got under way in 2005, in other words, would have been too late, and given the political climate, it probably would have been too little as well. Even so, it would have been a much better outcome than the one we got, in which most of us have spent the last ten years insisting that we don't have to worry about depleting oilfields because fracking was going to save us all. At this point, thirty years after the point at which we would have had to get started, it's all very well to talk about some sort of grand transition to sustainability, but the time when such a thing would have been possible came and went decades ago. We could have chosen that path, but we didn't, and insisting thirty years after the fact that we've changed our minds and want a different future than the one we chose isn't likely to make any kind of difference that matters.

So what options does that leave? In the minds of a great many people, at least in the United States, the choice that apparently comes first to mind involves buying farmland in some isolated rural area and setting up a homestead in the traditional style. Many of the people who talk enthusiastically about this option, to be sure, have never grown anything more demanding than a potted petunia, know nothing about the complex and demanding arts of farming and livestock raising, and aren't in anything like the sort of robust physical condition needed to handle the unremitting hard work of raising food without benefit of fossil fuels; thus it's a safe guess that in most of these cases, heading out to the country is simply a comforting daydream that serves to distract attention from the increasingly bleak prospects so many people are facing in the age of unraveling upon us.

There's a long history behind such daydreams. Since colonial times, the lure of the frontier has played a huge role in the American imagination, providing any number of colorful inkblots onto which fantasies of a better life could be projected. Those of my readers who are old enough to remember the aftermath of the Sixties counterculture, when a great many young people followed that dream to an assortment of hastily created rural communes, will also recall the head-on collision between middle-class fantasies of entitlement and the hard realities of rural subsistence farming that generally resulted. Some of the communes survived, though many more did not; that I know of, none of the surviving ones made it without a long and difficult period of readjustment in which romantic notions of easy living in the lap of nature got chucked in favor of a more realistic awareness of just how little in the way of goods and services a bunch of untrained ex-suburbanites can actually produce by their own labor.

In theory, that process of reassessment is still open. In practice, just at the moment, I'm far from sure it's an option for anyone who's not already traveled far along that road. The decline and fall of modern industrial civilization, it bears repeating, is not poised somewhere off in the indefinite future, waiting patiently for us to get ready for it before it puts in an appearance; it's already happening at the usual pace, and the points I've raised in posts here over the last few weeks suggest that the downward slope is probably going to get a lot steeper in the near future. As the collapse of the fracking bubble ripples out through the financial sphere, most of us are going to be scrambling to adapt, and the chances of getting everything lined up in time to move to rural property, get the necessary equipment and supplies to start farming, and get past the worst of the learning curve before crunch time arrives are not good.

If you're already on a rural farm, in other words, by all means pursue the strategy that put you there. If your plans to get the necessary property, equipment, and skills are well advanced at this point, you may still be able to make it, but you'd probably better get a move on. On the other hand, dear reader, if your rural retreat is still off there in the realm of daydreams and good intentions, it's almost certainly too late to do much about it, and where you are right now is probably where you'll be when the onrushing waves of crisis come surging up and break over your head.

That being the case, are there any options left other than hiding under the bed and hoping that the end will be relatively painless? As it happens, there are.

The point that has to be understood to make sense of those options is that in the real world, as distinct from Hollywood-style disaster fantasies, the end of a civilization follows the famous rule attributed to William Gibson: "The future is already here, it's just not evenly distributed yet." Put another way, the impacts of decline and fall aren't uniform; they vary in intensity over space and time, and they impact particular systems of a falling civilization at different times and in different ways. If you're in the wrong place at the wrong time, and depend on the wrong systems to support you, your chances aren't good, but the places, times, and systems that take the brunt of the collapse aren't random. To some extent, those can be anticipated, and some of them can also be avoided.

Here's an obvious example. Right now, if your livelihood depends on the fracking industry, the tar sands industry, or any of the subsidiary industries that feed into those, your chances of getting through 2015 with your income intact are pretty minimal. People in those industries who got to witness earlier booms and busts know this, and a good many of them are paying off their debts, settling any unfinished business they might have, and making sure they can cover a tank of gas or a plane ticket to get back home when the bottom falls out. People in those industries who don't have that experience to guide them, and are convinced that nothing bad can actually happen to them, are not doing these things, and are likely to end up in a world of hurt when their turn comes.

They're not the only ones who would benefit right now from taking such steps. A very large part of the US banking and finance industry has been flying high on bloated profits from an assortment of fracking-related scams, ranging from junk bonds through derivatives to exotic financial fauna such as volumetric production payments. Now that the goose that laid the golden eggs is bobbing feet upwards in a pond of used fracking fluid, the good times are coming to a sudden stop, and that means sharply reduced income for those junior bankers, brokers, and salespeople who can keep their jobs, and even more sharply reduced prospects for those who don't.

They've got plenty of company on the chopping block. The entire retail sector in the US is already in trouble, with big-box stores struggling for survival and shopping malls being abandoned, and the sharp economic downturn we can expect as the fracking bust unfolds will likely turn that decline into freefall, varying in intensity by region and a galaxy of other factors. Those who brace themselves for a hard landing now are a good deal more likely to make it than those who don't, and those who have the chance to jump to something more stable now would be well advised to make the leap.

That's one example; here's another. I've written here in some detail about how anthropogenic climate change will wallop North America in the centuries ahead of us. One thing that's been learned from the last few years of climate vagaries is that North America, at least, is shifting in exactly the way paleoclimatic data would suggest—more or less the same way it did during warm periods over the last ten or twenty million years. The short form is that the Southwest and mountain West are getting baked to a crackly crunch under savage droughts; the eastern Great Plains, Midwest, and most of the South are being hit by a wildly unstable climate, with bone-dry dry years alternating with exceptionally soggy wet ones; while the Appalachians and points eastward have been getting unsteady temperatures but reliable rainfall.

Line up your choice of subsistence strategies next to those climate shifts, and if you still have the time and resources to relocate, you have some idea where to go.

All this presumes, of course, that what we're facing has much more in common with the crises faced by other civilizations on their way to history's compost heap than it does with the apocalyptic fantasies so often retailed these days as visions of the immediate future. I expect to field a flurry of claims that it just ain't so, that everything I've just said is wasted breath because some vast and terrible whatsit will shortly descend on the whole world and squash us like bugs. I can utter that prediction with perfect confidence, because I've been fielding such claims over and over again since long before this blog got started. All the dates by which the world was surely going to end have rolled past without incident, and the inevitable cataclysms have pulled one no-show after another, but the shrill insistence that something of the sort really will happen this time around has shown no sign of letting up. Nor will it, since the unacceptable alternative consists of taking responsibility for doing something about the future.

Now of course I've already pointed out that there's not much that can be done about the future on the largest scale. As the fracking bubble implodes, the global economy shudders, the climate destabilizes, and a dozen other measures of imminent crisis head toward the red zone on the gauge, it's far too late in the day for much more than crisis management on a local and individual level. Even so, crisis management is a considerably more useful response than sitting on the sofa daydreaming about the grandiose project that's certain to save us or the grandiose cataclysm that's certain to annihilate us—though these latter options are admittedly much more comfortable in the short term.

What's more, there's no shortage of examples in relatively recent history to guide the sort of crisis management I have in mind. The tsunami of discontinuities that's rolling toward us out of the deep waters of the future may be larger than the waves that hit the Western world with the coming of the First World War in 1914, the Great Depression in 1929, or the Second World War in 1939, but from the perspective of the individual, the difference isn't as vast as it might seem. In fact, I'd encourage my readers to visit their local public libraries and pick up books about the lived experience of those earlier traumas. I'd also encourage those with elderly relatives who still remember the Second World War to sit down with them over a couple of cups of whatever beverage seems appropriate, and ask about what it was like on a day-by-day basis to watch their ordinary peacetime world unravel into chaos.

I've had the advantage of taking part in such conversations, and I've also done a great deal of reading about historical crises that have passed below the horizon of living memory. There are plenty of lessons to be gained from such sources, and one of the most important also used to be standard aboard sailing ships in the days before steam power. Sailors in those days had to go scrambling up the rigging at all hours and in all weathers to set, reef, or furl sails; it was not an easy job—imagine yourself up in the rigging of a tall ship in the middle of a howling storm at night, clinging to tarred ropes and slick wood and trying to get a mass of wet, heavy, wind-whipped canvas to behave, while below you the ship rolls from side to side and swings you out over a raging ocean and back again. If you slip and you're lucky, you land on deck with a pretty good chance of breaking bones or worse; if you slip and you're not lucky, you plunge straight down into churning black water and are never seen again.

The rule that sailors learned and followed in those days was simple: "One hand for yourself, one hand for the ship." Every chore that had to be done up there in the rigging could be done by a gang of sailors who each lent one hand to the effort, so the other could cling for dear life to the nearest rope or ratline. Those tasks that couldn't be done that way, such as hauling on ropes, took place down on the deck—the rigging was designed with that in mind. There were emergencies where that rule didn't apply, and even with the rule in place there were sailors who fell from the rigging to their deaths, but as a general principle it worked tolerably well.

I'd like to propose that the same rule might be worth pursuing in the crisis of our age. In the years to come, a great many of us will face the same kind of scramble for survival that so many others faced in the catastrophes of the early 20th century. Some of us won't make it, and some will have to face the ghastly choice between sheer survival and everything else they value in life. Not everyone, though, will land in one or the other of those categories, and many those who manage to stay out of them will have the chance to direct time and energy toward the broader picture.

Exactly what projects might fall into that latter category will differ from one person to another, for reasons that are irreducibly personal. I'm sure there are plenty of things that would motivate you to action in desperate times, dear reader, that would leave me cold, and of course the reverse is also true—and in times of crisis, of the kind we're discussing, it's personal factors of that sort that make the difference, not abstract considerations of the sort we might debate here. I'll be discussing a few of the options in upcoming posts, but I'd also encourage readers of this blog to reflect on the question themselves: in the wreck of industrial civilization, what are you willing to make an effort to accomplish, to defend, or to preserve?

In thinking about that, I'd encourage my readers to consider the traumatic years of the early 20th century as a model for what's approaching us. Those who were alive when the first great wave of dissolution hit in 1914 weren't facing forty years of continuous cataclysm; as noted here repeatedly, collapse is a fractal process, and unfolds in real time as a sequence of crises of various kinds separated by intervals of relative calm in which some level of recovery is possible. It's pretty clear that the first round of trouble here in the United States, at least, will be a major economic crisis; at some point not too far down the road, the yawning gap between our senile political class and the impoverished and disaffected masses promises the collapse of politics as usual and a descent into domestic insurgency or one of the other standard patterns by which former democracies destroy themselves; as already noted, there are plenty of other things bearing down on us—but after an interval, things will stabilize again.

Then it'll be time to sort through the wreckage, see what's been saved and what can be recovered, and go on from there. First, though, we have a troubled time to get through.

400: THE ONE WAY FORWARD

(Originally published 28 January 2015)

All things considered, 2015 just isn't shaping up to be a good year for believers in business as usual. Since last week's post here on *The Archdruid Report*, the anti-austerity party Syriza has swept the Greek elections, to the enthusiastic cheers of similar parties all over Europe and the discomfiture of the Brussels hierarchy. The latter have no one to blame for this turn of events but themselves; for more than a decade now, EU policies have effectively put sheltering banks and bondholders from the healthy discipline of the market ahead of all other considerations, including the economic survival of entire nations. It should be no surprise to anyone that this wasn't an approach with a long shelf life.

Meanwhile, the fracking bust continues unabated. The number of drilling rigs at work in American oilfields continues to drop vertically from week to week, layoffs in the nation's various oil patches are picking up speed, and the price of oil remains down at levels that make further fracking a welcome mat for the local bankruptcy judge. Those media pundits who are still talking the fracking industry's book keep insisting that the dropping price of oil proves that they were right and those dratted heretics who talk of peak oil must be wrong, but somehow those pundits never get around to explaining why iron ore, copper, and most other major commodities are dropping in price even faster than crude oil, nor why demand for petroleum products here in the US has been declining steadily as well.

The fact of the matter is that an industrial economy built to run on cheap conventional oil can't run on expensive oil for long without running itself into the ground. Since 2008, the world's industrial nations have tried to make up the difference by flooding their economies with cheap credit, in the hope that this would somehow make up for the sharply increased amounts of real wealth that have had to be diverted from other purposes into the struggle to keep liquid fuels flowing at their peak levels. Now, though, the laws of economics have called their bluff; the wheels are coming off one national economy after another, and the price of oil (and all those other commodities) has dropped to levels that won't cover the costs of fracked oil, tar sands, and the like, because all those frantic attempts to externalize the costs of energy production just meant that the whole global economy took the hit.

Now of course this isn't how governments and the media are spinning the emerging crisis. For that matter, there's no shortage of people outside the corridors of power, or for that matter of punditry, who ignore the general collapse of commodity prices, fixate on oil outside of the broader context of resource depletion in general, and insist that the change in the price of oil must be an act of economic warfare, or what have you. It's a logic that readers of this blog will have seen deployed many times in the past: whatever happens, it must have been decided and carried out by human beings. An astonishing number of people these days seem unable to imagine the possibility that such wholly impersonal factors as the laws of economics, geology, and thermodynamics could make things happen all by themselves.

The problem we face now is precisely that the unimaginable is now our reality. For just that little bit too long, too many people have insisted that we didn't need to worry about the absurdity of pursuing limitless growth on a finite and fragile planet, that "they'll think of something," or that chattering on internet forums about this or that or the other piece of technological vaporware was doing something concrete about our species' imminent collision with the limits to growth. For just that little bit too long, not enough people were willing to do anything that mattered, and now impersonal factors have climbed into the driver's seat, having mugged all seven billion of us and shoved us into the trunk.

As I noted in last week's post, that puts hard limits on what can be done in the short term. In all probability, at this stage of the game, each of us will be meeting the oncoming wave of crisis with whatever preparations we've made, however substantial or insubstantial those happen to be. I'm aware that a certain subset of my readers are unhappy with that suggestion, but that can't be helped; the future is under no obligation to wait patiently while we get ready for it. A few years back, when I posted an essay here whose title, "Collapse Now and Avoid the Rush," sums up the strategy I've been proposing, I probably should have put more stress on the most important word in that slogan: *now*. Still, that's gone wherever might-have-beens spend their time.

That doesn't mean the world is about to end. It means that in all probability, beginning at some point this year and continuing for several years after that, many of my readers will be busy coping with the multiple impacts of a thumping economic crisis on their own lives and those of their families, friends, communities, and employers, at a time when political systems over much of the industrial world have frozen up into gridlock, the simmering wars in the Middle East and much of the Third World seem more than usually likely to boil over, and the twilight of the Pax Americana is pushing both the US government and its enemies into an ever greater degree of brinksmanship. Exactly how that's going to play out is anyone's guess, but no matter what happens, it's unlikely to be pretty.

While we get ready for the first shocks to hit, though, it's worth talking a little bit about what comes afterwards. No matter how long a train of financial dominoes the collapse of the fracking bubble sets toppling, the last one fill fall eventually, and within a few years things will have found a "new normal," however far down the slope of contraction that turns out to be. No matter how many proxy wars, coups d'etat, covert actions, and manufactured insurgencies get launched by the United States or its global rivals in their struggle for supremacy, most of the places touched by that conflict will see a few years at most of actual warfare or the equivalent, with periods of relative peace before and after. The other driving forces of collapse act in much the same way; collapse is a fractal process, not a linear one.

Thus there's something on the far side of crisis besides more of the same. The discussion I'd like to start at this point centers on what might be worth doing once the various masses of economic, political, and military rubble stops bouncing. It's not too early to begin planning for that. If nothing else, it will give readers of this blog something to think about while standing in bread lines or hiding in the basement while riot police and insurgents duke it out in the streets. That benefit aside, the sooner we start thinking about the options that will be available once relative stability returns, the better chance we'll have of being ready to implement it, in our own lives or on a broader scale, once stability returns.

One of the interesting consequences of crisis, for that matter, is that what was unthinkable before a really substantial crisis may not be unthinkable afterwards. Read Barbara Tuchman's brilliant *The Proud Tower* and you'll see how many of the unquestioned certainties of 1914 were rotting in history's compost bucket by the time 1945 rolled around, and how many ideas that had been on the outermost fringes before the First World War that had become plain common sense after the Second. It's a common phenomenon, and I propose to get ahead of the curve here by proposing something that's utterly unthinkable today but may well be a matter of necessity ten or twenty or forty years from now.

What do I have in mind? Intentional technological regression as a matter of public policy.

Imagine, for a moment, that an industrial nation were to downshift its technological infrastructure to roughly what it was in 1950. That would involve a drastic decrease in energy consumption per capita, both directly — people used a lot less energy of all kinds in 1950 — and indirectly — goods and services took much less energy to produce then, too. It would involve equally sharp decreases in the per capita consumption of most resources. It would also involve a sharp *increase* in jobs for the working classes — a great many things currently done by robots were done by human beings in those days, and so there were a great many more paychecks going out of a Friday to pay for the goods and services that ordinary consumers buy. Since a steady flow of paychecks to the working classes is one of the major things that keep an economy stable and thriving, this has certain obvious advantages, but we can leave those alone for now.

Now of course the change just proposed would involve certain changes from the way we do things. Air travel in the 1950s was extremely expensive — the well-to-do in those days were called "the jet set," because that's who could afford tickets — and so everyone else had to put up with fast, reliable, energy-efficient railroads to get from place to place. Computers were rare and expensive, which meant once again that more people got hired to do jobs, and also meant that when you called a utility or a business, your chance of getting a human being who could help you with whatever problem you might have was considerably higher than it is today.

Lacking the internet, people had to make do instead with their choice of scores of AM and shortwave radio stations, thousands of general and specialized print periodicals, and local libraries bursting at the seams with books — in America, at least, the 1950s were the golden age of the public library, and most small towns had collections you can't always find in big cities these days. Oh, and the folks who like looking at pictures of people with their clothes off, and who play a large and usually unmentioned role in paying for the internet today, had to settle for monthly magazines, mail-order houses that shipped their products in plain brown wrappers, and tacky stores in the wrong end of town. (For what it's worth, this didn't seem to inconvenience them any.)

I'm quite aware that such a project is unthinkable today, and we'll get to the superstitious horror that lies behind that reaction in a bit. First, though, let's talk about the obvious objections. Would it be possible? Of course. Much of it could be done by simple changes in the tax code. Right now, in the United States, a galaxy of perverse tax incentives penalize employers for hiring people and reward them for replacing employees with machines. Change the tax code so that spending money on wages, salaries and benefits up to a certain comfortable threshold makes more financial sense for employers than using the money to automate, and you're halfway there already.

A revision in trade policy would do most of the rest of what's needed. What's jokingly called "free trade," despite the faith-based claims of economists, benefits the rich at everyone else's expense, and would best be replaced by sensible tariffs to support domestic production against the sort of predatory export-driven mercantilism that dominates the global economy these days. Add to that high tariffs on technology imports, and strip any technology beyond the 1950 level of the lavish subsidies that fatten the profit margins of the welfare-queen corporations in the Fortune 500, and you're basically there.

What's more, the process would involve far fewer unwelcome surprises and dead ends than trying to develop some new technological system. The huge advantage of technological regression is that it's easy to figure out what works, how to implement it, what will be needed and how much it will cost. All we have to do is glance back down memory lane, with the help of an abundance of surviving records and, in the case of 1950 technology, a fair amount of living memory. Thus it's wholly practicable, once the decision is made to do it.

Would there be downsides? Of course. Every technology and every set of policy options has its downsides. A common delusion these days claims, in effect, that it's unfair to take the downsides of new technologies or the corresponding upsides of old ones into consideration when deciding whether to replace an older technology with a newer one. An even more common delusion claims that you're not supposed to decide at all; once a new technology shows up, you're supposed to run bleating after it like everyone else, without asking any questions at all.

Current technology has immense downsides. Future technologies are going to have them, too — it's only in sales brochures and science fiction stories, remember, that any technology is without them. Thus the mere fact that 1950 technology has problematic features, too, is not a valid reason to dismiss technological retrogression. The question that needs to be asked, however unthinkable it might be, is whether, all things considered, it's wiser to accept the downsides of 1950 technology in order to have a working technological suite that can function on much smaller per capita inputs of energy and resources, and thus a much better chance to get through the age of limits ahead than today's far more extravagant and brittle technological infrastructure.

It's probably also necessary to talk about a particular piece of paralogic that comes up reliably any time somebody suggests technological regression: the notion that if you return to an older technology, you have to take the social practices and cultural mores of its heyday as well. I fielded a good many such comments last year when I suggested steam-powered Victorian technology powered by solar energy as a form the ecotechnics of the future might take. An astonishing number of people seemed unable to imagine that it was possible to have such a technology without also reintroducing Victorian habits such as child labor and sexual prudery. Silly as that claim is, it has deep roots in the modern imagination.

No doubt, as a result of those deep roots, there will be plenty of people who respond to the proposal just made by insisting that the social practices and cultural mores of 1950 were awful, and claiming that those habits can't be separated from the technologies I'm discussing. I could point out in response that 1950 didn't have a single set of social practices and cultural mores; even in the United States, a drive from Greenwich Village to rural Pennsylvania in 1950 would have met with remarkable cultural diversity among people using the same technology.

The point could be made even more strongly by noting that the same technology was in use that year in Paris, Djakarta, Buenos Aires, Tokyo, Tangiers, Novosibirsk, Guadalajara, and Lagos, and the social practices and cultural mores of 1950s middle America didn't follow the technology around to these distinctly diverse settings, you know. Pointing that out, though, will likely be wasted breath. To true believers in the religion of progress, the past is the bubbling pit of eternal damnation from which the surrogate messiah of progress is perpetually saving us, and the future is the radiant heaven into whose portals the faithful hope to enter in good time. Most people these days are no more willing to question those dubious classifications than a medieval peasant would be to question the miraculous powers that supposely emanated from the bones of St. Ethelfrith.

Nothing, but nothing, stirs up shuddering superstitious horror in the minds of the cultural mainstream these days as effectively as the thought of, heaven help us, "going back." Even if the technology of an earlier day is better suited to a future of energy and resource scarcity than the infrastructure we've got now, even if the technology of an earlier day actually does a better job of many things than what we've got today, "we can't go back!" is the anguished cry of the masses. They've been so thoroughly bamboozled by the propagandists of progress that they never stop to think that, why, yes, they can, and there are valid reasons why they might even decide that it's the best option open to them.

There's a very rich irony in the fact that alternative and avant-garde circles tend to be even more obsessively fixated on the dogma of linear progress than the supposedly more conformist masses. That's one of the sneakiest features of the myth of progress; when people get dissatisfied with the status quo, the myth convinces them that the only option they've got is to do exactly what everyone else is doing, and just take it a little further than anyone else has gotten yet. What starts off as rebellion thus gets coopted into perfect conformity, and society continues to march mindlessly along its current trajectory without ever asking the obvious questions about what might be waiting at the far end.

That's the thing about progress; all the word means is "continued movement in the same direction." If the direction was a bad idea to start with, or if it's passed the point at which it still made sense, continuing to trudge blindly onward into the gathering dark may not be the best idea in the world. Break out of that mental straitjacket, and the range of possible futures broadens out immeasurably.

It may be, for example, that technological regression to the level of 1950 turns out to be impossible to maintain over the long term. If the technologies of 1920 can be supported on the modest energy supply we can count on getting from renewable sources, for example, something like a 1920 technological suite might be maintained over the long term, without further regression. It might turn out instead that something like the solar steampower I mentioned earlier, an ecotechnic equivalent of 1880 technology, might be the most complex technology that can be supported on a renewable basis. It might be the case, for that matter, that something like the technological infrastructure the United States had in 1820, with windmills and water wheels as the prime movers of industry, canalboats as the core domestic transport technology, and most of the population working on small family farms to support very modest towns and cities, is the fallback level that can be sustained indefinitely.

Does that last option seem unbearably depressing? Compare it to another very likely scenario—what will happen if the world's industrial societies gamble their survival on a great leap forward to some unproven energy source, which doesn't live up to its billing, and leaves billions of people twisting in the wind without any working technological infrastructure at all—and you may find that it has its good points. If you've driven down a dead end alley and are sitting there with the front grill hard against a brick wall, it bears remembering, shouting "We can't go back!" isn't exactly a useful habit. In such a situation—and I'd like to suggest that that's a fair metaphor for the situation we're in right now—going back, retracing the route as far back as necessary, is the one way forward.

401: AS NIGHT CLOSES IN

(Originally published 4 February 2015)

I was saddened to learn a few days ago, via a phone call from a fellow author, that William R. Catton Jr. died early last month, just short of his 89th birthday. Some of my readers will have no idea who he was; others may dimly recall that I've mentioned him and his most important book, *Overshoot*, repeatedly in these essays. Those who've taken the time to read the book just named may be wondering why none of the sites in the peak oil blogosphere has put up an obituary, or even noted the man's passing. I don't happen to know the answer to that last question, though I have my suspicions.

I encountered *Overshoot* for the first time in a college bookstore in Bellingham, Washington in 1983. Red letters on a stark yellow spine spelled out the title, a word I already knew from my classes in ecology and systems theory; I pulled it off the shelf, and found the future staring me in the face. This is what's on the front cover:

> **carrying capacity:** maximum permanently supportable load.
> **cornucopian myth:** euphoric belief in limitless resources.
> **drawdown:** stealing resources from the future.
> **cargoism:** delusion that technology will always save us from
> **overshoot:** growth beyond an area's carrying capacity, leading to
> **crash:** die-off.

If you want to know where I got the core ideas I've been exploring in these essays for the last eight-going-on-nine years, in other words, now you know. I still have that copy of *Overshoot*; it's sitting on the desk in front of me right now, reminding me yet again just how many chances we had to turn away from the bleak future that's closing in around us now, like the night at the end of a long day.

Plenty of books in the 1970s and early 1980s applied the lessons of ecology to the future of industrial civilization and picked up at least part of the bad news that results. *Overshoot* was arguably the best of the lot, but it was pretty much guaranteed to land even deeper in the memory hole than the others. The difficulty was that Catton's book didn't pander to the standard mythologies that still beset any attempt to make sense of the predicament we've made for ourselves; it provided no encouragement to what he called cargoism, the claim that technological progress will inevitably allow us to have our planet and eat it too, without falling off the other side of the balance into the sort of apocalyptic daydreams that Hollywood loves to make into bad movies. Instead, in calm, crisp, thoughtful prose, he explained how industrial civilization was cutting its own throat, how far past the point of no return we'd already gone, and what had to be done in order to salvage anything from the approaching wreck.

As I noted in a post here in 2011, I had the chance to meet Catton at an ASPO conference, and tried to give him some idea of how much his book had meant to me. I did my best not to act like a fourteen-year-old fan meeting a rock star, but I'm by no means sure that I succeeded. We talked for fifteen minutes over dinner; he was very gracious; then things moved on, each of us left the conference to carry on with our lives, and now he's gone. As the old song says, that's the way it goes.

There's much more that could be said about William Catton, but that task should probably be left for someone who knew the man as a teacher, a scholar, and a human being. I didn't; except for that one fifteen-minute conversation, I knew him solely as the mind behind one of the books that helped me make sense of the world, and then kept me going on the long desert journey through the Reagan era, when most of those who claimed to be environmentalists over the previous decade cashed in their ideals and waved around the cornucopian myth as their excuse for that act. Thus I'm simply going to urge all of my readers who haven't yet read Overshoot to do so as soon as possible, even if they have to crawl on their bare hands and knees over abandoned fracking equipment to get a copy. Having said that, I'd like to go on to the sort of tribute I think he would have appreciated most: an attempt to take certain of his ideas a little further than he did.

The core of *Overshoot*, which is also the core of the entire world of appropriate technology and green alternatives that got shot through the head and shoved into an unmarked grave in the Reagan years, is the recognition that the principles of ecology apply to industrial society just as much as they do to other communities of living things. It's odd, all things considered, that this is such a controversial proposal. Most of us have no trouble grasping the fact that the law of gravity affects human beings the same way it affects rocks; most of us understand that other laws of nature really do apply to us; but quite a few of us seem to be incapable of extending that same sensible reasoning to one particular set of laws, the ones that govern how communities of living things relate to their environments.

If people treated gravity the way they treat ecology, you could visit a news website any day of the week and read someone insisting with a straight face that while it's true that rocks fall down when dropped, human beings don't—no, no, they fall straight up into the sky, and anyone who thinks otherwise is so obviously wrong that there's no point even discussing the matter. That degree of absurdity appears every single day in the American media, and in ordinary conversations as well, whenever ecological issues come up. Suggest that a finite planet must by definition contain a finite amount of fossil fuels, that dumping billions of tons of gaseous trash into the air every single year for centuries might change the way that the atmosphere retains heat, or that the law of diminishing returns might apply to technology the way it applies to everything else, and you can pretty much count on being shouted down by those who, for all practical purposes, might as well believe that the world is flat.

Still, as part of the ongoing voyage into the unspeakable in which this blog is currently engaged, I'd like to propose that, in fact, human societies are as subject to the laws of ecology as they are to every other dimension of natural law. That act of intellectual heresy implies certain conclusions that are acutely unwelcome in most circles just now; still, as my regular readers will have noticed long since, that's just one of the services this blog offers.

Let's start with the basics. Every ecosystem, in thermodynamic terms, is a process by which relatively concentrated energy is dispersed into diffuse background heat. Here on Earth, at least, the concentrated energy mostly comes from the Sun, in the form of solar radiation—there are a few ecosystems, in deep oceans and underground, that get their energy from chemical reactions driven by the Earth's internal heat instead. Ilya Prigogine showed some decades back that the flow of energy through a system of this sort tends to increase the complexity of the system; Jeremy England, a MIT physicist, has recently shown that the same process accounts neatly for the origin of life itself. The steady flow of energy from source to sink is the foundation on which everything else rests.

The complexity of the system, in turn, is limited by the rate at which energy flows through the system, and this in turn depends on the difference in concentration between the energy that enters the system, on the one hand, and the background into which waste heat diffuses when it leaves the system, on the other. That shouldn't be a difficult concept to grasp. Not only is it basic thermodynamics, it's basic physics—it's precisely equivalent, in fact, to pointing out that the rate at which water flows through any section of a stream depends on the difference in height between the place where the water flows into that section and the place where it flows out.

Simple as it is, it's a point that an astonishing number of people—including some who are scientifically literate—routinely miss. A while back on this blog, for example, I noted that one of the core reasons you can't power a modern industrial civilization on solar energy is that sunlight is relatively diffuse as an energy source, compared to the extremely concentrated energy we get from fossil fuels. I still field rants from people insisting that this is utter hogwash, since photons have exactly the same amount of energy they did when they left the Sun, and so the energy they carry is just as concentrated as it was when it left the Sun. You'll notice, though, that if this was the only variable that mattered, Neptune would be just as warm as Mercury, since each of the photons hitting the one planet pack on average the same energetic punch as those that hit the other.

It's hard to think of a better example of the blindness to whole systems that's pandemic in today's geek culture. Obviously, the difference between the temperatures of Neptune and Mercury isn't a function of the energy of individual photons hitting the two worlds; it's a function of differing concentrations of photons—the number of them, let's say, hitting a square meter of each planet's surface. This is also one of the two figures that matter when we're talking about solar energy here on Earth. The other? That's the background heat into which waste energy disperses when the system, eco- or solar, is done with it. On the broadest scale, that's deep space, but ecosystems don't funnel their waste heat straight into orbit, you know. Rather, they diffuse it into the ambient temperature at whatever height above or below sea level, and whatever latitude closer or further from the equator, they happen to be—and since that's heated by the Sun, too, the difference between input and output concentrations isn't very substantial.

Nature has done astonishing things with that very modest difference in concentration. People who insist that photosynthesis is horribly inefficient, and of course we can improve its efficiency, are missing a crucial point: something like half the energy that reaches the leaves of a green plant from the Sun is put to work lifting water up from the roots by an ingenious form of evaporative pumping, in which water sucked out through the leaf pores as vapor draws up more water through a network of tiny tubes in the plant's stems. Another few per cent goes into the manufacture of sugars by photosynthesis, and a variety of minor processes, such as the chemical reactions that ripen fruit, also depend to some extent on light or heat from the Sun. All told, a green plant is probably about as efficient in its total use of solar energy as the laws of thermodynamics will permit.

What's more, the Earth's ecosystems take the energy that flows through the green engines of plant life and put it to work in an extraordinary diversity of ways. The water pumped into the sky by what botanists call evapotranspiration—that's the evaporative pumping I mentioned a moment ago—plays critical roles in local, regional, and global water cycles. The production of sugars to store solar energy in chemical form kicks off an even more intricate set of changes, as the plant's cells are eaten by something, which is eaten by something, and so on through the lively but precise dance of the food web. Eventually all the energy the original plant scooped up from the Sun turns into diffuse waste heat and permeates slowly up through the atmosphere to its ultimate destiny warming some corner of deep space a bit above absolute zero, but by the time it gets there, it's usually had quite a ride.

That said, there are hard upper limits to the complexity of the ecosystem that these intricate processes can support. You can see that clearly enough by comparing a tropical rain forest to a polar tundra. The two environments may have approximately equal amounts of precipitation over the course of a year; they may have an equally rich or poor supply of nutrients in the soil; even so, the tropical rain forest can easily support fifteen or twenty thousand species of plants and animals, and the tundra will be lucky to support a few hundred. Why? The same reason Mercury is warmer than Neptune: the rate at which photons from the sun arrive in each place per square meter of surface.

Near the equator, the sun's rays fall almost vertically. Close to the poles, since the Earth is round, the Sun's rays come in at a sharp angle, and thus are spread out over more surface area. The ambient temperature's quite a bit warmer in the rain forest than it is on the tundra, but because the vast heat engine we call the atmosphere pumps heat from the equator to the poles, the difference in ambient temperature is not as great as the difference in solar input per cubic meter. Thus ecosystems near the equator have a greater difference in energy concentration between input and output than those near the poles, and the complexity of the two systems varies accordingly.

All this should be common knowledge. Of course it isn't, because the industrial world's notions of education consistently ignore what William Catton called "the processes that matter" — that is, the fundamental laws of ecology that frame our existence on this planet — and approach a great many of those subjects that do make it into the curriculum in ways that encourage the most embarrassing sort of ignorance about the natural processes that keep us all alive. Down the road a bit, we'll be discussing that in much more detail. For now, though, I want to take the points just made and apply them systematically, in much the way Catton did, to the predicament of industrial civilization.

A human society is an ecosystem. Like any other ecosystem, it depends for its existence on flows of energy, and as with any other ecosystem, the upper limit on its complexity depends ultimately on the difference in concentration between the energy that enters it and the background into which its waste heat disperses. (This last point is a corollary of White's Law, one of the fundamental principles of human ecology, which holds that a society's economic development is directly proportional to its consumption of energy per capita.) Until the beginning of the industrial revolution, that upper limit was not much higher than the upper limit of complexity in other ecosystems, since human ecosystems drew most of their energy from the same source as nonhuman ones: sunlight falling on green plants. As human societies figured out how to tap other flows of solar energy — windpower to drive windmills and send ships coursing over the seas, water power to turn mills, and so on — that upper limit crept higher, but not dramatically so.

The discoveries that made it possible to turn fossil fuels into mechanical energy transformed that equation completely. The geological processes that stockpiled half a billion years of sunlight into coal, oil, and natural gas boosted the concentration of the energy inputs available to industrial societies by an almost unimaginable factor, without warming the ambient temperature of the planet more than a few degrees, and the huge differentials in energy concentration that resulted drove an equally unimaginable increase in complexity. Choose any measure of complexity you wish — number of discrete occupational categories, average number of human beings involved in the production, distribution, and consumption of any given good or service, or what have you — and in the wake of the industrial revolution, it soared right off the charts. Thermodynamically, that's exactly what you'd expect.

The difference in energy concentration between input and output, it bears repeating, defines the upper limit of complexity. Other variables determine whether or not the system in question will achieve that upper limit. In the ecosystems we call human societies, knowledge is one of those other variables. If you have a highly concentrated energy source and don't yet know how to use it efficiently, your society isn't going to become as complex as it otherwise could. Over the three centuries of industrialization, as a result, the production of useful knowledge was a winning strategy, since it allowed industrial societies to rise steadily toward the upper limit of complexity defined by the concentration differential. The limit was never reached — the law of diminishing returns saw to that — and so, inevitably, industrial societies ended up believing that knowledge all by itself was capable of increasing the complexity of the human ecosystem. Since there's no upper limit to knowledge, in turn, that belief system drove what Catton called the cornucopian myth, the delusion that there would always be enough resources if only the stock of knowledge increased quickly enough.

That belief only seemed to work, though, as long as the concentration differential between energy inputs and the background remained very high. Once easily accessible fossil fuels started to become scarce, and more and more energy and other resources had to be invested in the extraction of what remained, problems started to crop up. Tar sands and oil shales in their natural form are not as concentrated an energy source as light sweet crude — once they're refined, sure, the differences are minimal, but a whole system analysis of energy concentration has to start at the moment each energy source enters the system. Take a cubic yard of tar sand fresh from the pit mine, with the sand still in it, or a cubic yard of oil shale with the oil still trapped in the rock, and you've simply got less energy per unit volume than you do if you've got a cubic yard of light sweet crude fresh from the well, or even a cubic yard of good permeable sandstone with light sweet crude oozing out of every pore.

It's an article of faith in contemporary culture that such differences don't matter, but that's just another aspect of our cornucopian myth. The energy needed to get the sand out of the tar sands or the oil out of the shale oil has to come from somewhere, and that energy, in turn, is not available for other uses. The result, however you slice it conceptually, is that the upper limit of complexity begins moving down. That sounds abstract, but it adds up to a great deal of very concrete misery, because as already noted, the complexity of a society determines such things as the number of different occupational specialties it can support, the number of employees who are involved in the production and distribution of a given good or service, and so on. There's a useful phrase for a sustained contraction in the usual measures of complexity in a human ecosystem: "economic depression."

The economic troubles that are shaking the industrial world more and more often these days, in other words, are symptoms of a disastrous mismatch between the level of complexity that our remaining concentration differential can support, and the level of complexity that our preferred ideologies insist we ought to have. As those two things collide, there's no question which of them is going to win. Adding to our total stock of knowledge won't change that result, since knowledge is a necessary condition for economic expansion but not a sufficient one: if the upper limit of complexity set by the laws of thermodynamics drops below the level that your knowledge base would otherwise support, further additions to the knowledge base simply mean that there will be a growing number of things that people know how to do in theory, but that nobody has the resources to do in practice.

Knowledge, in other words, is not a magic wand, a surrogate messiah, or a source of miracles. It can open the way to exploiting energy more efficiently than otherwise, and it can figure out how to use energy resources that were not previously being used at all, but it can't conjure energy out of thin air. Even if the energy resources are there, for that matter, if other factors prevent them from being used, the knowledge of how they might be used offers no consolation — quite the contrary.

That latter point, I think, sums up the tragedy of William Catton's career. He knew, and could explain with great clarity, why industrialism would bring about its own downfall, and what could be done to salvage something from its wreck. That knowledge, however, was not enough to make things happen; only a few people ever listened, most of them promptly plugged their ears and started chanting "La, la, la, I can't hear you" once Reagan made that fashionable, and the actions that might have spared all of us a vast amount of misery never happened. When I spoke to him in 2011, he was perfectly aware that his life's work had done essentially nothing to turn industrial society aside from its rush toward the abyss. That's got to be a bitter thing to contemplate in your final hours, and I hope his thoughts were on something else last month as the night closed in at last.

402: THE BUTLERIAN CARNIVAL

(Originally published 11 February 2015)

Over the last week or so, I've heard from a remarkable number of people who feel that a major crisis is in the offing. The people in question don't know each other, many of them have even less contact with the mass media than I do, and the sense they've tried to express to me is inchoate enough that they've been left fumbling for words, but they all end up reaching for the same metaphors: that something in the air just now seems reminiscent of the American colonies in 1775, France in 1789, America in 1860, Europe in 1914, or the world in 1939: a sense of being poised on the brink of convulsive change, with the sound of gunfire and marching boots coming ever more clearly from the dimly seen abyss ahead.

It's not an unreasonable feeling, all things considered. In Washington DC, Obama's flunkies are beating the war drums over Ukraine, threatening to send shipments of allegedly "defensive" weapons to join the mercenaries and military advisors we've already not-so-covertly got over there. Russian officials have responded to American saber-rattling by stating flatly that a US decision to arm Kiev will be the signal for all-out war. The current Ukrainian regime, installed by a US-sponsored coup and backed by NATO, means to Russia precisely what a hostile Canadian government installed by a Chinese-sponsored coup and backed by the People's Liberation Army would mean to the United States; if Obama's trademark cluelessness leads him to ignore that far from minor point and decide that the Russians are bluffing, we could be facing a European war within weeks.

Head south and west from the fighting around Donetsk, and another flashpoint is heating up toward an explosion of its own just now. Yes, that would be Greece, where the new Syriza government has refused to back down from the promises that got it into office: promises that center on the rejection of the so-called "austerity" policies that have all but destroyed the Greek economy since they were imposed in 2009. This shouldn't be news to anyone; those same policies, though they've been praised to the skies by neoliberal economists for decades now as a guaranteed ticket to prosperity, have had precisely the opposite effect in every single country where they've been put in place.

Despite that track record of unbroken failure, the EU — in particular, Germany, which has benefited handsomely from the gutting of southern European economies — continues to insist that Greece must accept what amounts to a perpetual state of debt peonage. The Greek defense minister noted in response in a recent speech that if Europe isn't willing to cut a deal, other nations might well do so. He's quite correct; it's probably a safe bet that cold-eyed men in Moscow and Beijing are busy right now figuring out how best to step through the window of opportunity the EU is flinging open for them. If they do so — well, I'll leave it to my readers to consider how the US is likely to respond to the threat of Russian air and naval bases in Greece, which would be capable of projecting power anywhere in the eastern and central Mediterranean basin. Here again, war is a likely outcome; I hope that the Greek government is braced for an attempt at regime change.

That is to say, the decline and fall of industrial civilization is proceeding in the normal way, at pretty much the normal pace. The thermodynamic foundations tipped over into decline first, as stocks of cheap abundant fossil fuels depleted steadily and the gap had to be filled by costly and much less abundant replacements, driving down net energy; the economy went next, as more and more real wealth had to be pulled out of all other economic activities to keep the energy supply more or less steady, until demand destruction cut in and made that increasingly frantic effort moot; now a global political and military superstructure dependent on cheap abundant fossil fuels, and on the economic arrangement that all of that surplus energy made possible, is cracking at the seams.

One feature of times like these is that the number of people who can have an influence on the immediate outcome declines steadily as crisis approaches. In the years leading up to 1914, for example, a vast number of people contributed to the rising spiral of conflict between the aging British Empire and its German rival, but the closer war came, the narrower the circle of decision-makers became, until a handful of politicians in Germany, France, and Britain had the fate of Europe in their hands. A few more bad decisions, and the situation was no longer under anybody's control; thereafter, the only option left was to let the juggernaut of the First World War roll mindlessly onward to its conclusion.

In the same way, as recently as the 1980s, many people in the United States and elsewhere had some influence on how the industrial age would end; unfortunately most of them backed politicians who cashed in the resources that could have built a better future on one last round of absurd extravagance, and a whole landscape of possibilities went by the boards. Step by step, as the United States backed itself further and further into a morass of short-term gimmicks with ghastly long-term consequences, the number of people who have had any influence on the trajectory we're on has narrowed steadily, and as we approach what may turn out to be the defining crisis of our time, a handful of politicians in a handful of capitals are left to make the last decisions that can shape the situation in any way at all, before the tanks begin to roll and the fighter-bombers rise up from their runways.

Out here on the fringes of the collective conversation of our time, where archdruids lurk and heresies get uttered, the opportunity to shape events as they happen is a very rare thing. Our role, rather, is to set agendas for the future, to take ideas that are unthinkable in the mainstream today and prepare them for their future role as the conventional wisdom of eras that haven't dawned yet. Every phrase on the lips of today's practical men of affairs, after all, was once a crazy notion taken seriously only by the lunatic fringe — yes, that includes democracy, free-market capitalism, and all the other shibboleths of our age.

With that in mind, while we wait to see whether today's practical men of affairs stumble into war the way they did in 1914, I propose to shift gears and talk about something else — something that may seem whimsical, even pointless, in the light of the grim martial realities just discussed. It's neither whimsical nor pointless, as it happens, but the implications may take a little while to dawn even on those of my readers who've been following the last few years of discussions most closely. Let's begin with a handful of data points.

Item: Britain's largest bookseller recently noted that sales of the Kindle e-book reader have dropped like a rock in recent months, while sales of old-fashioned printed books are up. Here in the more gizmocentric USA, e-books retain more of their erstwhile popularity, but the bloom is off the rose; among the young and hip, it's not hard at all to find people who got rid of their book collections in a rush of enthusiasm when e-books came out, regretted the action after it was too late, and now are slowly restocking their bookshelves while their e-book readers collect cobwebs or, at best, find use as a convenience for travel and the like.

Item: more generally, a good many of the hottest new trends in popular culture aren't new trends at all—they're old trends revived, in many cases, by people who weren't even alive to see them the first time around. Kurt B. Reighley's lively guide *The United States of Americana* was the first, and remains the best, introduction to the phenomenon, one that embraces everything from burlesque shows and homebrewed bitters to backyard chickens and the revival of Victorian martial arts. One pervasive thread that runs through the wild diversity of this emerging subculture is the simple recognition that many of these older things are better, in straightforwardly measurable senses, than their shiny modern mass-marketed not-quite-equivalents.

Item: within that subculture, a small but steadily growing number of people have taken the principle to its logical extreme and adopted the lifestyles and furnishings of an earlier decade wholesale in their personal lives. The 1950s are a common target, and so far as I know, adopters of 1950s culture are the furthest along the process of turning into a community, but other decades are increasingly finding the same kind of welcome among those less than impressed by what today's society has on offer. Meanwhile, the reenactment scene has expanded spectacularly in recent years from the standard hearty fare of Civil War regiments and the neo-medievalism of the Society for Creative Anachronism to embrace almost any historical period you care to name. These aren't merely dress-up games; go to a buckskinner's rendezvous or an outdoor SCA event, for example, and you're as likely as not to see handspinners turning wool into yarn with drop spindles, a blacksmith or two laboring over a portable forge, and the like.

Other examples of the same broad phenomenon could be added to the list, but these will do for now. I'm well aware, of course, that most people—even most of my readers—will have dismissed the things just listed as bizarre personal eccentricities, right up there with the goldfish-swallowing and flagpole-sitting of an earlier era. I'd encourage those of my readers who had that reaction to stop, take a second look, and tease out the mental automatisms that make that dismissal so automatic a part of today's conventional wisdom. Once that's done, a third look might well be in order, because the phenomenon sketched out here marks a shift of immense importance for our future.

For well over two centuries now, since it first emerged as the crackpot belief system of a handful of intellectuals on the outer fringes of their culture, the modern ideology of progress has taken it as given that new things were by definition better than whatever they replaced. That assumption stands at the heart of contemporary industrial civilization's childlike trust in the irreversible cumulative march of progress toward a future among the stars. Finding ways to defend that belief even when it obviously wasn't true—when the latest, shiniest products of progress turned out to be worse in every meaningful sense than the older products they elbowed out of the way—was among the great growth industries of the 20th century; even so, there were plenty of cases where progress really did seem to measure up to its billing. Given the steady increases of energy per capita in the world's industrial nations over the last century or so, that was a predictable outcome.

The difficulty, of course, is that the number of cases where new things really are better than what they replace has been shrinking steadily in recent decades, while the number of cases where old products are quite simply better than their current equivalents—easier to use, more effective, more comfortable, less prone to break, less burdened with unwanted side effects and awkward features, and so on—has been steadily rising. Back behind the myth of progress, like the little man behind the curtain in *The Wizard of Oz*, stand two unpalatable and usually unmentioned realities. The first is that profits, not progress, determines which products get marketed and which get roundfiled; the second is that making a cheaper, shoddier product and using advertising gimmicks to sell it anyway has been the standard marketing strategy across a vast range of American businesses for years now.

More generally, believers in progress used to take it for granted that progress would sooner or later bring about a world where everyone would live exciting, fulfilling lives brimfull of miracle products and marvelous experiences. You still hear that sort of talk from the faithful now and then these days, but it's coming to sound a lot like all that talk about the glorious worker's paradise of the future did right around the time the Iron Curtain came down for good. In both cases, the future that was promised didn't have much in common with the one that actually showed up. The one we got doesn't have some of the nastier features of the one the former Soviet Union and its satellites produced — well, not yet, at least — but the glorious consumer's paradise described in such lavish terms a few decades back got lost on the way to the spaceport, and what we got instead was a bleak landscape of decaying infrastructure, abandoned factories, prostituted media, and steadily declining standards of living for everyone outside the narrowing circle of the privileged, with the remnants of our once-vital democratic institutions hanging above it all like rotting scarecrows silhouetted against a darkening sky.

In place of those exciting, fulfilling lives mentioned above, furthermore, we got the monotony and stress of long commutes, cubicle farms, and would-you-like-fries-with that for the slowly shrinking fraction of our population who can find a job at all. *The Onion*, with its usual flair for packaging unpalatable realities in the form of deadpan humor, nailed it a few days ago with a faux health-news article announcing that the best thing office workers could do for their health is stand up at their desk, leave the office, and never go back. Joke or not, it's not bad advice; if you have a full-time job in today's America, the average medieval peasant had a less stressful job environment and more days off than you do; he also kept a larger fraction of the product of his labor than you'll ever see.

Then, of course, if you're like most Americans, you'll numb yourself once you get home by flopping down on the sofa and spending most of your remaining waking hours staring at little colored pictures on a glass screen. It's remarkable how many people get confused about what this action really entails. They insist that they're experiencing distant places, traveling in worlds of pure imagination, and so on through the whole litany of self-glorifying drivel the mass media likes to employ in its own praise. Let us please be real: when you watch a program about the Amazon rain forest, you're not experiencing the Amazon rain forest; you're experiencing colored pictures on a screen, and you're only getting as much of the experience as fits through the narrow lens of a video camera and the even narrower filter of the production process. The difference between experiencing something and watching it on TV or the internet, that is to say, is precisely the same as the difference between making love and watching pornography; in each case, the latter is a very poor substitute for the real thing.

For most people in today's America, in other words, the closest approach to the glorious consumer's paradise of the future they can expect to get is eight hours a day, five days a week of mindless, monotonous work under the constant pressure of management efficiency experts, if they're lucky enough to get a job at all, with anything up to a couple of additional hours commuting and any off-book hours the employer happens to choose to demand from them into the deal, in order to get a paycheck that buys a little less each month—inflation is under control, the government insists, but prices somehow keep going up—of products that get more cheaply made, more likely to be riddled with defects, and more likely to pose a serious threat to the health and well-being of their users, with every passing year. Then they can go home and numb their nervous systems with those little colored pictures on the screen, showing them bland little snippets of experiences they will never have, wedged in there between the advertising.

That's the world that progress has made. That's the shining future that resulted from all those centuries of scientific research and technological tinkering, all the genius and hard work and sacrifice that have gone into the project of progress. Of course there's more to the consequences of progress than that; progress has saved quite a few children from infectious diseases, and laced the environment with so many toxic wastes that childhood cancer, all but unheard of in 1850, is a routine event today; it's made impressive contributions to human welfare, while flooding the atmosphere with greenhouse gases that will soon make far more impressive contributions to human suffering and death—well, I could go on along these lines for quite a while. True believers in the ideology of perpetual progress like to insist that all the good things ought to be credited to progress while all the bad things ought to be blamed on something else, but that's not so plausible an article of faith as it once was, and it bids fair to become a great deal less common as the downsides of progress become more and more difficult to ignore.

The data points I noted earlier in this week's post, I've come to believe, are symptoms of that change, the first stirrings of wind that tell of the storm to come. People searching for a better way of living than the one our society offers these days are turning to the actual past, rather than to some imaginary future, in that quest. That's the immense shift I mentioned earlier. What makes it even more momentous is that by and large, it's not being done in the sort of grim Puritanical spirit of humorless renunciation that today's popular culture expects from those who want something other than what the consumer economy has on offer. It's being done, rather, in a spirit of celebration.

One of my readers responded to my post two weeks ago on deliberate technological regress by suggesting that I was proposing a Butlerian jihad of sorts. (Those of my readers who don't get the reference should pick up a copy of Frank Herbert's iconic SF novel *Dune* and read it.) I demurred, for two reasons. First, the Butlerian jihad in Herbert's novel was a revolt against computer technology, and I see no need for that; once the falling cost of human labor intersects the rising cost of energy and technology, and it becomes cheaper to hire file clerks and accountants than to maintain the gargantuan industrial machine that keeps computer technology available, computers will go away, or linger as a legacy technology for a narrowing range of special purposes until the hardware finally burns out.

The second reason, though, is the more important. I'm not a fan of jihads, or of holy wars of any flavor; history shows all too well that when you mix politics and violence with religion, any actual religious content vanishes away, leaving its castoff garments to cover the naked rule of force and fraud. If you want people to embrace a new way of looking at things, furthermore, violence, threats, and abusive language don't work, and it's even less effective to offer that new way as a ticket to virtuous misery, along the lines of the Puritanical spirit noted above. That's why so much of the green-lifestyle propaganda of the last thirty years has done so little good — so much of it has been pitched as a way to suffer self-righteously for the good of Gaia, and while that approach appeals to a certain number of wannabe martyrs, that's not a large enough fraction of the population to matter.

The people who are ditching their Kindles and savoring books as physical objects, brewing their own beer and resurrecting other old arts and crafts, reformatting their lives in the modes of a past decade, or spending their spare time reconnecting with the customs and technologies of an earlier time—these people aren't doing any of those things out of some passion for self-denial. They're doing them because these things bring them delights that the shoddy mass-produced lifestyles of the consumer economy can't match. What these first stirrings suggest to me is that the way forward isn't a Butlerian jihad, but a Butlerian carnival—a sensuous celebration of the living world outside the cubicle farms and the glass screens, which will inevitably draw most of its raw materials from eras, technologies, and customs of the past, which don't require the extravagant energy and resource inputs that the modern consumer economy demands, and so will be better suited to a future defined by scarce energy and resources.

The Butlerian carnival isn't the only way to approach the deliberate technological regression we need to carry out in the decades ahead, but it's an important one. In upcoming posts, I'll talk more about how this and other avenues to the same goal might be used to get through the mess immediately ahead, and start laying foundations for a future on the far side of the crises of our time.

403: WHAT PROGRESS MEANS

(Originally published 18 February 2015)

Last week's post here on *The Archdruid Report* appears to have hit a nerve. That didn't come as any sort of a surprise, admittedly. It's one thing to point out that going back to the simpler and less energy-intensive technologies of earlier eras could help extract us from the corner into which industrial society has been busily painting itself in recent decades; it's quite another to point out that doing this can also be great fun, more so than anything that comes out of today's fashionable technologies, and in a good many cases the results include an objectively better quality of life as well

That's not one of the canned speeches that opponents of progress are supposed to make. According to the folk mythology of modern industrial culture, since progress always makes things better, the foes of progress are assigned the role of putting on hair shirts and insisting that everyone has to suffer virtuously from a lack of progress for some reason based on sentimental superstition. The Pygmalion effect being what it is, it's not hard to find opponents of progress who say what they're expected to say, and thus fulfill their assigned role in contemporary culture, which is to stand there in their hair shirts bravely protesting until the steamroller of progress rolls right over them.

The grip of that particular bit of folk mythology on the collective imagination of our time is tight enough that when somebody brings up some other reason to oppose "progress" — we'll get into the ambiguities behind that familiar label in a moment — a great many people quite literally can't absorb what's actually being said, and respond instead to the canned speeches they expect to hear. Thus I had several people attempt to come charging into the comments on last week's post, castigating my readers with varying degrees of wrath and profanity for thinking that they had to sacrifice the delights of today's technology and go creeping mournfully back to the unsatisfying lifestyles of an earlier day.

That was all the more ironic in that none of the readers who were commenting on the post were saying anything of the kind. Most of them were enthusiastically talking about how much more durable, practical, repairable, enjoyable, affordable, and user-friendly older technologies are compared to the disposable plastic trash that fills the stores these days. They were discussing how much more fun it is to embrace the delights of outdated technologies than it would be to go creeping mournfully back — or perhaps forward — to the unsatisfying lifestyles of the present time. That heresy is far more than the alleged openmindness and intellectual diversity of our age is willing to tolerate, so it's not surprising that some people tried to pretend that nothing of the sort had been said at all. What was surprising to me, and pleasantly so, was the number of readers who were ready to don the party clothes of some earlier time and join in the Butlerian carnival.

There are subtleties to the project of deliberate technological regress that may not be obvious at first glance, though, and it seems sensible to discuss those here before we proceed. It's important, to begin with, to remember that when talking heads these days babble about technology in the singular, as a uniform, monolithic thing that progresses according to some relentless internal logic of its own, they're spouting balderdash on the grand scale. In the real world, there's no such monolith, no technology in the singular; instead, there are technologies in the plural, clustered more or less loosely in technological suites which may or may not have any direct relation to one another.

An example might be useful here. Consider the technologies necessary to build a steel-framed bicycle. The metal parts require the particular suite of technologies we use to smelt ores, combine the resulting metals into useful alloys, and machine and weld those into shapes that fit together to make a bicycle. The tires, inner tubes, brake pads, seat cushion, handlebar grips, and paint require a different suite of technologies drawing on various branches of applied organic chemistry, and a few other suites also have a place: for example, the one that's needed to make and apply lubricants The suites that make a bicycle have other uses; if you can build a bicycle, as Orville and Wilbur Wright demonstrated, you can also build an aircraft, and a variety of other interesting machines as well; that said, there are other technologies—say, the ones needed to manufacture medicines, or precision optics, or electronics—that require very different technological suites. You can have everything you need to build a bicycle and still be unable to make a telescope or a radio receiver, and vice versa.

Strictly speaking, therefore, nothing requires the project of deliberate technological regress to move in lockstep to the technologies of a specific past date and stay there. It would be wholly possible to dump certain items of modern technology while keeping others. It would be just as possible to replace one modern technological suite with an equivalent from one decade, another with an equivalent from a different decade and so on. Imagine, for example, a future America in which solar water heaters (worked out by 1920) and passive solar architecture (mostly developed in the 1960s and 1970s) were standard household features, canal boats (dating from before 1800) and tall ships (ditto) were the primary means of bulk transport, shortwave radio (developed in the early 20th century) was the standard long-range communications medium, ultralight aircraft (largely developed in the 1980s) were still in use, and engineers crunched numbers using slide rules (perfected around 1880).

There's no reason why such a pastiche of technologies from different eras couldn't work. We know this because what passes for modern technology is a pastiche of the same kind, in which (for example) cars whose basic design dates from the 1890s are gussied up with onboard computers invented a century later. Much of modern technology, in fact, is old technology with a new coat of paint and a few electronic gimmicks tacked on, and it's old technology that originated in many different eras, too. Part of what differentiates modern technology from older equivalents, in other words, is mere fashion. Another part, though, moves into more explosive territory.

In the conversation that followed last week's post, one of my readers—tip of the archdruid's hat to Cathy—recounted the story of the one and only class on advertising she took at college. The teacher invited a well-known advertising executive to come in and talk about the business, and one of the points he brought up was the marketing of disposable razors. The old-fashioned steel safety razor, the guy admitted cheerfully, was a much better product: it was more durable, less expensive, and gave a better shave than disposable razors. Unfortunately, it didn't make the kind of profits for the razor industry that the latter wanted, and so the job of the advertising company was to convince shavers that they really wanted to spend more money on a worse product instead.

I know it may startle some people to hear a luxuriantly bearded archdruid talk about shaving, but I do have a certain amount of experience with the process — though admittedly it's been a while. The executive was quite correct: an old-fashioned safety razor with interchangeable blades gives better shaves than a disposable. What's more, an old-fashioned safety razor combined with a shaving brush, a cake of shaving soap, a mug and a bit of hot water from the teakettle produces a shaving experience that's vastly better, in every sense, than what you'll get from squirting chemical-laced foam out of a disposable can and then scraping your face with a disposable razor; it takes the same amount of time, costs much less on a per-shave basis, and has a drastically smaller ecological footprint to boot.

Notice also the difference in the scale and complexity of the technological suites needed to maintain these two ways of shaving. To shave with a safety razor and shaving soap, you need the metallurgical suite that produces razors, the very simple household-chemistry suite that produces soap, the ability to make pottery and brushes, and some way to heat water. To shave with a disposable razor and a can of squirt-on shaving foam, you need fossil fuels for plastic feedstocks, chemical plants to manufacture the plastic and the foam, the whole range of technologies needed to manufacture and fill the pressurized can, and so on — all so that you can count on getting an inferior shave at a higher price, and the razor industry can boost its quarterly profits.

That's a small and arguably silly example of a vast and far from silly issue. These days, when you see the words "new and improved" on a product, rather more often than not, the only thing that's been improved is the bottom line of the company that's trying to sell it to you. When you hear equivalent claims about some technology that's being marketed to society as a whole, rather than sold to you personally, the same rule applies at least as often. That's one of the things that drove the enthusiastic conversations on this blog's comment page last week, as readers came out of hiding to confess that they, too, had stopped using this or that piece of cutting-edge, up-to-date, hypermodern trash, and replaced it with some sturdy, elegant, user-friendly device from an earlier decade which works better and lacks the downsides of the newer item.

What, after all, defines a change as "progress"? There's a wilderness of ambiguities hidden in that apparently simple word. The popular notion of progress presupposes that there's an inherent dynamic to history, that things change, or tend to change, or at the very least ought to change, from worse to better over time. That presupposition then gets flipped around into the even more dubious claim that just because something's new, it must be better than whatever it replaced. Move from there to specific examples, and all of a sudden it's necessary to deal with competing claims—if there are two hot new technologies on the market, is option A more progressive than option B, or vice versa? The answer, of course, is that whichever of them manages to elbow the other aside will be retroactively awarded the coveted title of the next step in the march of progress.

That was exactly the process by which the appropriate tech of the 1970s was shoved aside and buried in the memory hole of our culture. In its heyday, appropriate tech was as cutting-edge as anything you care to name, a rapidly advancing field pushed forward by brilliant young engineers and innovative startups, and it saw itself (and presented itself to the world) as the wave of the future. In the wake of the Reagan-Thatcher counterrevolution of the 1980s, though, it was retroactively stripped of its progressive label and consigned to the dustbin of the past. Technologies that had been lauded in the media as brilliantly innovative in 1978 were thus being condemned in the same media as Luddite throwbacks by 1988. If that abrupt act of redefinition reminds any of my readers of the way history got rewritten in George Orwell's *1984*—"Oceania has never been allied with Eurasia" and the like—well, let's just say the parallel was noticed at the time, too.

The same process on a much smaller scale can be traced with equal clarity in the replacement of the safety razor and shaving soap with the disposable razor and squirt-can shaving foam. In what sense is the latter, which wastes more resources and generates more trash in the process of giving users a worse shave at a higher price, more progressive than the former? Merely the fact that it's been awarded that title by advertising and the media. If razor companies could make more money by reintroducing the Roman habit of scraping beard hairs off the face with a chunk of pumice, no doubt that would quickly be proclaimed as the last word in cutting-edge, up-to-date hypermodernity, too.

Behind the mythological image of the relentless and inevitable forward march of technology-in-the-singular in the grand cause of progress, in other words, lies a murky underworld of crass commercial motives and no-holds-barred struggles over which of the available technologies will get the funding and marketing that will define it as the next great step in progress. That's as true of major technological programs as it is of shaving supplies. Some of my readers are old enough, as I am, to remember when supersonic airliners and undersea habitats were the next great steps in progress, until all of a sudden they weren't, and we may not be all that far from the point at which space travel and nuclear power will go the way of Sealab and the Concorde.

In today's industrial societies, we don't talk about that. It's practically taboo these days to mention the long, long list of waves of the future that abruptly stalled and rolled back out to sea without delivering on their promoters' overblown promises. Remind people that the same rhetoric currently being used to prop up faith in space travel, nuclear power, or some other grand technological project was lavished just as thickly on these earlier failures, and you can pretty much expect to have that comment shouted down as an irrelevancy if the other people in the conversation don't simply turn their backs and pretend they never heard you say anything at all.

They have to do something of the sort, because the alternative is to admit that what we call "progress" isn't the impersonal, unstoppable force of nature that industrial culture's ideology insists it must be. Pay attention to the grand technological projects that failed, compare them with those that are failing now, and it's impossible to keep ignoring certain crucial if hugely unpopular points. To begin with technological progress is a function of collective choices — do we fund Sealab or the Apollo program? Supersonic transports or urban light rail? Energy conservation and appropriate tech or an endless series of wars in the Middle East?

No impersonal force makes those decisions; individuals and institutions make them, and then use the rhetoric of impersonal progress to cloak the political and financial agendas that guide the decision-making process.

What's more, even if the industrial world chooses to invest its resources in a project, the laws of physics and economics determine whether the project is going to work. The Concorde is the poster child here, a technological success that was also a complete economic flop, a white elephant that could never even cover its own operating costs. Like nuclear power, it was only viable given huge and continuing government subsidies, and since the strategic benefits Britain and France got from having Concordes in the air were nothing like so great as those they got from having an independent source of raw material for nuclear weapons, it's not hard to see why the subsidies went where they did.

That is to say, when something is being lauded as the next great step forward in the glorious march of progress leading humanity to a better world someday, those who haven't drunk themselves tipsy on folk mythology need to keep three things in mind. The first is that the next great step (etc.) might not actually work when it's brought down out of the billowing clouds of overheated rhetoric into the cold hard world of everyday life. The second is that even if it does work, the next great step (etc.) may be an inferior product, and do a less effective job of meeting human needs than whatever it's supposed to replace. The third is that when it comes right down to it, to label something as the next great step (etc.) is just a sales pitch, an overblown and increasingly trite way of saying "You really ought to buy this."

Those necessary critiques, in turn, are all implicit in the project of deliberate technological regress. Get past the thoughtstopping rhetoric that insists "you can't turn back the clock" — to rephrase a comment of G.K. Chesterton's, most people turn back the clock every fall, so that's hardly a valid objection — and it becomes hard not to notice that "progress" is just a label for whatever choices happen to have been made by governments and corporations, with or without input from the rest of us, and that if we don't like the choices that have been made for us in the name of progress, we can choose something else.

Now of course it's possible to stuff that sort of thinking back into the straitjacket of progress, and claim that progress is chugging along just fine, and all we have to do is get it back on the proper track, or what have you. This is a very common sort of argument, and one that's been used over and over again by critics of this or that candidate for the next great step (etc.). The problem with that argument, as I see it, is that it may occasionally win battles but it pretty consistently loses the war; by failing to challenge the folk mythology of progress and the agendas enshrined by that mythology, it guarantees that no matter what technology or policy or program gets put into place, it'll end up leading the same place as all the others before it.

That's the trap hardwired into the contemporary faith in progress. Once you buy into the notion that the specific choices made by industrial societies over the last three centuries or so are something more than the projects that happened to win out in the struggle for wealth and power, once you let yourself believe that there's a teleology to it all — that there's some objectively definable goal called "progress" that these choices do a better or worse job of furthering — you've just made it much harder to ask the hard but necessary questions about where this thing called "progress" is going. The word "progress," remember, means going further in the same direction, and it's precisely questions about the direction that industrial society is going that most need to be asked.

I'd like to suggest, in fact, that going further in the direction we've been going isn't a particularly bright idea just now. Going further in the direction we've been going means trying to expand per capita energy consumption in an era when fossil fuel reserves are depleting fast and the global economy is creaking and shuddering under the burden of increasingly costly fuel extraction. It means dumping ever more waste into the biosphere when the consequences of previous dumping are already bidding fair to threaten the survival of entire nations. On a less global scale, it also means shoddier products with louder advertising in a race to the bottom that's already gone very far.

Look at a trend that affects your life right now, and extrapolate it out in a straight line; that's what going further in the same direction means. If that appeals to you, dear reader, then you're certainly welcome to it; I have to say it doesn't do much for me.

It's only from within the folk mythology of progress that we have no choice but to accept the endless prolongation of current trends. Right now, as individuals, we can choose to shrug and walk away from the latest hypermodern trash, and do something else instead. Later on, on the far side of the crisis of our time, it may be possible to take the same logic further, and make deliberate technological regress a recognized policy option for organizations, communities, and whole nations — but that will depend on whether individuals do the thing first, and show that it's a workable option. We'll talk more about where that strategy might lead in next week's post.

404: THE EXTERNALITY TRAP, OR, HOW PROGRESS COMMITS SUICIDE

(Originally published 25 February 2015)

I've commented more than once in these essays about the cooperative dimension of writing: the way that even the most solitary of writers inevitably takes part in what Mortimer Adler used to call the Great Conversation, the flow of ideas and insights across the centuries that's responsible for most of what we call culture. Sometimes that conversation takes place second- or third-hand— for example, when ideas from two old books collide in an author's mind and give rise to a third book, which will eventually carry the fusion to someone else further down the stream of time—but sometimes it's far more direct.

Last week's post here brought an example of the latter kind. My attempt to cut through the ambiguities surrounding that slippery word "progress" sparked a lively discussion on the comments page of my blog about just exactly what counted as progress, what factors made one change "progressive" while another was denied that label. In the midst of it all, one of my readers—tip of the archdruidical hat to Jonathan—proposed an unexpected definition: what makes a change qualify as progress, he suggested, is that it increases the externalization of costs.

I've been thinking about that definition since Jonathan proposed it, and it seems to me that it points up a crucial and mostly unrecognized dimension of the crisis of our time. To make sense of it, though, it's going to be necessary to delve briefly into economic jargon.

Economists use the term "externalities" to refer to the costs of an economic activity that aren't paid by either party in an exchange, but are pushed off onto somebody else. You won't hear a lot of talk about externalities these days; it many circles, it's considered impolite to mention them, but they're a pervasive presence in contemporary life, and play a very large role in some of the most intractable problems of our age. Some of those problems were discussed by Garret Hardin in his famous essay on the tragedy of the commons, and more recently by Elinor Ostrom in her studies of how that tragedy can be avoided; still, I'm not sure how often it's recognized that the phenomena they discussed applies not just to commons systems, but to societies as a whole—especially to societies like ours.

An example may be useful here. Let's imagine a blivet factory, which turns out three-prong, two-slot blivets in pallet loads for customers. The blivet-making process, like manufacturing of every other kind, produces waste as well as blivets, and we'll assume for the sake of the example that blivet waste is moderately toxic and causes health problems in people who ingest it. The blivet factory produces one barrel of blivet waste for every pallet load of blivets it ships. The cheapest option for dealing with the waste, and thus the option that economists favor, is to dump it into the river that flows past the factory.

Notice what happens as a result of this choice. The blivet manufacturer has maximized his own benefit from the manufacturing process, by avoiding the expense of finding some other way to deal with all those barrels of blivet waste. His customers also benefit, because blivets cost less than they would if the cost of waste disposal was factored into the price. On the other hand, the costs of dealing with the blivet waste don't vanish like so much twinkle dust; they are imposed on the people downstream who get their drinking water from the river, or from aquifers that receive water from the river, and who suffer from health problems because there's blivet waste in their water. The blivet manufacturer is externalizing the cost of waste disposal; his increased profits are being paid for at a remove by the increased health care costs of everyone downstream.

That's how externalities work. Back in the days when people actually talked about the downsides of economic growth, there was a lot of discussion of how to handle externalities, and not just on the leftward end of the spectrum. I recall a thoughtful book titled *TANSTAAFL*—that's an acronym, for those who don't know their Heinlein, for "There Ain't No Such Thing As A Free Lunch"—which argued, on solid libertarian-conservative grounds, that the environment could best be preserved by making sure that everyone paid full sticker price for the externalities they generated. Today's crop of pseudoconservatives, of course, turned their back on all this a long time ago, and insist at the top of their lungs on their allegedly God-given right to externalize as many costs as they possibly can. This is all the more ironic in that most pseudoconservatives claim to worship a God who said some very specific things about "what ye do to the least of these," but that's a subject for a different post.

Economic life in the industrial world these days can be described, without too much inaccuracy, as an arrangement set up to allow a privileged minority to externalize nearly all their costs onto the rest of society while pocketing as much as possible the benefits themselves. That's come in for a certain amount of discussion in recent years, but I'm not sure how many of the people who've participated in those discussions have given any thought to the role that technological progress plays in facilitating the internalization of benefits and the externalization of costs that drive today's increasingly inegalitarian societies. Here again, an example will be helpful.

Before the invention of blivet-making machinery, let's say, blivets were made by old-fashioned blivet makers, who hammered them out on iron blivet anvils in shops that were to be found in every town and village. Like other handicrafts, blivet-making was a living rather than a ticket to wealth; blivet makers invested their own time and muscular effort in their craft, and turned out enough in the way of blivets to meet the demand. Notice also the effect on the production of blivet waste. Since blivets were being made one at a time rather than in pallet loads, the total amount of waste was smaller; the conditions of handicraft production also meant that blivet makers and their families were more likely to be exposed to the blivet waste than anyone else, and so had an incentive to invest the extra effort and expense to dispose of it properly. Since blivet makers were ordinary craftspeople rather than millionaires, furthermore, they weren't as likely to be able to buy exemption from local health laws.

The invention of the mechanical blivet press changed that picture completely. Since one blivet press could do as much work as fifty blivet makers, the income that would have gone to those fifty blivet makers and their families went instead to one factory owner and his stockholders, with as small a share as possible set aside for the wage laborers who operate the blivet press. The factory owner and stockholders had no incentive to pay for the proper disposal of the blivet waste, either—quite the contrary, since having to meet the disposal costs cut into their profit, buying off local governments was much cheaper, and if the harmful effects of blivet waste were known, you can bet that the owner and shareholders all lived well upstream from the factory.

Notice also that a blivet manufacturer who paid a living wage to his workers and covered the costs of proper waste disposal would have to charge a higher price for blivets than one who did neither, and thus would be driven out of business by his more ruthless competitor. Externalities aren't simply made possible by technological progress, in other words; they're the inevitable result of technological progress in a market economy, because externalizing the costs of production is in most cases the most effective way to outcompete rival firms, and the firm that succeeds in externalizing the largest share of its costs is the most likely to prosper and survive.

Each further step in the progress of blivet manufacturing, in turn, tightened the same screw another turn. Today, to finish up the metaphor, the entire global supply of blivets is made in a dozen factories in distant Slobbovia, where sweatshop labor under ghastly working conditions and the utter absence of environmental regulations make the business of blivet fabrication more profitable than anywhere else. The blivets are as shoddily made as possible; the entire blivet supply chain from the open-pit mines worked by slave labor that provide the raw materials to the big box stores with part-time, poorly paid staff selling blivetronic technology to the masses is a human and environmental disaster. Every possible cost has been externalized, so that the two multinational corporations that dominate the global blivet industry can maintain their profit margins and pay absurdly high salaries to their CEOs.

That in itself is bad enough, but let's broaden the focus to include the whole systems in which blivet fabrication takes place: the economy as a whole, society as a whole, and the biosphere as a whole. The impact of technology on blivet fabrication in a market economy has predictable and well understood consequences for each of these whole systems, which can be summed up precisely in the language we've already used. In order to maximize its own profitability and return on shareholder investment, the blivet industry externalizes costs in every available direction. Since nobody else wants to bear those costs, either, most of them end up being passed onto the whole systems just named, because the economy, society, and the biosphere have no voice in today's economic decisions.

Like the costs of dealing with blivet waste, though, the other externalized costs of blivet manufacture don't go away just because they're externalized. As externalities increase, they tend to degrade the whole systems onto which they're dumped—the economy, society, and the biosphere. This is where the trap closes tight, because blivet manufacturing exists within those whole systems, and can't be carried out unless all three systems are sufficiently intact to function in their usual way. As those systems degrade, their ability to function degrades also, and eventually one or more of them breaks down—the economy plunges into a depression, the society disintegrates into anarchy or totalitarianism, the biosphere shifts abruptly into a new mode that lacks adequate rainfall for crops—and the manufacture of blivets stops because the whole system that once supported it has stopped doing so.

Notice how this works out from the perspective of someone who's benefiting from the externalization of costs by the blivet industry—the executives and stockholders in a blivet corporation, let's say. As far as they're concerned, until very late in the process, everything is fine and dandy: each new round of technological improvements in blivet fabrication increases their profits, and if each such step in the onward march of progress also means that working class jobs are eliminated or offshored, democratic institutions implode, toxic waste builds up in the food chain, or what have you, hey, that's not their problem—and after all, that's just the normal creative destruction of capitalism, right?

That sort of insouciance is easy for at least three reasons. First, the impacts of externalities on whole systems can pop up a very long way from the blivet factories. Second, in a market economy, everyone else is externalizing their costs as enthusiastically as the blivet industry, and so it's easy for blivet manufacturers (and everyone else) to insist that whatever's going wrong is not their fault. Third, and most crucially, whole systems as stable and enduring as economies, societies, and biospheres can absorb a lot of damage before they tip over into instability. The process of externalization of costs can thus run for a very long time, and become entrenched as a basic economic habit, long before it becomes clear to anyone that continuing along the same route is a recipe for disaster.

Even when externalized costs have begun to take a visible toll on the economy, society, and the biosphere, furthermore, any attempt to reverse course faces nearly insurmountable obstacles. Those who profit from the existing order of things can be counted on to fight tooth and nail for the right to keep externalizing their costs: after all, they have to pay the full price for any reduction in their ability to externalize costs, while the benefits created by not imposing those costs on whole systems are shared among all participants in the economy, society, and the biosphere respectively. Nor is it necessarily easy to trace back the causes of any given whole-system disruption to specific externalities benefiting specific people or industries. It's rather like loading hanging weights onto a chain; sooner or later, as the amount of weight hung on the chain goes up, the chain is going to break, but the link that breaks may be far from the last weight that pushed things over the edge, and every other weight on the chain made its own contribution to the end result

A society that's approaching collapse because too many externalized costs have been loaded onto on the whole systems that support it thus shows certain highly distinctive symptoms. Things are going wrong with the economy, society, and the biosphere, but nobody seems to be able to figure out why; the measurements economists use to determine prosperity show contradictory results, with those that measure the profitability of individual corporations and industries giving much better readings those that measure the performance of whole systems; the rich are convinced that everything is fine, while outside the narrowing circles of wealth and privilege, people talk in low voices about the rising spiral of problems that beset them from every side. If this doesn't sound familiar to you, dear reader, you probably need to get out more.

At this point it may be helpful to sum up the argument I've developed here:

a) Every increase in technological complexity tends also to increase the opportunities for externalizing the costs of economic activity;

b) Market forces make the externalization of costs mandatory rather than optional, since economic actors that fail to externalize costs will tend to be outcompeted by those that do;

c) In a market economy, as all economic actors attempt to externalize as many costs as possible, externalized costs will tend to be passed on preferentially and progressively to whole systems such as the economy, society, and the biosphere, which provide necessary support for economic activity but have no voice in economic decisions;

d) Given unlimited increases in technological complexity, there is no necessary limit to the loading of externalized costs onto whole systems short of systemic collapse;

e) Unlimited increases in technological complexity in a market economy thus necessarily lead to the progressive degradation of the whole systems that support economic activity;

f) Technological progress in a market economy is therefore self-terminating, and ends in collapse.

Now of course there are plenty of arguments that could be deployed against this modest proposal. For example, it could be argued that progress doesn't have to generate a rising tide of externalities. The difficulty with this argument is that externalization of costs isn't an accidental side effect of technology but an essential aspect—it's not a bug, it's a feature. Every technology is a means of externalizing some cost that would otherwise be borne by a human body. Even something as simple as a hammer takes the wear and tear that would otherwise affect the heel of your hand, let's say, and transfers it to something else: directly, to the hammer; indirectly, to the biosphere, by way of the trees that had to be cut down to make the charcoal to smelt the iron, the plants that were shoveled aside to get the ore, and so on.

For reasons that are ultimately thermodynamic in nature, the more complex a technology becomes, the more costs it generates. In order to outcompete a simpler technology, each more complex technology has to externalize a significant proportion of its additional costs, in order to compete against the simpler technology. In the case of such contemporary hypercomplex technosystems as the internet, the process of externalizing costs has gone so far, through so many tangled interrelationships, that it's remarkably difficult to figure out exactly who's paying for how much of the gargantuan inputs needed to keep the thing running. This lack of transparency feeds the illusion that large systems are cheaper than small ones, by making externalities of scale look like economies of scale.

It might be argued instead that a sufficiently stringent regulatory environment, forcing economic actors to absorb all the costs of their activities instead of externalizing them onto others, would be able to stop the degradation of whole systems while still allowing technological progress to continue. The difficulty here is that increased externalization of costs is what makes progress profitable. As just noted, all other things being equal, a complex technology will on average be more expensive in real terms than a simpler technology, for the simple fact that each additional increment of complexity has to be paid for by an investment of energy and other forms of real capital.

Strip complex technologies of the subsidies that transfer some of their costs to the government, the perverse regulations that transfer some of their costs to the rest of the economy, the bad habits of environmental abuse and neglect that transfer some of their costs to the biosphere, and so on, and pretty soon you're looking at hard economic limits to technological complexity, as people forced to pay the full sticker price for complex technologies maximize their benefits by choosing simpler, more affordable options instead. A regulatory environment sufficiently strict to keep technology from accelerating to collapse would thus bring technological progress to a halt by making it unprofitable.

Notice, however, the flipside of the same argument: a society that chose to stop progressing technologically could maintain itself indefinitely, so long as its technologies weren't dependent on nonrenewable resources or the like. The costs imposed by a stable technology on the economy, society, and the biosphere would be more or less stable, rather than increasing over time, and it would therefore be much easier to figure out how to balance out the negative effects of those externalities and maintain the whole system in a steady state. Societies that treated technological progress as an option rather than a requirement, and recognized the downsides to increasing complexity, could also choose to reduce complexity in one area in order to increase it in another, and so on—or they could just raise a monument to the age of progress, and go do something else instead.

The logic suggested here requires a comprehensive rethinking of most of the contemporary world's notions about technology, progress, and the good society. We'll begin that discussion in future posts—after, that is, we discuss a second dimension of progress that came out of last week's discussion.

405: PEAK MEANINGLESSNESS
(Originally published 4 March 2015)

Last week's discussion of externalities—costs of doing business that get dumped onto the economy, the community, or the environment, so that those doing the dumping can make a bigger profit—is, I'm glad to say, not the first time this issue has been raised recently. The long silence that closed around such things three decades ago is finally cracking; they're being mentioned again, and not just by archdruids. One of my readers—tip of the archdruidical hat to Jay McInerney—noted an article in *Grist* a while back that pointed out the awkward fact thatnone of the twenty biggest industries in today's world could break even, much less make a profit, if they had to pay for the damage they do to the environment.

Now of course the conventional wisdom these days interprets that statement to mean that it's unfair to make those industries pay for the costs they impose on the rest of us—after all, they have a God-given right to profit at everyone else's expense, right? That's certainly the attitude of fracking firms in North Dakota, who recently proposed that they ought to be exempted from the state's rules on dumping radioactive waste, because following the rules would cost them too much money. That the costs externalized by the fracking industry will sooner or later be paid by others, as radionuclides in fracking waste work their way up the food chain and start producing cancer clusters, is of course not something anyone in the industry or the media is interested in discussing.

Watch this sort of thing, and you can see the chasm opening up under the foundations of industrial society. Externalized costs don't just go away; one way or another, they're going to be paid, and costs that don't appear on a company's balance sheet still affect the economy. That's the argument of *The Limits to Growth*, still the most accurate (and thus inevitably the most reviled) of the studies that tried unavailingly to turn industrial society away from its suicidal path: on a finite planet, once an inflection point is passed, the costs of economic growth rise faster than growth does, and sooner or later force the global economy to its knees.

The tricks of accounting that let corporations pretend that their externalized costs vanish into thin air don't change that bleak prognosis. Quite the contrary, the pretense that externalities don't matter just makes it harder for a society in crisis to recognize the actual source of its troubles. I've come to think that that's the unmentioned context behind a dispute currently roiling those unhallowed regions where economists lurk in the shrubbery: the debate over secular stagnation.

Secular stagnation? That's the concept, unmentionable until recently, that the global economy could stumble into a rut of slow, no, or negative growth, and stay there for years. There are still plenty of economists who insist that this can't happen, which is rather funny, really, when you consider that this has basically been the state of the global economy since 2009. (My back-of-the-envelope calculations suggest, in fact, that if you subtract the hallucinatory paper wealth manufactured by derivatives and similar forms of financial gamesmanship from the world's GDP, the production of nonfinancial goods and services worldwide has actually been declining since before the 2008 housing crash.)

Even among those who admit that what's happening can indeed happen, there's no consensus as to how or why such a thing could occur. On the off chance that any mainstream economists are lurking in the shrubbery in the even more unhallowed regions where archdruids utter unspeakable heresies, and green wizards clink mugs of homebrewed beer together and bay at the moon, I have a suggestion to offer: the most important cause of secular stagnation is the increasing impact of externalities on the economy. The dishonest macroeconomic bookkeeping that leads economists to think that externalized costs go away because they're not entered into anyone's ledger books doesn't actually make them disappear; instead, they become an unrecognized burden on the economy as a whole, an unfelt headwind blowing with hurricane force in the face of economic growth.

Thus there's a profound irony in the insistence by North Dakota fracking firms that they ought to be allowed to externalize even more of their costs in order to maintain their profit margin. If I'm right, the buildup of externalized costs is what's causing the ongoing slowdown in economic activity worldwide that's driving down commodity prices, forcing interest rates in many countries to zero or below, and resurrecting the specter of deflationary depression. The fracking firms in question thus want to respond to the collapse in oil prices — a result of secular stagnation — by doing even more of what's causing secular stagnation. To say that this isn't likely to end well is to understate the case considerably.

In the real world, of course, mainstream economists don't listen to suggestions from archdruids, and fracking firms, like every other business concern these days, can be expected to put their short-term cash flow ahead of the survival of their industry, or for that matter of industrial civilization as a whole. Thus I propose to step aside from the subject of economic externalities for a moment — though I'll be returning to it at intervals as we proceed with this sequence of posts — in order to discuss a subtler and less crassly financial form of the same phenomenon.

That form came in for discussion in the same post two weeks ago that brought the issue of externalities into this blog's ongoing conversation. Quite a few readers commented about the many ways in which things labeled "more advanced," "more progressive," and the like were actually less satisfactory and less effective at meeting human needs than the allegedly more primitive technologies they replaced. Some of those comments focused, and quite sensibly, on the concrete examples, but others pondered the ways that today's technology fails systematically at meeting certain human needs, and reflected on the underlying causes for that failure. One of my readers — tip of the archdruidical hat here to Ruben — gave an elegant frame for that discussion by suggesting that the peak of technological complexity in our time may also be described as peak meaninglessness.

I'd like to take the time to unpack that phrase. In the most general sense, technologies can be divided into two broad classes, which we can respectively call tools and prosthetics. The difference is a matter of function. A tool expands human potential, giving people the ability to do things they couldn't otherwise do. A prosthetic, on the other hand, replaces human potential, doing something that under normal circumstances, people can do just as well for themselves. Most discussions of technology these days focus on tools, but the vast majority of technologies that shape the lives of people in a modern industrial society are not tools but prosthetics.

Prosthetics have a definite value, to be sure. Consider an artificial limb, the sort of thing on which the concept of technology-as-prosthetic is modeled. If you've lost a leg in an accident, say, an artificial leg is well worth having; it replaces a part of ordinary human potential that you don't happen to have any more, and enables you to do things that other people can do with their own leg. Imagine, though, that some clever marketer were to convince people to have their legs cut off so that they could be fitted for artificial legs. Imagine, furthermore, that the advertising for artificial legs became so pervasive, and so successful, that nearly everybody became convinced that human legs were hopelessly old-fashioned and ugly, and rushed out to get their legs amputated so they could walk around on artificial legs.

Then, of course, the manufacturers of artificial arms got into the same sort of marketing, followed by the makers of sex toys. Before long you'd have a society in which most people were gelded quadruple amputees fitted with artificial limbs and rubber genitals, who spent all their time talking about the wonderful things they could do with their prostheses. Only in the darkest hours of the night, when the TV was turned off, might some of them wonder why it was that a certain had-to-define numbness had crept into all their interactions with other people and the rest of the world.

In a very real sense, that's the way modern industrial society has reshaped and deformed human life for its more privileged inmates. Take any human activity, however humble or profound, and some clever marketer has found a way to insert a piece of technology in between the person and the activity. You can't simply bake bread—a simple, homely, pleasant activity that people have done themselves for thousands of years using their hands and a few simple handmade tools; no, you have to have a bread machine, into which you dump a prepackaged mix and some liquid, push a button, and stand there being bored while it does the work for you, if you don't farm out the task entirely to a bakery and get the half-stale industrially extruded product that passes for bread these days.

Now of course the bread machine manufacturers and the bakeries pitch their products to the clueless masses by insisting that nobody has time to bake their own bread any more. Ivan Illich pointed out in *Energy and Equity* a long time ago the logical fallacy here, which is that using a bread machine or buying from a bakery is only faster if you don't count the time you have to spend earning the money needed to pay for it, power it, provide it with overpriced prepackaged mixes, repair it, clean it, etc., etc., etc. Illich's discussion focused on automobiles; he pointed out that if you take the distance traveled by the average American auto in a year, and divide that by the total amount of time spent earning the money to pay for the auto, fuel, maintenance, insurance, etc., plus all the other time eaten up by tending to the auto in various ways, the average American car goes about 3.5 miles an hour: about the same pace, that is, that an ordinary human being can walk.

If this seems somehow reminiscent of last week's discussion of externalities, dear reader, it should. The claim that technology saves time and labor only seems to make sense if you ignore a whole series of externalities—in this case, the time you have to put into earning the money to pay for the technology and into coping with whatever requirements, maintenance needs, and side effects the technology has. Have you ever noticed that the more "time-saving technologies" you bring into your life, the less free time you have? This is why—and it's also why the average medieval peasant worked shorter hours, had more days off, and kept a larger fraction of the value of his labor than you do.

Something else is being externalized by prosthetic technology, though, and it's that additional factor that gives Ruben's phrase "peak meaninglessness" its punch. What are you doing, really, when you use a bread machine? You're not baking bread; the machine is doing that. You're dumping a prepackaged mix and some water into a machine, closing the lid, pushing a button, and going away to do something else. Fair enough—but what is this "something else" that you're doing? In today's industrial societies, odds are you're going to go use another piece of prosthetic technology, which means that once again, you're not actually doing anything. A machine is doing something for you. You can push that button and walk away, but again, what are you going to do with your time? Use another machine?

The machines that industrial society uses to give this infinite regress somewhere to stop—televisions, video games, and computers hooked up to the internet—simply take the same process to its ultimate extreme. Whatever you think you're doing when you're sitting in front of one of these things, what you're actually doing is staring at little colored pictures on a glass screen and pushing some buttons. All things considered, this is a profoundly boring activity, which is why the little colored pictures jump around all the time; that's to keep your nervous system so far off balance that you don't notice just how tedious it is to spend hours at a time staring at little colored pictures on a screen.

I can't help but laugh when people insist that the internet is an information-rich environment. It's quite the opposite, actually: all you get from it is the very narrow trickle of verbal, visual, and auditory information that can squeeze through the digital bottleneck and turn into little colored pictures on a glass screen. The best way to experience this is to engage in a media fast—a period in which you deliberately cut yourself off from all electronic media for a week or more, preferably in a quiet natural environment. If you do that, you'll find that it can take two or three days, or even more, before your numbed and dazzled nervous system recovers far enough that you can begin to tap in to the ocean of sensory information and sensual delight that surrounds you at every moment. It's only then, furthermore, that you can start to think your own thoughts and dream your own dreams, instead of just rehashing whatever the little colored pictures tell you.

A movement of radical French philosophers back in the 1960s, the Situationists, argued that modern industrial society is basically a scheme to convince people to hand over their own human capabilities to the industrial machine, so that imitations of those capabilities can be sold back to them at premium prices. It was a useful analysis then, and it's even more useful now, when the gap between realities and representations has become even more drastic than it was back then. These days, as often as not, what gets sold to people isn't even an imitation of some human capability, but an abstract representation of it, an arbitrary marker with only the most symbolic connection to what it represents.

This is one of the reasons why I think it's deeply mistaken to claim that Americans are materialistic. Americans are arguably the least materialistic people in the world; no actual materialist—no one who had the least appreciation for actual physical matter and its sensory and sensuous qualities—could stand the vile plastic tackiness of America's built environment and consumer economy for a fraction of a second. Americans don't care in the least about matter; they're happy to buy even the most ugly, uncomfortable, shoddily made and absurdly overpriced consumer products you care to imagine, so long as they've been convinced that having those products symbolizes some abstract quality they want, such as happiness, freedom, sexual pleasure, or what have you.

Then they wonder, in the darkest hours of the night, why all the things that are supposed to make them happy and satisfied somehow never manage to do anything of the kind. Of course there's a reason for that, too, which is that happy and satisfied people don't keep on frantically buying products in a quest for happiness and satisfaction. Still, the little colored pictures keep showing them images of people who are happy and satisfied because they guzzle the right brand of tasteless fizzy sugar water, and pay for the right brand of shoddily made half-disposable clothing, and keep watching the little colored pictures: that last above all else. "Tune in tomorrow" is the most important product that every media outlet sells, and they push it every minute of every day on every stop and key.

That is to say, between my fantasy of voluntary amputees eagerly handing over the cash for the latest models of prosthetic limbs, and the reality of life in a modern industrial society, the difference is simply in the less permanent nature of the alterations imposed on people here and now. It's easier to talk people into amputating their imaginations than it is to convince them to amputate their limbs, but it's also a good deal easier to reverse the surgery.

What gives this even more importance than it would otherwise have, in turn, is that all this is happening in a society that's hopelessly out of touch with the realities that support its existence, and that relies on bookkeeping tricks of the sort discussed toward the beginning of this essay to maintain the fantasy that it's headed somewhere other than history's well-used compost bin. The externalization of the mind and the imagination plays just as important a role in maintaining that fantasy as the externalization of costs— and the cold mechanical heart of the externalization of the mind and imagination is *mediation*, the insertion of technological prosthetics into the space between the individual and the world. We'll talk more about that in next week's post.

406: THE PROSTHETIC IMAGINATION

(Originally published 11 March 2015)

Two news stories and an op-ed piece in the media in recent days provide a useful introduction to the theme of this week's post here on *The Archdruid Report*. The first news story followed the official announcement that the official unemployment rate here in the United States dropped to 5.5% last month. This was immediately hailed by pundits and politicians as proof that the recession we weren't in is over at last, and the happy days that never went away are finally here again.

This jubilation makes perfect sense so long as you don't happen to know that the official unemployment rate in the United States doesn't actually depend on the number of people who are out of work. What it indicates is the percentage of US residents who are officially classified as looking for work. Right now there are a huge number of Americans who have spent years trying to find work without success, and would count as unemployed by any measure except the one used by the US government these days. As far as officialdom is concerned, they are nonpersons in very nearly an Orwellian sense, their existence erased to preserve a politically expedient fiction of prosperity.

How many of these economic nonpersons are there in the United States today? That figure's not easy to find amid the billowing statistical smokescreens. Still, it's worth noting that 92,898,000 Americans of working age are not currently in the work force—that is, more than 47 per cent of the working age population. If you spend time around people who don't belong to this nation's privileged classes, you already know that a lot of those people would gladly take jobs if there were jobs to be had, but again, that's not something that makes it through the murk.

We could spend quite a bit of time talking about the galaxy

of ways in which economic statistics are finessed and/or fabricated these days, but the points already raised are enough for the present purpose. Let's move on. The op-ed piece comes from erstwhile environmentalist Stewart Brand, whose long journey from editing *CoEvolution Quarterly* to channeling Bjorn Lomborg is as perfect a microcosm of the moral collapse of 20th century American environmentalism as you could hope to find. Brand's latest piece claims that despite all evidence to the contrary—and of course there's quite a bit of that these days—the environment is doing just fine: the economy has decoupled from resource use in recent decades, at least here in America, and so we can continue to wallow in high-tech consumer goodies without worrying about what we're doing to the planet.

There's a savage irony in the fact that in 1975, when his magazine was the go-to place to read about the latest ideas in systems theory and environmental science, Brand could have pointed out the gaping flaw in that argument in a Sausalito minute. Increasing prosperity in the United States has "decoupled" from resource use for two reasons: first, only a narrowing circle of privileged Americans get to see any of the paper prosperity we're discussing—the standard of living for most people in this country has been contracting steadily for four decades—and second, the majority of consumer goods used in the United States are produced overseas, and so the resource use and environmental devastation involved in manufacturing the goodies we consume so freely takes place somewhere else.

That is to say, what Brand likes to call decoupling is our old friend, the mass production of ecological externalities. Brand can boast about prosperity without environmental cost because the great majority of the costs are being carried by somebody else, somewhere else, and so don't find their way into his calculations. The poor American neighborhoods where people struggle to get by without jobs are as absent from his vision of the world as they are from the official statistics; the smokestacks, outflow pipes, toxic-waste dumps, sweatshopped factories, and open-pit mines worked by slave labor that prop up his high-tech lifestyle are overseas, so they don't show up on US statistics either. As far as Brand is concerned, that means they don't count.

We could talk more about the process by which a man who first became famous for pressuring NASA into releasing a photo of the whole earth is now insisting that the only view that matters is the one from his living room window, but let's go on. The other news item is the simplest and, in a bleak sort of way, the funniest of the lot. According to recent reports, state government officials in Florida are being forbidden from using the phrase "climate change" when discussing the effects of, whisper it, climate change.

This is all the more mordantly funny because Florida is on the front lines of climate change right now. Even the very modest increases in sea level we've seen so far, driven by thermal expansion and the first rounds of Greenland and Antarctic meltwater, are sending seawater rushing out of the storm sewers into the streets of low-lying parts of coastal Florida towns whenever the tide is high and an onshore wind blows hard enough. As climate change accelerates—and despite denialist handwaving, it does seem to be doing that just now—a lot of expensive waterfront property in Florida is going to end up underwater in more than a financial sense. The state government's response to this clear and present danger? Prevent state officials from talking about it.

We could look at a range of other examples of this same kind, but these three will do for now. What I want to discuss now is what's going on here, and what it implies.

Let's begin with the obvious. In all three of the cases I've cited, an uncomfortable reality is being dismissed by manipulating abstractions. An abstraction called "the unemployment rate" has been defined so that the politicians and bureaucrats who cite it don't have to deal with just how many Americans these days can't get paid employment; an abstraction called "decoupling" and a range of equally abstract (and cherrypicked) measures of environmental health are being deployed so that Brand and his readers don't have to confront the soaring ecological costs of computer technology in particular and industrial society in general; an abstraction called "climate change," finally, is being banned from use by state officials because it does too good a job of connecting certain dots that, for political reasons, Florida politicians don't want people to connect.

To a very real extent, this sort of thing is pervasive in human interaction, and has been since the hoots and grunts of hominin vocalization first linked up with a few crude generalizations in the dazzled mind of an eccentric australopithecine. Human beings everywhere use abstract categories and the words that denote them as handles by which to grab hold of unruly bundles of experience. We do it far more often, and far more automatically, than most of us ever notice. It's only under special circumstances — waking up at night in an unfamiliar room, for example, and finding that the vague somethings around us take a noticeable amount of time to coalesce into ordinary furniture — that the mind's role in assembling the fragmentary data of sensation into the objects of our experience comes to light.

When you look at a tree, for example, it's common sense to think that the tree is sitting out there, and your eyes and mind are just passively receiving a picture of it — but then it's common sense to think that the sun revolves around the earth. In fact, as philosophers and researchers into the psychophysics of sensation both showed a long time ago, what happens is that you get a flurry of fragmentary sense data — green, brown, line, shape, high contrast, low contrast — and your mind constructs a tree out of it, using its own tree-concept (as well as a flurry of related concepts such as "leaf," "branch," "bark," and so on) as a template. You do that with everything you see, and the reason you don't notice it is that it was the very first thing you learned how to do, as a newborn infant, and you've practiced it so often you don't have to think about it any more.

You do the same thing with every representation of a sensory object. Let's take visual art for an example. Back in the 1880s, when the Impressionists first started displaying their paintings, it took many people a real effort to learn how to look at them, and a great many never managed the trick at all. Among those who did, though, it was quite common to hear comments about how this or that painting had taught them to see a landscape, or what have you, in a completely different way. That wasn't just hyperbole: the Impressionists had learned how to look at things in a way that brought out features of their subjects that other people in late 19th century Europe and America had never gotten around to noticing, and highlighted those things in their paintings so forcefully that the viewer had to notice them.

The relation between words and the things they denote is thus much more complex, and much more subjective, than most people ever quite get around to realizing. That's challenging enough when we're talking about objects of immediate experience, where the concept in the observer's mind has the job of fitting fragmentary sense data into a pattern that can be verified by other forms of sense data — in the example of the tree, by walking up to it and confirming by touch that the trunk is in fact where the sense of sight said it was. It gets far more difficult when the raw material that's being assembled by the mind consists of concepts rather than sensory data: when, let's say, you move away from your neighbor Joe, who can't find a job and is about to lose his house, start thinking about all the people in town who are in a similar predicament, and end up dealing with abstract concepts such as unemployment, poverty, the distribution of wealth, and so on.

Difficult or not, we all do this, all the time. There's a common notion that dealing in abstractions is the hallmark of the intellectual, but that puts things almost exactly backwards; it's the ordinary unreflective person who thinks in abstractions most of the time, while the thinker's task is to work back from the abstract category to the raw sensory data on which it's based. That's what the Impressionists did: staring at a snowbank as Monet did, until he could see the rainbow play of colors behind the surface impression of featureless white, and then painting the colors into the representation of the snowbank so that the viewer was shaken out of the trance of abstraction ("snow" = "white") and saw the colors too — first in the painting, and then when looking at actual snow.

Human thinking, and human culture, thus dance constantly between the concrete and the abstract, or to use a slightly different terminology, between immediate experience and a galaxy of forms that reflect experience back in mediated form. It's a delicate balance: too far into the immediate and experience disintegrates into fragmentary sensation; too far from the immediate and experience vanishes into an echo chamber of abstractions mediating one another. The most successful and enduring creations of human culture have tended to be those that maintain the balance. Representational painting is one of those; another is literature. Read the following passage closely:

"Eastward the Barrow-downs rose, ridge behind ridge into the morning, and vanished out of eyesight into a guess: it was no more than a guess of blue and a remote white glimmer blending with the hem of the sky, but it spoke to them, out of memory and old tales, of the high and distant mountains."

By the time you finished reading it, you likely had a very clear sense of what Frodo Baggins and his friends were seeing as they looked off to the east from the hilltop behind Tom Bombadil's house. So did I, as I copied the sentence, and so do most people who read that passage—but no two people see the same image, because the image each of us sees is compounded out of bits of our own remembered experiences. For me, the image that comes to mind has always drawn heavily on the view eastwards from the suburban Seattle neighborhoods where I grew up, across the rumpled landscape to the stark white-topped rampart of the Cascade Mountains. I know for a fact that that wasn't the view that Tolkien himself had in mind when he penned that sentence; I suspect he was thinking of the view across the West Midlands toward the Welsh mountains, which I've never seen; and I wonder what it must be like for someone to read that passage whose concept of ridges and mountains draws on childhood memories of the Urals, the Andes, or Australia's Great Dividing Range instead.

That's one of the ways that literature takes the reader through the mediation of words back around to immediate experience. If I ever do have the chance to stand on a hill in the West Midlands and look off toward the Welsh mountains, Tolkien's words are going to be there with me, pointing me toward certain aspects of the view I might not otherwise have noticed, just as they did in my childhood. It's the same trick the Impressionists managed with a different medium: stretching the possibilities of experience by representing (literally re-presenting) the immediate in a mediated form.

Now think about what happens when that same process is hijacked, using modern technology, for the purpose of behavioral control.

That's what advertising does, and more generally what the mass media do. Think about the fast food company that markets its product under the slogan "I'm loving it," complete with all those images of people sighing with post-orgasmic bliss as they ingest some artificially flavored and colored gobbet of processed pseudofood. Are they loving it? Of course not; they're hack actors being paid to go through the motions of loving it, so that the imagery can be drummed into your brain and drown out your own recollection of the experience of not loving it. The goal of the operation is to keep you away from immediate experience, so that a deliberately distorted mediation can be put in its place.

You can do that with literature and painting, by the way. You can do it with any form of mediation, but it's a great deal more effective with modern visual media, because those latter short-circuit the journey back to immediate experience. You see the person leaning back with the sigh of bliss after he takes a bite of pasty bland bun and tasteless gray mystery-meat patty, and you see it over and over and over again. If you're like most Americans, and spend four or five hours a day staring blankly at little colored images on a glass screen, a very large fraction of your total experience of the world consists of this sort of thing: distorted imitations of immediate experience, intended to get you to think about the world in ways that immediate experience won't justify.

The externalization of the human mind and imagination via the modern mass media has no shortage of problematic features, but the one I want to talk about here is the way that it feeds into the behavior discussed at the beginning of this post: the habit, pervasive in modern industrial societies just now, of responding to serious crises by manipulating abstractions to make them invisible. That kind of thing is commonplace in civilizations on their way out history's exit door, for reasons I've discussed in an earlier sequence of posts here, but modern visual media make it an even greater problem in the present instance. These latter function as a prosthetic for the imagination, a device for replacing the normal image-making functions of the human mind with electromechanical equivalents. What's more, you don't control the prosthetic imagination; governments and corporations control it, and use it to shape your thoughts and behavior in ways that aren't necessarily in your best interests.

The impact on the prosthetic imagination on the crisis of our time is almost impossible to overstate. I wonder, for example, how many of my readers have noticed just how pervasive references to science fiction movies and TV shows have become in discussions of the future of technology. My favorite example just now is the replicator, a convenient gimmick from the Star Trek universe: you walk up to it and order something, and the replicator pops it into being out of nothing.

It's hard to think of a better metaphor for the way that people in the privileged classes of today's industrial societies like to think of the consumer economy. It's also hard to think of anything that's further removed from the realities of the consumer economy. The replicator is the ultimate wet dream of externalization: it has no supply chains, no factories, no smokestacks, no toxic wastes, just whatever product you want any time you happen to want it. That's exactly the kind of thinking that lies behind Stewart Brand's fantasy of "decoupling"—and it's probably no accident that more often than not, when I've had conversations with people who think that 3-D printers are the solution to everything, they bring Star Trek replicators into the discussion.

3-D printers are not replicators. Their supply chains and manufacturing costs include the smokestacks, outflow pipes, toxic-waste dumps, sweatshopped factories, and open-pit mines worked by slave labor mentioned earlier, and the social impacts of their widespread adoption would include another wave of mass technological unemployment—remember, it's only in the highly mediated world of current economic propaganda that people who lose their jobs due to automation automatically get new jobs in some other field; in the immediate world, that's become increasingly uncommon. As long as people look at 3-D printers through minds full of little pictures of *Star Trek* replicators, though, those externalized ecological and social costs are going to be invisible to them.

That, in turn, defines the problem with the externalization of the human mind and imagination: no matter how frantically you manipulate abstractions, the immediate world is still what it is, and it can still clobber you. Externalizing a cost doesn't make it go away; it just guarantees that you won't see it in time to do anything but suffer the head-on impact.

407: THE VIEW FROM OUTSIDE

(Originally published 18 February 2015)

Recently I've been reacquainting myself with the stories of Clark Ashton Smith. Though he's largely forgotten today, Smith was one of the leading lights of *Weird Tales* magazine during its 1930s golden age, ranking with H.P Lovecraft and Robert Howard as a craftsman of fantasy fiction. Like Lovecraft, Howard, and most of the other authors in the *Weird Tales* stable, Smith was an outsider; he spent his life in a small town in rural California; he was roundly ignored by the literary scene of his day, and returned the favor with gusto. With the twilight of the pulps, Smith's work was consigned to the dustbin of literary history. It was revived briefly during the fantasy boom of the 1970, only to sink from sight again when the fantasy genre drowned in a swamp of faux-medieval clichés thereafter.

There's no shortage of reasons to give Smith another look today, starting with his mastery of image and atmosphere and the wry humor that shaped the best of his mature work. Still, that's a theme for another time, and possibly another forum. The theme that's relevant to this blog is woven into one of Smith's classic stories, "The Dark Age." First published in 1938, it's among the earliest science fiction stories I know of that revolves around an organized attempt to preserve modern science through a future age of barbarism.

The story's worth reading in its own right, so I won't hand out spoilers here. Still, I don't think it will give away anything crucial to mention that one of the mainsprings of the story is the inability of the story's scientists to find or make common ground with the neo-barbarian hill tribes around them. That aspect of the story has been much on my mind of late. Despite the rockets and rayguns that provide so much of its local color, science fiction is always about the present, which it displays in an unfamiliar light by showing a view from outside, from the distant perspective of an imaginary future.

That's certainly true of Smith's tale, which drew much of its force at the time of its composition from the widening chasm between the sciences and the rest of human culture that C.P. Snow discussed two decades later in his famous work "The Two Cultures." That chasm has opened up a good deal further since Smith's time, and its impact on the future deserves discussion here, not least because it's starting to come into sight even through the myopic lenses of today's popular culture.

I'm thinking here, for example, of a recent blog post by Scott Adams, the creator of the "Dilbert" comic strip. There's a certain poetic justice in seeing popular culture's acknowledged expert on organizational failure skewer one of contemporary science's more embarrassing habits, but there's more to the spectacle than a Dilbertesque joke. As Adams points out, there's an extreme mismatch between the way that science works and the way that scientists expect their claims to be received by the general public. Within the community of researchers, the conclusions of the moment are, at least in theory, open to constant challenge—but only from within the scientific community.

The general public is not invited to take part in those challenges. Quite the contrary, it's supposed to treat the latest authoritative pronouncement as truth pure and simple, even when that contradicts the authoritative pronouncements of six months before. Now of course there are reasons why scientists might not want to field a constant stream of suggestions and challenges from people who don't have training in relevant disciplines, but the fact remains that expecting people to blindly accept whatever scientists say about nutrition, when scientific opinion on that subject has been whirling around like a weathercock for decades now, is not a strategy with a long shelf life. Sooner or later people start asking why they should take the latest authoritative pronouncement seriously, when so many others landed in the trash can of discarded opinions a few years further on.

There's another, darker reason why such questions are increasingly common just now. I'm thinking here of the recent revelation that the British scientists tasked by the government with making dietary recommendations have been taking payola of various kinds from the sugar industry. That's hardly a new thing these days. Especially but not only in those branches of science concerned with medicine, pharmacology, and nutrition, the prostitution of the scientific process by business interests has become an open scandal. When a scientist gets behind a podium and makes a statement about the safety or efficacy of a drug, a medical treatment, or what have you, the first question asked by an ever-increasing number of people outside the scientific community these days is "Who's paying him?"

It would be bad enough if that question was being asked because of scurrilous rumors or hostile propaganda. Unfortunately, it's being asked because there's nothing particularly unusual about the behavior of the British scientists mentioned above. These days, in any field where science comes into contact with serious money, scientific studies are increasingly just another dimension of marketing. From influential researchers being paid to put their names on dubious studies to give them unearned credibility to the systematic concealment of "outlying" data that doesn't support the claims made for this or that lucrative product, the corruption of science is an ongoing reality, and one that existing safeguards within the scientific community are not effectively countering.

Scientists have by and large treated the collapse in scientific ethics as an internal matter. That's a lethal mistake, because the view that matters here is the view from outside. What looks to insiders like a manageable problem that will sort itself out in time, looks from outside the laboratory and the faculty lounge like institutionalized corruption on the part of a self-proclaimed elite whose members cover for each other and are accountable to no one. It doesn't matter, by the way, how inaccurate that view is in specific cases, how many honest men and women are laboring at lab benches, or how overwhelming the pressure to monetize research that's brought to bear on scientists by university administrations and corporate sponsors: none of that finds its way into the view from outside, and in the long run, the view from outside is the one that counts..

The corruption of science by self-interest is an old story, and unfortunately it's most intense in those fields where science impacts the lives of nonscientists most directly: yes, those would be medicine, pharmacology, and nutrition. I mentioned in an earlier blog post here a friend whose lifelong asthma, which landed her in the hospital repeatedly and nearly killed her twice, was cured at once by removing a common allergen from her diet. Mentioning this to her physician led to the discovery that he'd known about the allergy issue all along, but as he explained, "We prefer to medicate for that." Understandably so, as a patient who's cured of an ailment is a good deal less lucrative for the doctor than one who has to keep on receiving regular treatments and prescriptions—but as a result of that interaction among others, the friend in question has lost most of what respect she once had for mainstream medicine, and is now learning herbalism to meet her health care needs.

It's an increasingly common story these days, and I could add plenty of other accounts here. The point I want to make, though, is that it's painfully obvious that the physician who preferred to medicate never thought about the view from outside. I have no way of knowing what combination of external pressures and personal failings led him to conceal a less costly cure from my friend, and keep her on expensive and ineffective drugs with a gallery of noxious side effects instead, but from outside the walls of the office, it certainly looked like a callous betrayal of whatever ethics the medical profession might still have left—and again, the view from outside is the one that counts.

It counts because institutional science only has the authority and prestige it possesses today because enough of those outside the scientific community accept its claim to speak the truth about nature. Not that many years ago, all things considered, scientists didn't have the authority or the prestige, and no law of nature or of society guarantees that they'll keep either one indefinitely. Every doctor who would rather medicate than cure, every researcher who treats conflicts of interest as just another detail of business as usual, every scientist who insists in angry tones that nobody without a Ph.D. in this or that discipline is entitled to ask why this week's pronouncement should be taken any more seriously than the one it just disproved—and let's not even talk about the increasing, and increasingly public, problem of overt scientific fraud in the pharmaceutical field among others—is hastening the day when modern science is taken no more seriously by the general public than, say, academic philosophy is today.

That day may not be all that far away. That's the message that should be read, and is far too rarely read, in the accelerating emergence of countercultures that reject the authority of science in one field. As a recent and thoughtful essay in Slate pointed out, that crisis of authority is what gives credibility to such movements as climate denialists and "anti-vaxxers" (the growing number of parents who refuse to have their children vaccinated). A good many any people these days, when the official voices of the scientific community say this or that, respond by asking "Why should we believe you?" — and too many of them don't get a straightforward answer that addresses their concerns.

A bit of personal experience from a different field may be relevant here. Back in the late 1980s and early 1990s, when I lived in Seattle, I put a fair amount of time into collecting local folklore concerning ghosts and other paranormal phenomena. I wasn't doing this out of any particular belief, or for that matter any particular unbelief; I was seeking a sense of the mythic terrain of the Puget Sound region, the landscapes of belief and imagination that emerged from the experiences of people on the land, with an eye toward the career writing fiction that I then hoped to launch. While I was doing this research, when something paranormal was reported anywhere in the region, I generally got to hear about it fairly quickly, and in the process I got to watch a remarkable sequence of events that repeated itself like a broken record in more cases than I can count.

Whether the phenomenon that was witnessed was an unusual light in the sky, a seven-foot-tall hairy biped in the woods, a visit from a relative who happened to be dead at the time, or what have you, two things followed promptly once the witness went public. The first was the arrival of a self-proclaimed skeptic, usually a member of CSICOP (the Committee for Scientific Investigation of Claims of the Paranormal), who treated the witness with scorn and condescension, made dogmatic claims about what must have happened, and responded to any disagreement with bullying and verbal abuse. The other thing that followed was the arrival of an investigator from one of the local paranormal-research organizations, who was invariably friendly and supportive, listened closely to the account of the witness, and took the incident seriously. I'll let you guess which of the proposed explanations the witness usually ended up embracing, not to mention which organization he or she often joined.

The same process on a larger and far more dangerous scale is shaping attitudes toward science across a wide and growing sector of American society. Notice that unlike climate denialism, the anti-vaxxer movement isn't powered by billions of dollars of grant money, but it's getting increasing traction. The reason is as simple as it is painful: parents are asking physicians and scientists, "How do I know this substance you want to put into my child is safe?"—and the answers they're getting are not providing them with the reassurance they need.

It's probably necessary here to point out that I'm no fan of the anti-vaxxer movement. Since epidemic diseases are likely to play a massive role in the future ahead of us, I've looked into anti-vaxxer arguments with some care, and they don't convince me at all. It's clear from the evidence that vaccines do far more often than not provide protection against dangerous diseases; while some children are harmed by the side effects of vaccination, that's true of every medical procedure, and the toll from side effects is orders of magnitude smaller than the annual burden of deaths from these same diseases in the pre-vaccination era.

Nor does the anti-vaxxer claim that vaccines cause autism hold water. (I have Aspergers syndrome, so the subject's of some personal interest to me.) The epidemiology of autism spectrum disorders simply doesn't support that claim; to my educated-layperson's eyes, at least, it matches that of an autoimmune disease instead, complete with the rapid increase in prevalence in recent years. The hypothesis I'd be investigating now, if I'd gone into biomedical science rather than the history of ideas, is that autism spectrum disorders are sequelae of an autoimmune disease that strikes in infancy or early childhood, and causes damage to any of a variety of regions in the central nervous system—thus the baffling diversity of neurological deficits found in those of us on the autism spectrum.

Whether that's true or not will have to be left to trained researchers. The point that I want to make here is that I don't share the beliefs that drive the anti-vaxxer movement. Similarly, I'm sufficiently familiar with the laws of thermodynamics and the chemistry of the atmosphere to know that when the climate denialists insist that dumping billions of tons of carbon dioxide into the atmosphere can't change its capacity to retain heat, they're smoking their shorts. I've retained enough of a childhood interest in paleontology, and studied enough of biology and genetics since then, to be able to follow the debates between evolutionary biology and so-called "creation science," and I'm solidly on Darwin's side of the bleachers. I could go on; I have my doubts about a few corners of contemporary scientific theory, but then so do plenty of scientists.

That is to say, I don't agree with the anti-vaxxers, the climate denialists, the creationists, or their equivalents, but I think I understand why they've rejected the authority of science, and it's not because they're ignorant cretins, much as though the proponents and propagandists of science would like to claim that. It's because they've seen far too much of the view from outside. Parents who encounter a medical industry that would rather medicate than heal are more likely to listen to anti-vaxxers; Americans who watch climate change activists demand that the rest of the world cut its carbon footprint, while the activists themselves get to keep cozy middle-class lifestyles, are more likely to believe that global warming is a politically motivated hoax; Christians who see atheists using evolution as a stalking horse for their ideology are more likely to turn to creation science—and all three, and others, are not going to listen to scientists who insist that they're wrong, until and unless the scientists stop and take a good hard look at how they and their proclamations look when viewed from outside.

I'm far from sure that anybody in the scientific community is willing to take that hard look. It's possible; these days, even committed atheists are starting to notice that whenever Richard Dawkins opens his mouth, twenty people who were considering atheism decide to give God a second chance. The arrogant bullying that used to be standard practice among the self-proclaimed skeptics and "angry atheists" has taken on a sullen and defensive tone recently, as though it's started to sink in that yelling abuse at people who disagree with you might not be the best way to win their hearts and minds. Still, for that same act of reflection to get any traction in the scientific community, a great many people in that community are going to have to rethink the way they handle dealing with the public, especially when science, technology, and medicine cause harm. That, in turn, is only going to happen if enough of today's scientists remember the importance of the view from outside.

In the light of the other issues I've tried to discuss over the years in this blog, that view has another dimension, and it's a considerably harsher one. Among the outsiders whose opinion of contemporary science matters most are some that haven't been born yet: our descendants, who will inhabit a world shaped by science and the technologies that have resulted from scientific research. It's still popular to insist that their world will be a Star Trek fantasy of limitlessness splashed across the galaxy, but I think most people are starting to realize just how unlikely that future actually is.

Instead, the most likely futures for our descendants are those in which the burdens left behind by today's science and technology are much more significant than the benefits. Those most likely futures will be battered by unstable climate and rising oceans due to anthropogenic climate change, stripped of most of its topsoil, natural resources, and ecosystems, strewn with the radioactive and chemical trash that our era produced in such abundance and couldn't be bothered to store safely—and most of today's advanced technologies have long since rusted into uselessness, because the cheap abundant energy and other nonrenewable resources that were needed to keep them running all got used up in our time.

People living in such a future aren't likely to remember that a modest number of scientists signed petitions and wrote position papers protesting some of these things. They're even less likely to recall the utopian daydreams of perpetual progress and limitless abundance that encouraged so many other people in the scientific community to tell themselves that these things didn't really matter—and if by chance they do remember those daydreams, their reaction to them won't be pretty. That science today, like every other human institution in every age, combines high ideals and petty motives in the usual proportions will not matter to them in the least.

Unless something changes sharply very soon, their view from outside may well see modern science—all of it, from the first gray dawn of the scientific revolution straight through to the flamelit midnight when the last laboratory was sacked and burned by a furious mob—as a wicked dabbling in accursed powers that eventually brought down just retribution upon a corrupt and arrogant age. So long as the proponents and propagandists of science ignore the view from outside, and blind themselves to the ways that their own defense of science is feeding the forces that are rising against it, the bleak conclusion of the Clark Ashton Smith story cited at the beginning of this post may yet turn out to be far more prophetic than the comfortable fantasies of perpetual scientific advancement cherished by so many people today.

408: PLANET OF THE SPACE BATS

(Originally published 25 March 2015)

As my regular readers know, I've been talking for quite a while now here about the speculative bubble that's built up around the fracking phenomenon, and the catastrophic bust that's guaranteed to follow so vast and delusional a boom. Over the six months or so, I've noted the arrival of one warning sign after another of the impending crash. As the saying has it, though, it's not over 'til the fat lady sings, so I've been listening for the first notes of the metaphorical aria that, in the best Wagnerian style, will rise above the orchestral score as the fracking industry's surrogate Valhalla finally bursts into flames and goes crashing down into the Rhine.

I think I just heard those first high notes, though, in an improbable place: the email inbox of the Ancient Order of Druids in America (AODA), the Druid order I head.

I have no idea how many of my readers know the first thing about my unpaid day job as chief executive—the official title is Grand Archdruid—of one of the two dozen or so Druid orders in the western world. Most of what goes into that job, and the admittedly eccentric minority religious tradition behind it, has no relevance to the present subject. Still, I think most people know that Druids revere the natural world, and take ecology seriously even when that requires scrapping some of the absurd extravagances that pass for a normal lifestyle these days. Thus a Druid order is arguably the last place that would come to mind if you wanted to sell stock in a fracking company.

Nonetheless, that's what happened. The bemused AODA office staff the other day fielded a solicitation from a stock firm trying to get Druids to invest their assets in the fracking industry.

Does that sound like a desperation move to you, dear reader?

It certainly does to me—and there's good reason to think that it probably sounds that way to the people who are trying to sell shares in fracking firms to one final round of clueless chumps, too. A recent piece in the Wall Street Journal (available outside the paywall here) noted that American banks have suddenly found themselves stuck with tens of millions of dollars' worth of loans to fracking firms which they hoped to package up and sell to investors—but suddenly nobody's buying. Bankruptcies and mass layoffs are becoming an everyday occurrence in the fracking industry, and the price of oil continues to lurch down as producers maximize production for the sake of immediate cash flow.

Why, though, isn't the drop in the price of oil being met by an upsurge in consumption that drives the price back up, as the accepted rules of economics would predict? That's the cream of the jest. Here in America, and to a lesser extent elsewhere in the industrial world, four decades of enthusiastically bipartisan policies that benefited the rich at everyone else's expense managed to prove Henry Ford's famous argument: if you don't pay your own employees enough that they can afford to buy your products, sooner or later, you're going to go broke.

By driving down wages and forcing an ever larger fraction of the US population into permanent unemployment and poverty, the movers and shakers of America's political class have managed to trigger < a classic crisis of overproduction, in which goods go begging for buyers because too few people can afford to buy them at any price. It's not just oil that's affected, either: scores of other commodities are plunging in price as the global economy tips over into depression. There's a specter haunting the industrial world; it's the ghost of Karl Marx, laughing with mordant glee as the soi-disant masters of the universe, having crushed his misbegotten Soviet stepchildren, go all out to make his prophecy of capitalism's self-immolation look remarkably prescient.

The soaring price of crude oil in the wake of the 2005 global peak of conventional oil production should have served notice to the industrial world that, to adapt the title of Richard Heinberg's excellent 2003 summary of the situation, the party was over: the long era in which energy supplies had increased year over year was giving way to an unwelcome new reality in which decreasing energy supplies and increasing environmental blowback were the defining themes. As my readers doubtless noticed, though, the only people who willing to grasp that were out here on the fringes where archdruids lurk. Closer to the mainstream of our collective thinking, most people scrunched shut their eyes, plugged their ears with their fingers, and shouted "La, la, la, I can't hear you" at the top of their lungs, in a desperate attempt to keep reality from getting a word in edgewise.

For the last five years or so, any attempt to talk about the impending twilight of the age of oil thus ran headfirst into a flurry of pro-fracking propaganda. Fatuous twaddle about America's inevitable future as the world's new energy superpower took the place of serious discussions of the predicament into which we've backed ourselves — and not for the first time, either. That's what makes the attempt to get Druids to invest their life savings in fracking so funny, in a bleak sort of way: it's an attempt to do for the fracking boom what the fracking boom attempted to do for industrial civilization as a whole — to pretend, in the teeth of the facts, that the unsustainable can be sustained for just a little while longer.

A few months back, I decided to celebrate this sort of thinking by way of the grand old Druid custom of satire. The Great Squirrel Case Challenge of 2015 solicited mock proposals for solving the world's energy problems that were even nuttier than the ones in the mainstream media. That was no small challenge — a detail some of my readers pointed up by forwarding any number of clueless stories from the mainstream media loudly praising energy boondoggles of one kind or another.

I'm delighted to say, though, that the response was even better than I'd hoped for. The contest fielded more than thirty entries, ranging from the merely very good to the sidesplittingly funny. There were two winners, one chosen by the members of the Green Wizards forum, one chosen by me; in both cases, it was no easy choice, and if I had enough author's copies of my new book *After Progress*, I'd probably just up and given prizes to all the entries, they were that good. Still, it's my honor to announce the winners:

My choice for best squirrel case — drumroll, please — goes to Steve Morgan, for his fine gosh-wow sales prospectus for, ahem, "*Shares of Hydrocarbons Imported from Titan.*" The Green Wizards forum choice — drumroll again — goes to Jason Heppenstall for his hilarious parody of a sycophantic media story, "King Solomon's Miners." Please join me in congratulating them. (Steve and Jason, drop me a comment with your mailing addresses, marked not for posting, and I'll get your prizes on the way.)

Their hard-won triumph probably won't last long. In the months and years ahead, I expect to see claims even more ludicrous being taken oh-so-seriously by the mainstream media, because the alternative is to face up to just how badly we've bungled the opportunities of the last four decades or so and just how rough a road we have ahead of us as a result. What gave the fracking bubble whatever plausibility it ever had, after all, was the way it fed on one of the faith-based credos at the heart of contemporary popular culture: the insistence, as pervasive as it is irrational, that the universe is somehow obligated to hand us abundant new energy sources to replace the ones we've already used so profligately. Lacking that blind faith, it would have been obvious to everyone — as it was to those of us in the peak oil community — that the fracking industry was scraping the bottom of the barrel and pretending that this proved the barrel was full.

Read the morning news with eyes freed from the deathgrip of the conventional wisdom and it's brutally obvious that that's what happened, and that the decline and fall of our civilization is well under way. Here in the US, a quarter of the country is in the fourth year of record drought, with snowpack on California's Sierra Nevada mountains about 9% of normal; the Gulf Stream is slowing to a crawl due to the rapid melting of the Greenland ice sheets; permanent joblessness and grinding poverty have become pervasive in this country; the national infrastructure is coming apart after decades of malign neglect — well, I could go on; if you want to know what life is like in a falling civilization, go look out the window.

In the mainstream media, on the occasions when such things are mentioned at all, they're treated as disconnected factoids irrelevant to the big picture. Most people haven't yet grasped that these things *are* the big picture — that while we're daydreaming about an assortment of shiny futures that look more or less like the present with more toys, climate change, resource depletion, collapsing infrastructure, economic contraction, and the implosion of political and cultural institutions are creating the future we're going to inhabit. Too many of us suffer from a weird inability to imagine a future that isn't simply a continuation of the present, even when such a future stands knocking at our own front doors.

So vast a failure of imagination can't be overcome by the simple expedient of pointing out the ways that it's already failed to explain the world in which we live. That said, there are other ways to break the grip of the conventional wisdom, and I'm pleased to say that one of those other ways seems to be making modest but definite headway just now.

Longtime readers here will remember that in 2011, this blog launched a contest for short stories about the kind of future we can actually expect—a future in which no *deus ex machina* saves industrial civilization from the exhaustion of its resource base, the deterioration of the natural systems that support it, and the normal process of decline and fall. That contest resulted in an anthology, *After Oil: SF Stories of a Post-Petroleum Future*, which found a surprisingly large audience. On the strength of its success, I ran a second contest in 2014, which resulted in two more volumes—*After Oil 2: The Years of Crisis*, which is now available, and *After Oil 3: The Years of Rebirth,* which is in preparation. Demand for the original volume has remained steady, and the second is selling well; after a conversation with the publisher, I'm pleased to announce that we're going to do it again, with a slight twist.

The basic rules are mostly the same as before:

Stories should be between 2500 and 7500 words in length;

They should be entirely the work of their author or authors, and should not borrow characters or setting from someone else's work;

They should be in English, with correct spelling, grammar and punctuation;

They should be stories—narratives with a plot and characters—and not simply a guided tour of some corner of the future as the author imagines it;

They should be set in our future, not in an alternate history or on some other planet;

They should be works of realistic fiction or science fiction, not magical or supernatural fantasy—that is, the setting and story should follow the laws of nature as those are presently understood;

They should take place in settings subject to thermodynamic, ecological, and economic limits to growth; and as before,

They must not rely on "alien space bats" — that is, *dei ex machina* inserted to allow humanity to dodge the consequences of the limits to growth.

This time, though, I'm adding an additional rule:

Stories submitted for this contest must be set at least one thousand years in the future — that is, after March 25, 3015 in our calendar.

That's partly a reflection of a common pattern in entries for the two previous contests, and partly something deeper. The common pattern? A great many authors submitted stories that were set during or immediately after the collapse of industrial civilization; there's certainly room for those, enough so that the entire second volume is basically devoted to them, but tales of surviving decline and fall are only a small fraction of the galaxy of potential stories that would fit within the rules listed above. I'd like to encourage entrants to consider telling something different, at least this time.

The deeper dimension? That's a reflection of the blindness of the imagination discussed earlier in this post, the inability of so many people to think of a future that isn't simply a prolongation of the present. Stories set in the immediate aftermath of our civilization don't necessarily challenge that, and I think it's high time to start talking about futures that are genuinely *other* — neither utopia nor oblivion, but different, radically different, from the linear extrapolations from the present that fill so many people's imaginations these days, and have an embarrassingly large role even in science fiction.

You have to read SF from more than a few decades back to grasp just how tight the grip of a single linear vision of the future has become on what used to be a much more freewheeling literature of ideas. In book after book, and even more in film after film, technologies that are obviously derived from ours, ideologies that are indistinguishable from ours, political and economic arrangements that could pass for ours, and attitudes and ideas that belong to this or that side of today's cultural struggles get projected onto the future as though they're the only imaginable options. This takes place even when there's very good reason to think that the linear continuation of current trends isn't an option at all—for example, the endlessly regurgitated, done-to-death trope of interstellar travel.

Let us please be real: we aren't going to the stars—not in our lifetimes, not in the lifetime of industrial civilization, not in the lifetime of our species. There are equally good thermodynamic and economic reasons to believe that many of the other standard tropes of contemporary science fiction are just as unreachable—that, for example, limitless energy from gimmicks of the dilithium-crystal variety, artificial intelligences capable of human or superhuman thought, and the like belong to fantasy, not to the kind of science fiction that has any likelihood of becoming science fact. Any of my readers who want to insist that human beings can create anything they can imagine, by the way, are welcome to claim that, just as soon as they provide me with a working perpetual motion machine.

It's surprisingly common to see people insist that the absence of the particular set of doodads common to today's science fiction would condemn our descendants to a future of endless boredom. This attitude shows a bizarre stunting of the imagination—not least because stories about interstellar travel normally end up landing the protagonists in a world closely modeled on some past or present corner of the Earth. If our genus lasts as long as the average genus of vertebrate megafauna, we've got maybe ten million years ahead of us, or roughly two thousand times as long as all of recorded human history to date: more than enough time for human beings to come up with a dazzling assortment of creative, unexpected, radically different societies, technologies, and ways of facing the universe and themselves.

That's what I'd like to see in submissions to this year's Space Bats challenge—yes, it'll be an annual thing from here on out, as long as the market for such stories remains lively. A thousand years from now, industrial civilization will be as far in the past as the Roman Empire was at the time of the Renaissance, and new human societies will have arisen to pass their own judgment on the relics of our age. Ten thousand years from now, or ten million? Those are also options. Fling yourself into the far future, far enough that today's crises are matters for the history books, or tales out of ancient myth, or forgotten as completely as the crises and achievements of the Neanderthal people are today, and tell a story about human beings (or, potentially, post-human beings) confronting the challenges of their own time in their own way. Do it with verve and a good readable style, and your story may be be one of the ones chosen to appear in the pages of *After Oil 4: The Future's Distant Shores*.

The mechanics are pretty much the same as before. Write your story and post it to the internet — if you don't have a blog, you can get one for free from Blogspot or Wordpress. Post a link to it in the comments to *The Archdruid Report*. You can write more than one story, but please let me know which one you want entered in the competition — there will be only one entry accepted per author this time. Stories must be written and posted online, and a link posted to this blog, by August 30, 2015 to be eligible for inclusion in the anthology.

409: THE BURDEN OF DENIAL

(Originally published 8 April 2015)

It occurred to me the other day that quite a few of the odder features of contemporary American culture make perfect sense if you assume that everybody knows exactly what's wrong and what's coming as our society rushes, pedal to the metal, toward its face-first collision with the brick wall of the future. It's not that they don't get it; they get it all too clearly, and they just wish that those of us on the fringes would quit reminding them of the imminent impact, so they can spend whatever time they've got left in as close to a state of blissful indifference as they can possibly manage.

I grant that this realization probably had a lot to do with the context in which it came to me. I was sitting in a restaurant, as it happens, with a vanload of fellow Freemasons. We'd carpooled down to Baltimore, some of us to receive one of the higher degrees of Masonry and the rest to help with the ritual work, and we stopped for dinner on the way back home. I'll spare you the name of the place we went; it was one of those currently fashionable beer-and-burger joints where the waitresses have all been outfitted with skirts almost long enough to cover their underwear, bare midriffs, and the sort of push-up bras that made them look uncomfortably like inflatable dolls—an impression that their too obviously scripted jiggle-and-smile routines did nothing to dispell.

Still, that wasn't the thing that made the restaurant memorable. It was the fact that every wall in the place had television screens on it. By this I don't mean that there was one screen per wall; I mean that they were lined up side by side right next to each other, covering the upper part of every single wall in the place, so that you couldn't raise your eyes above head level without looking at one. They were all over the interior partitions of the place, too. There must have been forty of them in one not too large restaurant, each one blaring something different into the thick air, while loud syrupy music spattered down on us from speakers on the ceiling and the waitresses smiled mirthlessly as they went through their routines. My burger and fries were tolerably good, and two tall glasses of Guinness will do much to ameliorate even so charmless a situation; still, I was glad to get back on the road.

The thing I'd point out is that all this is quite recent. Not that many years ago, it was tolerably rare to see a TV screen in an American restaurant, and even those bars that had a television on the premises for the sake of football season generally had the grace to leave the thing off the rest of the time. Within the last decade, I've watched televisions sprout in restaurants and pubs I used to enjoy like buboes on the body of a plague victim: first one screen, then several, then one on each wall, then metastatizing across the remaining space. Meanwhile, along the same lines, people who used to go to coffee shops and the like to read the papers, talk with other patrons, or do anything else you care to name are now sitting in the same coffee shops in total silence, hunched over their allegedly smart phones like so many scowling gargoyles on the walls of a medieval cathedral.

Yes, there were people in the restaurant crouched in the classic gargoyle pose over their allegedly smart phones, too, and that probably also had something to do with my realization that evening. It so happens that the evening before my Baltimore trip, I'd recorded a podcast interview with Chris Martenson on his Peak Prosperity show, and he'd described to me a curious response he'd been fielding from people who attended his talks on the end of the industrial age and the unwelcome consequences thereof. He called it "the iPhone moment" — the point at which any number of people in the audience pulled that particular technological toy out of their jacket pockets and waved it at him, insisting that its mere existence somehow disproved everything he was saying.

You've got to admit, as modern superstitions go, this one is pretty spectacular. Let's take a moment to look at it rationally. Do iPhones produce energy? Nope. Will they refill our rapidly depleting oil and gas wells, restock the ravaged oceans with fish, or restore the vanishing topsoil from the world's fields? Of course not. Will they suck carbon dioxide from the sky, get rid of the vast mats of floating plastic that clog the seas, or do something about the steadily increasing stockpiles of nuclear waste that are going to sicken and kill people for the next quarter of a million years unless the waste gets put someplace safe — if there is any-where safe to put it at all? Not a chance. As a response to any of the predicaments that are driving the crisis of our age, iPhones are at best irrelevant. Since they consume energy and resources, and the sprawling technosystems that make them function con-sume energy and resources at a rate orders of magnitude greater, they're part of the problem, not any sort of a solution

Now of course the people waving their iPhones at Chris Mar-tenson aren't thinking about any of these things. A good case could be made that they're not actually thinking at all. Their rea-soning, if you want to call it that, seems to be that the existence of iPhones proves that progress is still happening, and this in turn somehow proves that progress will inevitably bail us out from the impacts of every one of the predicaments we face. To call this magical thinking is an insult to honest sorcerers; rath-er, it's another example of the arbitrary linkage of verbal noises to emotional reactions that all too often passes for thinking in today's America. Readers of classic science fiction may find all this weirdly reminiscent of a scene from some edgily updated version of H.G. Wells' *The Island of Doctor Moreau*: "Not to doubt Progress: that is the Law. Are we not Men?"

Seen from a certain perspective, though, there's a definite if unmentionable logic to "the iPhone moment," and it has much in common with the metastatic spread of television screens across pubs and restaurants in recent years. These allegedly smart phones don't do anything to fix the rising spiral of problems be-setting industrial civilization, but they make it easier for people to distract themselves from those problems for a little while lon-ger. That, I'd like to suggest, is also what's driving the metastasis of television screens in the places that people used to go to enjoy a meal, a beer, or a cup of coffee and each other's company. These days, that latter's too risky; somebody might mention a friend who lost his job and can't get another one, a spouse who gets sicker with each overpriced prescription the medical industry pushes on her, a kid who didn't come back from Afghanistan, or the like, and then it's right back to the reality that everyone's trying to avoid. It's much easier to sit there in silence staring at little colored pictures on a glass screen, from which all such troubles have been excluded.

Of course that habit has its own downsides. To begin with, those who are busy staring at the screens have to know, on some level, that sooner or later it's going to be their turn to lose their jobs, or have their health permanently wrecked by the side effects their doctors didn't get around to telling them about, or have their kids fail to come back from whatever America's war du jour happens to be just then, or the like. That's why so many people these days put so much effort into insisting as loudly as possible that the poor and vulnerable are to blame for their plight. The people who say this know perfectly well that it's not true, but repeating such claims over and over again is the only defense they've got against the bitter awareness that their jobs, their health, and their lives or those of the people they care about could all too easily be next on the chopping block.

What makes this all the more difficult for most Americans to face is that none of these events are happening in a vacuum. They're part of a broader process, the decline and fall of modern industrial society in general and the United States of America in particular. Outside the narrowing circles of the well-to-do, standards of living for most Americans have been declining since the 1970s, along with standards of education, public health, and most of the other things that make for a prosperous and stable society. Today, a nation that once put human bootprints on the Moon can't afford to maintain its roads and bridges or keep its cities from falling into ruin. Hiding from that reality in an imaginary world projected onto glass screens may be comforting in the short term; the mere fact that realities don't go away just because they're ignored does nothing to make this choice any less tempting.

What's more, the world into which that broader process of decline is bringing us is not one in which staring at little colored pictures on a glass screen will count for much. Quite the contrary, it promises to be a world in which raw survival, among other things, will depend on having achieved at least a basic mastery of one or more of a very different range of skills. There's no particular mystery about those latter skills; they were, in point of fact, the standard set of basic human survival skills for thousands of years before those glass screens were invented, and they'll still be in common use when the last of the glass screens has weathered away into sand; but they have to be learned and practiced before they're needed, and there may not be all that much time left to learn and practice them before hard necessity comes knocking at the door.

I think a great many people who claim that everything's fine are perfectly aware of all this. They know what the score is; it's doing something about it that's the difficulty, because taking meaningful action at this very late stage of the game runs head-long into at least two massive obstacles. One of them is practical in nature, the other psychological, and human nature being what it is, the psychological dimension is far and away the most difficult of the two.

Let's deal with the practicalities first. The non-negotiable foundation of any meaningful response to the crisis of our time, as I've pointed out more than once here, can be summed up conveniently with the acronym L.E.S.S. — that is, Less Energy, Stuff, and Stimulation. We are all going to have much less of these things at our disposal in the future. Using less of them now frees up time, money, and other resources that can be used to get ready for the inevitable transformations. It also makes for decreased dependence on systems and resources that in many cases are already beginning to fail, and in any case will not be there indefinitely in a future of hard limits and inevitable scarcities.

On the other hand, using L.E.S.S. flies in the face of two powerful forces in contemporary culture. The first is the ongoing barrage of advertising meant to convince people that they can't possibly be happy without the latest time-, energy-, and resource-wasting trinket that corporate interests want to push on them. The second is the stark shivering terror that seizes most Americans at the thought that anybody might think that they're poorer than they actually are. Americans like to think of themselves as proud individualists, but like so many elements of the American self-image, that's an absurd fiction; these days, as a rule, Americans are meek conformists who shudder with horror at the thought that they might be caught straying in the least particular from whatever other people expect of them.

That's what lies behind the horrified response that comes up the moment someone suggests that using L.E.S.S. might be a meaningful part of our response to the crises of our age. When people go around insisting that not buying into the latest over-hyped and overpriced lump of technogarbage is tantamount to going back to the caves — and yes, I field such claims quite regularly — you can tell that what's going on in their minds has nothing to do with the realities of the situation and everything to do with stark unreasoning fear. Point out that a mere thirty years ago, people got along just fine without email and the internet, and you're likely to get an even more frantic and abusive reaction, precisely because your listener knows you're right and can't deal with the implications.

This is where we get into the psychological dimension. What James Howard Kunstler has usefully termed the psychology of previous investment is a massive cultural force in today's America. The predicaments we face today are in very large part the product of a long series of really bad decisions that were made over the last four decades or so. Most Americans, even those who had little to do with making those decisions, enthusiastically applauded them, and treated those who didn't with no small amount of abuse and contempt. Admitting just how misguided those decisions turned out to be thus requires a willingness to eat crow that isn't exactly common among Americans these days. Thus there's a strong temptation to double down on the bad decisions, wave those iPhones in the air, and put a few more television screens on the walls to keep the cognitive dissonance at bay for a little while longer.

That temptation isn't an abstract thing. It rises out of the raw emotional anguish woven throughout America's attempt to avoid looking at the future it's made for itself. The intensity of that anguish can be measured most precisely, I think, in one small but telling point: the number of people whose final response to the lengthening shadow of the future is, "I hope I'll be dead before it happens."

Think about those words for a moment. It used to be absolutely standard, and not only in America, for people of every social class below the very rich to work hard, save money, and do without so that their children could have a better life than they had. That parents could say to their own children, "I got mine, Jack; too bad your lives are going to suck," belonged in the pages of lurid dime novels, not in everyday life. Yet that's exactly what the words "I hope I'll be dead before it happens" imply. The destiny that's overtaking the industrial world isn't something imposed from outside; it's not an act of God or nature or callous fate; rather, it's unfolding with mathematical exactness from the behavior of those who benefit from the existing order of things. It could be ameliorated significantly if those same beneficiaries were to let go of the absurd extravagance that characterizes what passes for a normal life in the modern industrial world these days—it's just that the act of letting go involves an emotional price that few people are willing to pay.

Thus I don't think that anyone says "I hope I'll be dead before it happens" lightly. I don't think the people who are consigning their own children and grandchildren to a ghastly future, and placing their last scrap of hope on the prospect that they themselves won't live to see that future arrive, are making that choice out of heartlessness or malice. The frantic concentration on glass screens, the bizarre attempts to banish unwelcome realities by waving iPhones in their faces, and the other weird behavior patterns that surround American society's nonresponse to its impending future, are signs of the enormous strain that so many Americans these days are under as they try to keep pretending that nothing is wrong in the teeth of the facts.

Denying a reality that's staring you in the face is an immensely stressful process, and the stress gets worse as the number of things that have to be excluded from awareness mounts up. These days, that list is getting increasingly long. Look away from the pictures on the glass screens, and the United States is visibly a nation in rapid decline: its cities collapsing, its infrastructure succumbing to decades of malign neglect, its politics mired in corruption and permanent gridlock, its society frayed to breaking, and the natural systems that support its existence passing one tipping point after another and lurching through chaotic transitions.

Oklahoma has passed California as the most seismically active state in the Union as countless gallons of fracking fluid pumped into deep disposal wells remind us that nothing ever really "goes away." It's no wonder that so many shrill voices these days are insisting that nothing is wrong, or that it's all the fault of some scapegoat or other, or that Jesus or the Space Brothers or somebody will bail us out any day now, or that we're all going to be wiped out shortly by some colorful Hollywood cataclysm that, please note, is never our fault.

There is, of course, another option.

Over the years since this blog first began to attract an audience, I've spoken to quite a few people who broke themselves out of that trap, or were popped out of it willy-nilly by some moment of experience just that little bit too forceful to yield to the exclusionary pressure; many of them have talked about how the initial burst of terror—no, no, you can't say that, you can't think that!—gave way to an immense feeling of release and freedom, as the burden of keeping up the pretense dropped away and left them able to face the world in front of them at last.

I suspect, for what it's worth, that a great many more people are going to be passing through that transformative experience in the years immediately ahead. A majority? Almost certainly not; to judge by historical precedents, the worse things get, the more effort will go into the pretense that nothing is wrong at all, and the majority will cling like grim death to that pretense until it drags them under. That said, a substantial minority might make a different choice: to let go of the burden of denial soon enough to matter, to let themselves plunge through those moments of terror and freedom, and to haul themselves up, shaken but alive, onto the unfamiliar shores of the future.

When they get there, there will be plenty of work for them to do. I've discussed some of the options in previous posts on this blog, but there's at least one that hasn't gotten a detailed examination yet, and it's one that I've come to think may be of crucial importance in the decades ahead. We'll talk about that next week.

410: THE RETRO FUTURE

(Originally published 15 April 2015)

Is it just me, or has the United States taken yet another great leap forward into the surreal over the last few days? Glancing through the news, I find another round of articles babbling about how fracking has guaranteed America a gaudy future as a petroleum and natural gas exporter. Somehow none of these articles get around to mentioning that the United States is a major net importer of both commodities, that most of the big-name firms in the fracking industry have been losing money at a rate of billions a year since the boom began, and that the pileup of bad loans to fracking firms is pushing the US banking industry into a significant credit crunch, but that's just par for the course nowadays.

Then there's the current tempest in the media's teapot, Hillary Clinton's presidential run. I've come to think of Clinton as the Khloe Kardashian of American politics, since she owed her original fame to the mere fact that she's related to someone else who once caught the public eye. Since then she's cycled through various roles because, basically, that's what Famous People do, and the US presidency is just the next reality-TV gig on her bucket list. I grant that there's a certain wry amusement to be gained from watching this child of privilege, with the help of her multimillionaire friends, posturing as a champion of the downtrodden, but I trust that none of my readers are under the illusion that this rhetoric will amount to anything more than all that chatter about hope and change eight years ago.

Let us please be real: whoever mumbles the oath of office up there on the podium in 2017, whether it's Clinton or the interchangeably Bozoesque figures currently piling one by one out of the GOP's clown car to contend with her, we can count on more of the same: more futile wars, more giveaways to the rich at everyone else's expense, more erosion of civil liberties, more of all the other things Obama's cheerleaders insisted back in 2008 he would stop as soon as he got into office. As Arnold Toynbee pointed out a good many years ago, one of the hallmarks of a nation in decline is that the dominant elite sinks into senility, becoming so heavily invested in failed policies and so insulated from the results of its own actions that nothing short of total disaster will break its deathgrip on the body politic.

While we wait for the disaster in question, though, those of us who aren't part of the dominant elite and aren't bamboozled by the spectacle du jour might reasonably consider what we might do about it all. By that, of course, I don't mean that it's still possible to save industrial civilization in general, and the United States in particular, from the consequences of their history. That possibility went whistling down the wind a long time ago. Back in 2005, the Hirsch Report showed that any attempt to deal with the impending collision with the hard ecological limits of a finite planet had to get under way at least twenty years before the peak of global conventional petroleum reserves, if there was to be any chance of avoiding massive disruptions. As it happens, 2005 also marked the peak of conventional petroleum production worldwide, which may give you some sense of the scale of the current mess.

Consider, though, what happened in the wake of that announcement. Instead of dealing with the hard realities of our predicament, the industrial world panicked and ran the other way, with the United States well in the lead. Strident claims that ethanol—er, solar—um, biodiesel—okay, wind—well, fracking, then—would provide a cornucopia of cheap energy to replace the world's rapidly depleting reserves of oil, coal, and natural gas took the place of a serious energy policy, while conservation, the one thing that might have made a difference, was as welcome as garlic aioli at a convention of vampires.

That stunningly self-defeating response had a straightforward cause, which was that everyone except a few of us on the fringes treated the whole matter as though the issue was how the privileged classes of the industrial world could maintain their current lifestyles on some other resource base. Since that question has no meaningful answer, questions that could have been answered—for example, how do we get through the impending mess with at least some of the achievements of the last three centuries intact? — never got asked at all. At this point, as a result, ten more years have been wasted trying to come up with answers to the wrong question, and most of the doors that were still open in 2005 have been slammed shut by events since that time.

Fortunately, there are still a few possibilities for constructive action open even this late in the game. More fortunate still, the ones that will likely matter most don't require Hillary Clinton, or any other member of America's serenely clueless ruling elite, to do something useful for a change. They depend, rather, on personal action, beginning with individuals, families, and local communities and spiraling outward from there to shape the future on wider and wider scales.

I've talked about two of these possibilities at some length in posts here. The first can be summed up simply enough in a cheery sentence: "Collapse now and avoid the rush!" In an age of economic contraction — and behind the current facade of hallucinatory paper wealth, we're already in such an age — nothing is quite so deadly as the attempt to prop up extravagant lifestyles that the real economy of goods and services will no longer support. Those who thrive in such times are those who downshift ahead of the economy, take the resources that would otherwise be wasted on attempts to sustain the unsustainable, and apply them to the costs of transition to less absurd ways of living. The acronym L.E.S.S. — "Less Energy, Stuff, and Stimulation" — provides a good first approximation of the direction in which such efforts at controlled collapse might usefully move.

The point of this project isn't limited to its advantages on the personal scale, though these are fairly substantial. It's been demonstrated over and over again that personal example is far more effective than verbal rhetoric at laying the groundwork for collective change. A great deal of what keeps so many people pinned in the increasingly unsatisfying and unproductive lifestyles sold to them by the media is simply that they can't imagine a better alternative. Those people who collapse ahead of the rush and demonstrate that it's entirely possible to have a humane and decent life on a small fraction of the usual American resource footprint are already functioning as early adopters; with every month that passes, I hear from more people — especially young people in their teens and twenties — who are joining them, and helping to build a bridgehead to a world on the far side of the impending crisis.

The second possibility is considerably more complex, and resists summing up so neatly. In a series of posts here in 2010 and 2011, and then in my book Green Wizardry, I sketched out the toolkit of concepts and approaches that were central to the appropriate technology movement back in the 1970s, where I had my original education in the subjects central to this blog. I argued then, and still believe now, that by whatever combination of genius and sheer dumb luck, the pioneers of that movement managed to stumble across a set of approaches to the work of sustainability that are better suited to the needs of our time than anything that's been proposed since then.

Among the most important features of what I've called the "green wizardry" of appropriate tech is the fact that those who want to put it to work don't have to wait for the Hillary Clintons of the world to lift a finger. Millions of dollars in government grants and investment funds aren't necessary, or even particularly useful. From its roots in the Sixties counterculture, the appropriate tech scene inherited a focus on do-it-yourself projects that could be done with hand tools, hard work, and not much money. In an age of economic contraction, that makes even more sense than it did back in the day, and the ability to keep yourself and others warm, dry, fed, and provided with many of the other needs of life without potentially lethal dependencies on today's baroque technostructures has much to recommend it.

Nor, it has to be said, is appropriate tech limited to those who can afford a farm in the country; many of the most ingenious and useful appropriate tech projects were developed by and for people living in ordinary homes and apartments, with a small backyard or no soil at all available for gardening. The most important feature of appropriate tech, though, is that the core elements of its toolkit—intensive organic gardening and small-scale animal husbandry, homescale solar thermal technologies, energy conservation, and the like—are all things that will still make sense long after the current age of fossil fuel extraction has gone the way of the dinosaurs. Getting these techniques into as many hands as possible now is thus not just a matter of cushioning the impacts of the impending era of crisis; it's also a way to start building the sustainable world of the future right now.

Those two strategies, collapsing ahead of the rush and exploring the green wizardry of appropriate technology, have been core themes of this blog for quite a while now. There's a third project, though, that I've been exploring in a more abstract context here for a while now, and it's time to talk about how it can be applied to some of the most critical needs of our time.

In the early days of this blog, I pointed out that technological progress has a feature that's not always grasped by its critics, much less by those who've turned faith in progress into the established religion of our time. Very few new technologies actually meet human needs that weren't already being met, and so the arrival of a new technology generally leads to the abandonment of an older technology that did the same thing. The difficulty here is that new technologies nowadays are inevitably more dependent on global technostructures, and the increasingly brittle and destructive economic systems that support them, than the technologies they replace. New technologies look more efficient than old ones because more of the work is being done somewhere else, and can therefore be ignored—for now.

This is the basis for what I've called the externality trap. As technologies get more complex, that complexity allows more of their costs to be externalized—that is to say, pushed onto someone other than the makers or users of the technology. The pressures of a market economy guarantee that those economic actors who externalize more of their costs will prosper at the expense of those who externalize less. The costs thus externalized, though, don't go away; they get passed from hand to hand like hot potatoes and finally pile up in the whole systems—the economy, the society, the biosphere itself—that have no voice in economic decisions, but are essential to the prosperity and survival of every economic actor, and sooner or later those whole systems will break down under the burden. Unlimited technological progress in a market economy thus guarantees the economic, social, and/or environmental destruction of the society that fosters it.

The externality trap isn't just a theoretical possibility. It's an everyday reality, especially but not only in the United States and other industrial societies. There are plenty of forces driving the rising spiral of economic, social, and environmental disruption that's shaking the industrial world right down to its foundations, but among the most important is precisely the unacknowledged impact of externalized costs on the whole systems that support the industrial economy. It's fashionable these days to insist that increasing technological complexity and integration will somehow tame that rising spiral of crisis, but the externality trap suggests that exactly the opposite is the case — that the more complex and integrated technologies become, the more externalities they will generate. It's precisely because technological complexity makes it easy to ignore externalized costs that progress becomes its own nemesis.

Yes, I know, suggesting that progress isn't infallibly beneficent is heresy, and suggesting that progress will necessarily terminate itself with extreme prejudice is heresy twice over. I can't help that; it so happens that in most declining civilizations, ours included, the things that most need to be said are the things that, by and large, nobody wants to hear. That being the case, I might as well make it three for three and point out that the externality trap is a problem rather than a predicament. The difference, as longtime readers know, is that problems can be solved, while predicaments can only be faced. We don't have to keep loading an ever-increasing burden of externalized costs on the whole systems that support us — which is to say, we don't have to keep increasing the complexity and integration of the technologies that we use in our daily lives. We can stop adding to the burden; we can even go the other way.

Now of course suggesting that, even thinking it, is heresy on the grand scale. I'm reminded of a bit of technofluff in the Canadian media a week or so back that claimed to present a radically pessimistic view of the next ten years. Of course it had as much in common with actual pessimism as lite beer has with a pint of good brown ale; the worst thing the author, one Douglas Coupland, is apparently able to imagine is that industrial society will keep on doing what it's doing now — though the fact that more of what's happening now apparently counts as radical pessimism these days is an interesting point, and one that deserves further discussion.

The detail of this particular Dystopia Lite that deserves attention here, though, is Coupland's dogmatic insistence that "you can never go backward to a lessened state of connectedness." That's a common bit of rhetoric out of the mouths of tech geeks these days, to be sure, but it isn't even remotely true. I know quite a few people who used to be active on social media and have dropped the habit. I know others who used to have allegedly smart phones and went back to ordinary cell phones, or even to a plain land line, because they found that the costs of excess connectedness outweighed the benefits. Technological downshifting is already a rising trend, and there are very good reasons for that fact.

Most people find out at some point in adolescence that there really is such a thing as drinking too much beer. I think a lot of people are slowly realizing that the same thing is true of connectedness, and of the other prominent features of today's fashionable technologies. One of the data points that gives me confidence in that analysis is the way that people like Coupland angrily dismiss the possibility. Part of his display of soi-disant pessimism is the insistence that within a decade, people who don't adopt the latest technologies will be dismissed as passive-aggressive control freaks. Now of course that label could be turned the other way just as easily, but the point I want to make here is that nobody gets that bent out of shape about behaviors that are mere theoretical possibilities. Clearly, Coupland and his geek friends are already contending with people who aren't interested in conforming to the technosphere.

It's not just geek technologies that are coming in for that kind of rejection, either. These days, in the town where I live, teenagers whose older siblings used to go hotdogging around in cars ten years ago are doing the same thing on bicycles today. Granted, I live in a down-at-the-heels old mill town in the north central Appalachians, but there's more to it than that. For a lot of these kids, the costs of owning a car outweigh the benefits so drastically that cars aren't cool any more. One consequence of that shift in cultural fashion is that these same kids aren't contributing anything like so much to the buildup of carbon dioxide in the atmosphere, or to the other externalized costs generated by car ownership.

I've written here already about deliberate technological regression as a matter of public policy. Over the last few months, though, it's become increasingly clear to me that deliberate technological regression as a matter of personal choice is also worth pursuing. Partly this is because the deathgrip of failed policies on the political and economic order of the industrial world, as mentioned earlier, is tight enough that any significant change these days has to start down here at the grassroots level, with individuals, families, and communities, if it's going to get anywhere at all; partly, it's because technological regression, like anything else that flies in the face of the media stereotypes of our time, needs the support of personal example in order to get a foothold; partly, it's because older technologies, being less vulnerable to the impacts of whole-system disruptions, will still be there meeting human needs when the grid goes down, the economy freezes up, or something really does break the internet, and many of them will still be viable when the fossil fuel age is a matter for the history books.

Still, there's another aspect, and it's one that the essay by Douglas Coupland mentioned above managed to hit squarely: the high-tech utopia ballyhooed by the first generation or so of internet junkies has turned out in practice to be a good deal less idyllic, and in fact a good deal more dystopian, than its promoters claimed. All the wonderful things we were supposedly going to be able to do turned out in practice to consist of staring at little pictures on glass screens and pushing buttons, and these are not exactly the most interesting activities in the world, you know. The people who are dropping out of social media and ditching their allegedly smart phones for a less connected lifestyle have noticed this.

What's more, a great many more people — the kids hotdogging on bikes here in Cumberland are among them — are weighing the costs and benefits of complex technologies with cold eyes, and deciding that an older, simpler technology less dependent on global technosystems is not just more practical, but also, and importantly, more fun. True believers in the transhumanist cyberfuture will doubtless object to that last point, but the deathgrip of failed ideas on societies in decline isn't limited to the senile elites mentioned toward the beginning of this post; it can also afflict the fashionable intellectuals of the day, and make them proclaim the imminent arrival of the future's rising waters when the tide's already turned and is flowing back out to sea.

I'd like to suggest, in fact, that it's entirely possible that we could be heading toward a future in which people will roll their eyes when they think of Twitter, texting, 24/7 connectivity, and the rest of today's overblown technofetishism — like, dude, all that stuff is *so* twenty-teens! Meanwhile, those of us who adopt the technologies and habits of earlier eras, whether that adoption is motivated by mere boredom with little glass screens or by some more serious set of motives, may actually be on the cutting edge: the early adopters of the Retro Future. We'll talk about that more in the weeks ahead.

411: A FIELD GUIDE TO NEGATIVE PROGRESS

(Originally published 22 April 2015)

I've commented before in these posts that writing is always partly a social activity. What Mortimer Adler used to call the Great Conversation, the dance of ideas down the corridors of the centuries, shapes every word in a writer's toolkit; you can hardly write a page in English without drawing on a shade of meaning that Geoffrey Chaucer, say, or William Shakespeare, or Jane Austen first put into the language. That said, there's also a more immediate sense in which any writer who interacts with his or her readers is part of a social activity, and one of the benefits came my way just after last week's post.

That post began with a discussion of the increasingly surreal quality of America's collective life these days, and one of my readers—tip of the archdruidical hat to Anton Mett—had a fine example to offer. He'd listened to an economic report on the media, and the talking heads were going on and on about the US economy's current condition of, ahem, "negative growth." Negative growth? Why yes, that's the opposite of growth, and it's apparently quite a common bit of jargon in economics just now.

Of course the English language, as used by the authors named earlier among many others, has no shortage of perfectly clear words for the opposite of growth. "Decline" comes to mind; so does "decrease," and so does "contraction." Would it have been so very hard for the talking heads in that program, or their many equivalents in our economic life generally, to draw in a deep breath and actually come right out and say "The US economy has contracted," or "GDP has decreased," or even "we're currently in a state of economic decline"? Come on, economists, you can do it!

But of course they can't. Economists in general are supposed to provide, shall we say, negative clarity when discussing certain aspects of contemporary American economic life, and talking heads in the media are even more subject to this rule than most of their peers. Among the things about which they're supposed to be negatively clear, two are particularly relevant here; the first is that economic contraction happens, and the second is that that letting too much of the national wealth end up in too few hands is a very effective way to cause economic contraction. The logic here is uncomfortably straightforward — an economy that depends on consumer expenditures only prospers if consumers have plenty of money to spend — but talking about that equation would cast an unwelcome light on the culture of mindless kleptocracy entrenched these days at the upper end of the US socioeconomic ladder. So we get to witness the mass production of negative clarity about one of the main causes of negative growth.

It's entrancing to think of other uses for this convenient mode of putting things. I can readily see it finding a role in health care — "I'm sorry, ma'am," the doctor says, "but your husband is negatively alive;" in sports — "Well, Joe, unless the Orioles can cut down that negative lead of theirs, they're likely headed for a negative win;" and in the news — "The situation in Yemen is shaping up to be yet another negative triumph for US foreign policy." For that matter, it's time to update one of the more useful proverbs of recent years: what do you call an economist who makes a prediction? Negatively right.

Come to think of it, we might as well borrow the same turn of phrase for the subject of last week's post, the deliberate adoption of older, simpler, more independent technologies in place of today's newer, more complex, and more interconnected ones. I've been talking about that project so far under the negatively mealy-mouthed label "intentional technological regress," but hey, why not be cool and adopt the latest fashion? For this week, at least, we'll therefore redefine our terms a bit, and describe the same thing as "negative progress." Since negative growth sounds like just another kind of growth, negative progress ought to pass for another kind of progress, right?

With this in mind, I'd like to talk about some of the reasons that individuals, families, organizations, and communities, as they wend their way through today's cafeteria of technological choices, might want to consider loading up their plates with a good hearty helping of negative progress.

Let's start by returning to one of the central points raised here in earlier posts, the relationship between progress and the production of externalities. By and large, the more recent a technology is, the more of its costs aren't paid by the makers or the users of the technology, but are pushed off onto someone else. As I pointed out in a post two months ago, this isn't accidental; quite the contrary, as noted in the post just cited, it's hardwired into the relationship between progress and market economics, and bids fair to play a central role in the unraveling of the entire project of industrial civilization.

The same process of increasing externalities, though, has another face when seen from the point of view of the individual user of any given technology. When you externalize any cost of a technology, you become dependent on whoever or whatever picks up the cost you're not paying. What's more, you become dependent on the system that does the externalizing, and on whoever controls that system. Those dependencies aren't always obvious, but they impose costs of their own, some financial and some less tangible. What's more, unlike the externalized costs, a great many of these secondary costs land directly on the user of the technology.

It's interesting, and may not be entirely accidental, that there's no commonly used term for the entire structure of externalities and dependencies that stand behind any technology. Such a term is necessary here, so for the present purpose, we'll call the structure just named the technology's *externality system*. Given that turn of phrase, we can restate the point about progress made above: by and large, the more recent a technology is, the larger the externality system on which it depends.

An example will be useful here, so let's compare the respective externality systems of a bicycle and an automobile. Like most externality systems, these divide up more or less naturally into three categories: manufacture, maintenance, and use. Everything that goes into fabricating steel parts, for instance, all the way back to the iron ore in the mine, is an externality of manufacture; everything that goes into making lubricating oil, all the way back to drilling for the oil well, is an externality of maintenance; everything that goes into building roads suitable for bikes and cars is an externality of use.

Both externality systems are complex, and include a great many things that aren't obvious at first glance. The point I want to make here, though, is that the car's externality system is far and away the more complex of the two. In fact, the bike's externality system is a subset of the car's, and this reflects the specific historical order in which the two technologies were developed. When the technologies that were needed for a bicycle's externality system came into use, the first bicycles appeared; when all the additional technologies needed for a car's externality system were added onto that foundation, the first cars followed. That sort of incremental addition of externality-generating technologies is far and away the most common way that technology progresses.

We can thus restate the pattern just analyzed in a way that brings out some of its less visible and more troublesome aspects: by and large, each new generation of technology imposes more dependencies on its users than the generation it replaces. Again, a comparison between bicycles and automobiles will help make that clear. If you want to ride a bike, you've committed yourself to dependence on all the technical, economic, and social systems that go into manufacturing, maintaining, and using the bike; you can't own, maintain, and ride a bike without the steel mills that produce the frame, the chemical plants that produce the oil you squirt on the gears, the gravel pits that provide raw material for roads and bike paths, and so on.

On the other hand, you're not dependent on a galaxy of other systems that provide the externality system for your neighbor who drives. You don't depend on the immense network of pipelines, tanker trucks, and gas stations that provide him with fuel; you don't depend on the interstate highway system or the immense infrastructure that supports it; if you did the sensible thing and bought a bike that was made by a local craftsperson, your dependence on vast multinational corporations and all of their infrastructure, from sweatshop labor in Third World countries to financial shenanigans on Wall Street, is considerably smaller than that of your driving neighbor. Every dependency you have, your neighbor also has, but not vice versa.

Whether or not these dependencies matter is a complex thing. Obviously there's a personal equation—some people like to be independent, others are fine with being just one more cog in the megamachine—but there's also a historical factor to consider. In an age of economic expansion, the benefits of dependency very often outweigh the costs; standards of living are rising, opportunities abound, and it's easy to offset the costs of any given dependency. In a stable economy, one that's neither growing nor contracting, the benefits and costs of any given dependency need to be weighed carefully on a case by case basis, as one dependency may be worth accepting while another costs more than it's worth.

On the other hand, in an age of contraction and decline—or, shall we say, negative expansion?—most dependencies are problematic, and some are lethal. In a contracting economy, as everyone scrambles to hold onto as much as possible of the lifestyles of a more prosperous age, your profit is by definition someone else's loss, and dependency is just another weapon in the Hobbesian war of all against all. By many measures, the US economy has been contracting since before the bursting of the housing bubble in 2008; by some—in particular, the median and modal standards of living—it's been contracting since the 1970s, and the unmistakable hissing sound as air leaks out of the fracking bubble just now should be considered fair warning that another round of contraction is on its way.

With that in mind, it's time to talk about the downsides of dependency.

First of all, **dependency is expensive**. In the struggle for shares of a shrinking pie in a contracting economy, turning any available dependency into a cash cow is an obvious strategy, and one that's already very much in play. Consider the conversion of freeways into toll roads, an increasingly popular strategy in large parts of the United States. Consider, for that matter, the soaring price of health care in the US, which hasn't been accompanied by any noticeable increase in quality of care or treatment outcomes. In the dog-eat-dog world of economic contraction, commuters and sick people are just two of many captive populations whose dependencies make them vulnerable to exploitation. As the spiral of decline continues, it's safe to assume that any dependency that can be exploited will be exploited, and the more dependencies you have, the more likely you are to be squeezed dry.

The same principle applies to power as well as money; thus, **whoever owns the systems on which you depend, owns you**. In the United States, again, laws meant to protect employees from abusive behavior on the part of employers are increasingly ignored; as the number of the permanently unemployed keeps climbing year after year, employers know that those who still have jobs are desperate to keep them, and will put up with almost anything in order to keep that paycheck coming in. The old adage about the inadvisability of trying to fight City Hall has its roots in this same phenomenon; no matter what rights you have on paper, you're not likely to get far with them when the other side can stop picking up your garbage and then fine you for creating a public nuisance, or engage in some other equally creative use of their official prerogatives. As decline accelerates, expect to see dependencies increasingly used as levers for exerting various kinds of economic, political, and social power at your expense.

Finally, and crucially, if you're dependent on a failing system, **when the system goes down, so do you**. That's not just an issue for the future; it's a huge if still largely unmentioned reality of life in today's America, and in most other corners of the industrial world as well. Most of today's permanently unemployed got that way because the job on which they depended for their livelihood got offshored or automated out of existence; much of the rising tide of poverty across the United States is a direct result of the collapse of political and social systems that once countered the free market's innate tendency to drive the gap between rich and poor to Dickensian extremes. For that matter, how many people who never learned how to read a road map are already finding themselves in random places far from help because something went wrong with their GPS units?

It's very popular among those who recognize the problem with being shackled to a collapsing system to insist that it's a problem for the future, not the present. They grant that dependency is going to be a losing bet someday, but everything's fine for now, so why not enjoy the latest technological gimmickry while it's here? Of course that presupposes that you enjoy the latest technological gimmicry, which isn't necessarily a safe bet, and it also ignores the first two difficulties with dependency outlined above, which are very much present and accounted for right now. We'll let both those issues pass for the moment, though, because there's another factor that needs to be included in the calculation.

A practical example, again, will be useful here. In my experience, it takes around five years of hard work, study, and learning from your mistakes to become a competent vegetable gardener. If you're transitioning from buying all your vegetables at the grocery store to growing them in your backyard, in other words, you need

to start gardening about five years before your last trip to the grocery store. The skill and hard work that goes into growing vegetables is one of many things that most people in the world's industrial nations externalize, and those things don't just pop back to you
when you leave the produce section of the store for the last time.
There's a learning curve that has to be undergone.

Not that long ago, there used to be a subset of preppers who
grasped the fact that a stash of cartridges and canned wieners in a
locked box at their favorite deer camp cabin wasn't going to get them
through the downfall of industrial civilization, but hadn't factored
in the learning curve. Businesses targeting the prepper market thus
used to sell these garden-in-a-box kits, which had seed packets for
vegetables, a few tools, and a little manual on how to grow a garden. It's a good thing that Y2K, 2012, and all those other dates when
doom was supposed to arrive turned out to be wrong, because I
met a fair number of people who thought that having one of those
kits would save them even though they last grew a plant from seed
in fourth grade. If the apocalypse had actually arrived, survivors
a few years later would have gotten used to a landscape scattered
with empty garden-in-a-box kits, overgrown garden patches, and
the skeletal remains of preppers who starved to death because the
learning curve lasted just that much longer than they did.

The same principle applies to every other set of skills that has
been externalized by people in today's industrial society, and will
be coming back home to roost as economic contraction starts to cut
into the viability of our externality systems. You can adopt them
now, when you have time to get through the learning curve while
there's still an industrial society around to make up for the mistakes and failures that are inseparable from learning, or you can
try to adopt them later, when those same inevitable mistakes and
failures could very well land you in a world of hurt. You can also
adopt them now, when your dependencies haven't yet been used
to empty your wallet and control your behavior, or you can try to
adopt them later, when a much larger fraction of the resources and
autonomy you might have used for the purpose will have been extracted from you by way of those same dependencies.

This is a point I've made in previous posts here, but it applies
with particular force to negative progress — that is, to the deliberate adoption of older, simpler, more independent technologies in
place of the latest, dependency-laden offerings from the corporate

machine. As decline—or, shall we say, negative growth—becomes an inescapable fact of life in postprogress America, decreasing your dependence on sprawling externality systems is going to be an essential tactic.

Those who become early adopters of the retro future, to use an edgy term from last week's post, will have at least two, and potentially three, significant advantages. The first, as already noted, is that they'll be much further along the learning curve by the time rising costs, increasing instabilities, and cascading systems failures either put the complex technosystems out of reach or push the relationship between costs and benefits well over into losing-proposition territory. The second is that as more people catch onto the advantages of older, simpler, more sustainable technologies, surviving examples will become harder to find and more expensive to buy; in this case as in many others, collapsing first ahead of the rush is, among other things, the more affordable option.

The third advantage? Depending on exactly which old technologies you happen to adopt, and whether or not you have any talent for basement-workshop manufacture and the like, you may find yourself on the way to a viable new career as most other people will be losing their jobs—and their shirts. As the global economy comes unraveled and people in the United States lose their current access to shoddy imports from Third World sweatshops, there will be a demand for a wide range of tools and simple technologies that still make sense in a deindustrializing world. Those who already know how to use such technologies will be prepared to teach others how to use them; those who know how to repair, recondition, or manufacture those technologies will be prepared to barter, or to use whatever form of currency happens to replace today's mostly hallucinatory forms of money, to good advantage.

My guess, for what it's worth, is that salvage trades will be among the few growth industries in the 21st century, and the crafts involved in turning scrap metal and antique machinery into tools and machines that people need for their homes and workplaces will be an important part of that economic sector. To understand how that works, though, it's probably going to be necessary to get a clearer sense of the way that today's complex technostructures are likely to come apart. Next week, with that in mind, we'll spend some time thinking about the unthinkable—the impending death of the internet.

412: THE DEATH OF THE INTERNET: A PRE-MORTEM

(Originally published 29 April 2015)

The mythic role assigned to progress in today's popular culture has any number of odd effects, but one of the strangest is the blindness to the downside that clamps down on the collective imagination of our time once people become convinced that something or other is the wave of the future. It doesn't matter in the least how many or obvious the warning signs are, or how many times the same tawdry drama has been enacted. Once some shiny new gimmick gets accepted as the next glorious step in the invincible march of progress, most people lose the ability to imagine that the wave of the future might just do what waves generally do: that is to say, crest, break, and flow back out to sea, leaving debris scattered on the beach in its wake.

It so happens that I grew up in the middle of just such a temporary wave of the future, in the south Seattle suburbs in the 1960s, where every third breadwinner worked for Boeing. The wave in question was the supersonic transport, SST for short: a jetliner that would fly faster than sound, cutting hours off long flights. The inevitability of the SST was an article of faith locally, and not just because Boeing was building one; an Anglo-French consortium was in the lead with the Concorde, and the Soviets were working on the Tu-144, but the Boeing 2707 was expected to be the biggest and baddest of them all, a 300-seat swing-wing plane that was going to make commercial supersonic flight an everyday reality.

Long before the 2707 had even the most ghostly sort of reality, you could buy model kits of the plane, complete with Pan Am decals, at every hobby store in the greater Seattle area. For that matter, take Interstate 5 south from downtown Seattle past the sprawling Boeing plant just outside of town, and you'd see the image of the 2707 on the wall of one of the huge assembly buildings, a big delta-winged shape in white and gold winging its way through the imagined air toward the gleaming future in which so many people believed back then.

There was, as it happened, a small problem with the 2707, a problem it shared with all the other SST projects; it made no economic sense at all. It was, to be precise, what an earlier post here called a subsidy dumpster: that is, a project that was technically feasible but economically impractical, and existed mostly as a way to pump government subsidies into Boeing's coffers. Come 1971, the well ran dry: faced with gloomy numbers from the economists, worried calculations from environmental scientists, and a public not exactly enthusiastic about dozens of sonic booms a day rattling plates and cracking windows around major airports, Congress cut the project's funding.

That happened right when the US economy generally, and the notoriously cyclical airplane industry in particular, were hitting downturns. Boeing was Seattle's biggest employer in those days, and when it laid off employees en masse, the result was a local depression of legendary severity. You heard a lot of people in those days insisting that the US had missed out on the next aviation boom, and Congress would have to hang its head in shame once Concordes and Tu-144s were hauling passengers all over the globe. Of course that's not what happened; the Tu-144 flew a handful of commercial flights and then was grounded for safety reasons, and the Concorde lingered on, a technical triumph but an economic white elephant, until the last plane retired from service in 2003.

All this has been on my mind of late as I've considered the future of the internet. The comparison may seem far-fetched, but then that's what supporters of the SST would have said if anyone had compared the Boeing 2707 to, say, the zeppelin, another wave of the future that turned out to make too little economic sense to matter. Granted, the internet isn't a subsidy dumpster, and it's also much more complex than the SST; if anything, it might be compared to the entire system of commercial air travel, which we still have with us or the moment. Nonetheless, a strong case can be made that the internet, like the SST, doesn't actually make economic sense; it's being propped up by a set of financial gimmickry with a distinct resemblance to smoke and mirrors; and when those go away — and they will — much of what makes the internet so central a part of pop culture will go away as well.

It's probably necessary to repeat here that the reasons for this are economic, not technical. Every time I've discussed the hard economic realities that make the internet's lifespan in the deindustrial age roughly that of a snowball in Beelzebub's back yard, I've gotten a flurry of responses fixating on purely technical issues. Those issues are beside the point. No doubt it would be possible to make something like the internet technically feasible in a society on the far side of the Long Descent, but that doesn't matter; what matters is that the internet has to cover its operating costs, and it also has to compete with other ways of doing the things that the internet currently does.

It's a source of wry amusement to me that so many people seem to have forgotten that the internet doesn't actually do very much that's new. Long before the internet, people were reading the news, publishing essays and stories, navigating through unfamiliar neighborhoods, sharing photos of kittens with their friends, ordering products from faraway stores for home delivery, looking at pictures of people with their clothes off, sending anonymous hate-filled messages to unsuspecting recipients, and doing pretty much everything else that they do on the internet today. For the moment, doing these things on the internet is cheaper and more convenient than the alternatives, and that's what makes the internet so popular. If that changes — if the internet becomes more costly and less convenient than other options — its current popularity is unlikely to last.

Let's start by looking at the costs. Every time I've mentioned the future of the internet on this blog, I've gotten comments and emails from readers who think that the price of their monthly internet service is a reasonable measure of the cost of the internet as a whole. For a useful corrective to this delusion, talk to people who work in data centers. You'll hear about trucks pulling up to the loading dock every single day to offload pallet after pallet of brand new hard drives and other components, to replace those that will burn out that same day. You'll hear about power bills that would easily cover the electricity costs of a small city. You'll hear about many other costs as well. Data centers are not cheap to run, there are many thousands of them, and they're only one part of the vast infrastructure we call the internet: by many measures, the most gargantuan technological project in the history of our species.

Your monthly fee for internet service covers only a small portion of what the internet costs. Where does the rest come from? That depends on which part of the net we're discussing. The basic structure is paid for by internet service providers (ISPs), who recoup part of the costs from your monthly fee, part from the much larger fees paid by big users, and part by advertising. Content providers use some mix of advertising, pay-to-play service fees, sales of goods and services, packaging and selling your personal data to advertisers and government agencies, and new money from investors and loans to meet their costs. The ISPs routinely make a modest profit on the deal, but many of the content providers do not. Amazon may be the biggest retailer on the planet, for example, and its cash flow has soared in recent years, but its expenses have risen just as fast, and it rarely makes a profit. Many other content provider firms, including fish as big as Twitter, rack up big losses year after year.

How do they stay in business? A combination of vast amounts of investment money and ultracheap debt. That's very common in the early decades of a new industry, though it's been made a good deal easier by the Fed's policy of next-to-zero interest rates. Investors who dream of buying stock in the next Microsoft provide venture capital for internet startups, banks provide lines of credit for existing firms, the stock and bond markets snap up paper of various kinds churned out by internet businesses, and all that money goes to pay the bills. It's a reasonable gamble for the investors; they know perfectly well that a great many of the firms they're funding will go belly up within a few years, but the few that don't will either be bought up at inflated prices by one of the big dogs of the online world, or will figure out how to make money and then become big dogs themselves.

Notice, though, that this process has an unexpected benefit for ordinary internet users: a great many services are available for free, because venture-capital investors and lines of credit are footing the bill for the time being. Boosting the number of page views and clickthroughs is far more important for the future of an internet company these days than making a profit, and so the usual business plan is to provide plenty of free goodies to the public without worrying about the financial end of things. That's very convenient just now for internet users, but it fosters the illusion that the internet costs nothing.

As mentioned earlier, this sort of thing is very common in the early decades of a new industry. As the industry matures, markets become saturated, startups become considerably riskier, and venture capital heads for greener pastures. Once this happens, the companies that dominate the industry have to stay in business the old-fashioned way, by earning a profit, and that means charging as much as the market will bear, monetizing services that are currently free, and cutting service to the lowest level that customers will tolerate. That's business as usual, and it means the end of most of the noncommercial content that gives the internet so much of its current role in popular culture.

All other things being equal, in other words, the internet can be expected to follow the usual trajectory of a maturing industry, becoming more expensive, less convenient, and more tightly focused on making a quick buck with each passing year. Governments have already begun to tax internet sales, removing one of the core "stealth subsidies" that boosted the internet at the expense of other retail sectors, and taxation of the internet will only increase as cash-starved officials contemplate the tidal waves of money sloshing back and forth online. None of these changes will kill the internet, but they'll slap limits on the more utopian fantasies currently burbling about the web, and provide major incentives for individuals and businesses to back away from the internet and do things in the real world instead.

Then there's the increasingly murky world of online crime, espionage, and warfare, which promises to push very hard in the same direction in the years ahead. I think most people are starting to realize that on the internet, there's no such thing as secure data, and the costs of conducting business online these days include a growing risk of having your credit cards stolen, your bank accounts looted, your identity borrowed for any number of dubious purposes, and the files on your computer encrypted without your knowledge, so that you can be forced to pay a ransom for their release — this latter, or so I've read, is the latest hot new trend in internet crime.

Online crime is one of the few fields of criminal endeavor in which raw cleverness is all you need to make out, as the saying goes, like a bandit. In the years ahead, as a result, the internet may look less like an information superhighway and more like one of those grim inner city streets where not even the muggers go alone. Trends in online espionage and warfare are harder to track, but either or both could become a serious burden on the internet as well.

Online crime, espionage, and warfare aren't going to kill the internet, any more than the ordinary maturing of the industry will. Rather, they'll lead to a future in which costs of being online are very often greater than the benefits, and the internet is by and large endured rather than enjoyed. They'll also help drive the inevitable rebound away from the net. That's one of those things that always happens and always blindsides the cheerleaders of the latest technology: a few decades into its lifespan, people start to realize that they liked the old technology better, thank you very much, and go back to it. The rebound away from the internet has already begun, and will only become more visible as time goes on, making a great many claims about the future of the internet look as absurd as those 1950s articles insisting that in the future, every restaurant would inevitably be a drive-in.

To be sure, the resurgence of live theater in the wake of the golden age of movie theaters didn't end cinema, and the revival of bicycling in the aftermath of the automobile didn't make cars go away. In the same way, the renewal of interest in offline practices and technologies isn't going to make the internet go away. It's simply going to accelerate the shift of avant-garde culture away from an increasingly bleak, bland, unsafe, and corporate- and government-controlled internet and into alternative venues. That won't kill the internet, though once again it will put a stone marked R.I.P. atop the grave of a lot of the utopian fantasies that have clustered around today's net culture.

All other things being equal, in fact, there's no reason why the internet couldn't keep on its present course for years to come. Under those circumstances, it would shed most of the features that make it popular with today's avant-garde, and become one more centralized, regulated, vacuous mass medium, packed to the bursting point with corporate advertising and lowest-common-denominator content, with dissenting voices and alternative culture shut out or shoved into corners where nobody ever looks. That's the normal trajectory of an information technology in today's industrial civilization, after all; it's what happened with radio and television in their day, as the gaudy and grandiose claims of the early years gave way to the crass commercial realities of the mature forms of each medium.

But all other things aren't equal.

Radio and television, like most of the other familiar technologies that define life in a modern industrial society, were born and grew to maturity in an expanding economy. The internet, by contrast, was born during the last great blowoff of the petroleum age — the last decades of the twentieth century, during which the world's industrial nations took the oil reserves that might have cushioned the transition to sustainability, and blew them instead on one last orgy of over-the-top conspicuous consumption — and it's coming to maturity in the early years of an age of economic contraction and ecological blowback.

The rising prices, falling service quality, and relentless monetization of a maturing industry, together with the increasing burden of online crime and the inevitable rebound away from internet culture, will thus be hitting the internet in a time when the global economy no longer has the slack it once did, and the immense costs of running the internet in anything like its present form will have to be drawn from a pool of real wealth that has many other demands on it. What's more, quite a few of those other demands will be far more urgent than the need to provide consumers with a convenient way to send pictures of kittens to their friends. That stark reality will add to the pressure to monetize internet services, and provide incentives to those who choose to send their kitten pictures by other means.

It's crucial to remember here, as noted above, that the internet is simply a cheaper and more convenient way of doing things that people were doing long before the first website went live, and a big part of the reason why it's cheaper and more convenient right now is that internet users are being subsidized by the investors and venture capitalists who are funding the internet industry. That's not the only subsidy on which the internet depends, though. Along with the rest of industrial society, it's also subsidized by half a billion years of concentrated solar energy in the form of fossil fuels. As those deplete, the vast inputs of energy, labor, raw materials, industrial products, and other forms of wealth that sustain the internet will become increasingly expensive to provide, and ways of distributing kitten pictures that don't require the same inputs will prosper in the resulting competition.

There are also crucial issues of scale. Most pre-internet communications and information technologies scale down extremely well. A community of relatively modest size can have its own public library, its own small press, its own newspaper, and its own radio station running local programming, and could conceivably keep all of these functioning and useful even if the rest of humanity suddenly vanished from the map. Internet technology doesn't have that advantage. It's orders of magnitude more complex and expensive than a radio transmitter, not to mention the 14th-century technology of printing presses and card catalogs; what's more, on the scale of a small community, the benefits of using internet technology instead of simpler equivalents wouldn't come close to justifying the vast additional cost.

Now of course the world of the future isn't going to consist of a single community surrounded by desolate wasteland. That's one of the reasons why the demise of the internet won't happen all at once. Telecommunications companies serving some of the more impoverished parts of rural America are already letting their networks in those areas degrade, since income from customers doesn't cover the costs of maintenance. To my mind, that's a harbinger of the internet's future—a future of uneven decline punctuated by local and regional breakdowns, some of which will be fixed for a while.

That said, it's quite possible that there will still be an internet of some sort fifty years from now. It will connect government agencies, military units, defense contractors, and the handful of universities that survive the approaching implosion of the academic industry here in the US, and it may provide email and a few other services to the very rich, but it will otherwise have a lot more in common with the original DARPAnet than with the 24/7 virtual cosmos imagined by today's more gullible netheads.

Unless you're one of the very rich or an employee of one of the institutions just named, furthermore, you won't have access to the internet of 2065. You might be able to hack into it, if you have the necessary skills and are willing to risk a long stint in a labor camp, but unless you're a criminal or a spy working for the insurgencies flaring in the South or the mountain West, there's not much point to the stunt. If you're like most Americans in 2065, you live in Third World conditions without regular access to electricity or running water, and you've got other ways to buy things, find out what's going on in the world, find out how to get to the next town and, yes, look at pictures of people with their clothes off. What's more, in a deindustrializing world, those other ways of doing things will be cheaper, more resilient, and more useful than reliance on the baroque intricacies of a vast computer net.

Exactly when the last vestiges of the internet will sputter to silence is a harder question to answer. Long before that happens, though, it will have lost its current role as one of the poster children of the myth of perpetual progress, and turned back into what it really was all the time: a preposterously complex way to do things most people have always done by much simpler means, which only seemed to make sense during that very brief interval of human history when fossil fuels were abundant and cheap.

413: THE WHISPER OF THE SHUTOFF VALVE

(Originally published 6 May 2015)

Last week's post on the impending decline and fall of the internet fielded a great many responses. That was no surprise, to be sure; nor was I startled in the least to find that many of them rejected the thesis of the post with some heat. Contemporary pop culture's strident insistence that technological progress is a clock that never runs backwards made such counterclaims inevitable.

Still, it's always educational to watch the arguments fielded to prop up the increasingly shaky edifice of the modern mythology of progress, and the last week was no exception. A response I found particularly interesting from that standpoint appeared on one of the many online venues where *Archdruid Report* posts appear. One of the commenters insisted that my post should be rejected out of hand as mere doom and gloom; after all, he pointed out, it was ridiculous for me to suggest that fifty years from now, a majority of the population of the United States might be without reliable electricity or running water.

I've made the same prediction here and elsewhere a good many times. Each time, most of my readers or listeners seem to have taken it as a piece of sheer rhetorical hyperbole. The electrical grid and the assorted systems that send potable water flowing out of faucets are so basic to the rituals of everyday life in today's America that their continued presence is taken for granted. At most, it's conceivable that individuals might choose not to connect to them; there's a certain amount of talk about off-grid living here and there in the alternative media, for example. That people who want these things might not have access to them, though, is pretty much unthinkable.

Meanwhile, in Detroit and Baltimore, tens of thousands of residents are in the process of losing their access to water and electricity. The situation in both cities is much the same, and there's every reason to think that identical headlines will shortly appear in reference to other cities around the nation. Not that many decades ago, Detroit and Baltimore were important industrial centers with thriving economies. Along with more than a hundred other cities in America's Rust Belt, they were thrown under the bus with the first wave of industrial offshoring in the 1970s. The situation for both cities has only gotten worse since that time, as the United States completed its long transition from a manufacturing economy producing goods and services to a bubble economy that mostly produces unpayable IOUs.

These days, the middle-class families whose tax payments propped up the expansive urban systems of an earlier day have long since moved out of town. Most of the remaining residents are poor, and the ongoing redistribution of wealth in America toward the very rich and away from everyone else has driven down the income of the urban poor to the point that many of them can no longer afford to pay their water and power bills. City utilities in Detroit and Baltimore have been sufficiently sensitive to political pressures that large-scale utility shutoffs have been delayed, but shifts in the political climate in both cities are bringing the delays to an end; water bills have increased steadily, more and more people have been unable to pay them, and the result is as predictable as it is brutal.

The debate over the Detroit and Baltimore shutoffs has followed the usual pattern, as one side wallows in bash-the-poor rhetoric while the other side insists plaintively that access to utilities is a human right. Neither side seems to be interested in talking about the broader context in which these disputes take shape. There are two aspects to that broader context, and it's a tossup which is the more threatening.

The first aspect is the failure of the US economy to recover in any meaningful sense from the financial crisis of 2008. Now of course politicians from Obama on down have gone overtime grandstanding about the alleged recovery we're in. I invite any of my readers who bought into that rhetoric to try the following simple experiment. Go to your favorite internet search engine and look up how much the fracking industry has added to the US gross domestic product each year from 2009 to 2014. Now subtract that figure from the US gross domestic product for each of those years, and see how much growth there's actually been in the rest of the economy since the real estate bubble imploded.

What you'll find, if you take the time to do that, is that the rest of the US economy has been flat on its back gasping for air for the last five years. What makes this even more problematic, as I've noted in several previous posts here, is that the great fracking boom about which we've heard so much for the last five years was never actually the game-changing energy revolution its promoters claimed; it was simply another installment in the series of speculative bubbles that has largely replaced constructive economic activity in this country over the last two decades or so.

What's more, it's not the only bubble currently being blown, and it may not even be the largest. We've also got a second tech-stock bubble, with money-losing internet corporations racking up absurd valuations in the stock market while they burn through millions of dollars of venture capital; we've got a student loan bubble, in which billions of dollars of loans that will never be paid back have been bundled, packaged, and sold to investors just like all those no-doc mortgages were a decade ago; car loans are getting the same treatment; the real estate market is fizzing again in many urban areas as investors pile into another round of lavishly marketed property investments—well, I could go on for some time. It's entirely possible that if all the bubble activity were to be subtracted from the last five years or so of GDP, the result would show an economy in freefall.

Certainly that's the impression that emerges if you take the time to check out those economic statistics that aren't being systematically jiggered by the US government for PR purposes. The number of long-term unemployed in America is at an all-time high; roads, bridges, and other basic infrastructure is falling to pieces; measurements of US public health—generally considered a good proxy for the real economic condition of the population—are well below those of other industrial countries, heading toward Third World levels; abandoned shopping malls litter the landscape while major retailers announce more than 6000 store closures. These are not things you see in an era of economic expansion, or even one of relative stability; they're markers of decline.

The utility shutoffs in Detroit and Baltimore are further symptoms of the same broad process of economic unraveling. It's true, as pundits in the media have been insisting since the story broke, that utilities get shut off for nonpayment of bills all the time. It's equally true that shutting off the water supply of 20,000 or 30,000 people all at once is pretty much unprecedented. Both cities, please note, have had very large populations of poor people for many decades now. Those who like to blame a "culture of poverty" for the tangled relationship between US governments and the American poor, and of course that trope has been rehashed by some of the pundits just mentioned, haven't yet gotten around to explaining how the culture of poverty all at once inspired tens of thousands of people who had been paying their utility bills to stop doing so.

There are plenty of good reasons, after all, why poor people who used to pay their bills can't do so any more. Standard business models in the United States used to take it for granted that the best way to run the staffing dimensions of any company, large or small, was to have as many full-time positions as possible and to use raises and other practical incentives to encourage employees who were good at their jobs to stay with the company. That approach has been increasingly unfashionable in today's America, partly due to perverse regulatory incentives that penalize employers for offering full-time positions, partly to the emergence of attitudes in corner offices that treat employees as just another commodity. (I doubt it's any kind of accident that most corporations nowadays refer to their employment offices as "human resource departments." What do you do with a resource? You exploit it.)

These days, most of the jobs available to the poor are part-time, pay very little, and include nasty little clawbacks in the form of requirements that employees pay out of pocket for uniforms, equipment, and other things that employers used to provide as a matter of course. Meanwhile housing prices and rents are rising well above their post-2008 dip, and a great many other necessities are becoming more costly — inflation may be under control, or so the official statistics say, but anyone who's been shopping at the same grocery store for the last eight years knows perfectly well that prices kept on rising anyway.

So you've got falling incomes running up against rising costs for food, rent, and utilities, among other things. In the resulting collision, something's got to give, and for tens of thousands of poor Detroiters and Baltimoreans, what gave first was the ability to keep current on their water bills. Expect to see the same story playing out across the country as more people on the bottom of the income pyramid find themselves in the same situation. What you won't hear in the media, though it's visible enough if you know where to look and are willing to do so, is that people above the bottom of the income pyramid are also losing ground, being forced down toward economic nonpersonhood. From the middle classes down, everyone's losing ground.

That process doesn't continue any further than the middle class, to be sure. It's been pointed out repeatedly that over the last four decades or so, the distribution of wealth in America has skewed further and further out of balance, with the top 20% of incomes taking a larger and larger share at the expense of everybody else. That's an important factor in bringing about the collision just described. Some thinkers on the radical fringes of American society, which is the only place in the US you can talk about such things these days, have argued that the raw greed of the well-to-do is the sole reason why so many people lower down the ladder are being pushed further down still.

Scapegoating rhetoric of that sort is always comforting, because it holds out the promise — theoretically, if not practically — that something can be done about the situation. If only the thieving rich could be lined up against a convenient brick wall and removed from the equation in the time-honored fashion, the logic goes, people in Detroit and Baltimore could afford to pay their water bills! I suspect we'll hear such claims increasingly often as the years pass and more and more Americans find their access to familiar comforts and necessities slipping away. Simple answers are always popular in such times, not least when the people being scapegoated go as far out of their way to make themselves good targets for such exercises as the American rich have done in recent decades.

John Kenneth Galbraith's equation of the current US political and economic elite with the French aristocracy on the eve of revolution rings even more true than it did when he wrote it back in 1992, in the pages of *The Culture of Contentment*. The unthinking extravagances, the casual dismissal of the last shreds of *noblesse oblige*, the obsessive pursuit of personal advantages and private feuds without the least thought of the potential consequences, the bland inability to recognize that the power, privilege, wealth, and sheer survival of the aristocracy depended on the system the aristocrats themselves were destabilizing by their actions—it's all there, complete with sprawling overpriced mansions that could just about double for Versailles. The urban mobs that played so large a role back in 1789 are warming up for their performances as I write these words; the only thing left to complete the picture is a few tumbrils and a guillotine, and those will doubtless arrive on cue.

The senility of the current US elite, as noted in a previous post here, is a massive political fact in today's America. Still, it's not the only factor in play here. Previous generations of wealthy Americans recognized without too much difficulty that their power, prosperity, and survival depended on the willingness of the rest of the population to put up with their antics. Several times already in America's history, elite groups have allied with populist forces to push through reforms that sharply weakened the power of the wealthy elite, because they recognized that the alternative was a social explosion even more destructive to the system on which elite power depends.

I suppose it's possible that the people currently occupying the upper ranks of the political and economic pyramid in today's America are just that much more stupid than their equivalents in the Jacksonian, Progressive, and New Deal eras. Still, there's at least one other explanation to hand, and it's the second of the two threatening contextual issues mentioned earlier.

Until the nineteenth century, fresh running water piped into homes for everyday use was purely an affectation of the very rich in a few very wealthy and technologically adept societies. Sewer pipes to take dirty water and human wastes out of the house belonged in the same category. This wasn't because nobody knew how plumbing works—the Romans had competent plumbers, for example, and water faucets and flush toilets were to be found in Roman mansions of the imperial age. The reason those same things weren't found in every Roman house was economic, not technical.

Behind that economic issue lay an ecological reality. White's Law, one of the foundational principles of human ecology, states that economic development is a function of energy per capita. For a society before the industrial age, the Roman Empire had an impressive amount of energy per capita to expend; control over the agricultural economy of the Mediterranean basin, modest inputs from sunlight, water and wind, and a thriving slave industry fed by the expansion of Roman military power all fed into the capacity of Roman society to develop itself economically and technically. That's why rich Romans had running water and iced drinks in summer, while their equivalents in ancient Greece a few centuries earlier had to make do without either one.

Fossil fuels gave industrial civilization a supply of energy many orders of magnitude greater than any previous human civilization has had—a supply vast enough that the difference remains huge even after the vast expansion of population that followed the industrial revolution. There was, however, a catch—or, more precisely, two catches. To begin with, fossil fuels are finite, nonrenewable resources; no matter how much handwaving is employed in the attempt to obscure this point—and whatever else might be in short supply these days, that sort of handwaving is not—every barrel of oil, ton of coal, or cubic foot of natural gas that's burnt takes the world one step closer to the point at which there will be no economically extractable reserves of oil, coal, or natural gas at all.

That's catch #1. Catch #2 is subtler, and considerably more dangerous. Oil, coal, and natural gas don't leap out of the ground on command. They have to be extracted and processed, and this takes energy. Companies in the fossil fuel industries have always targeted the deposits that cost less to extract and process, for obvious economic reasons. What this means, though, is that over time, a larger and larger fraction of the energy yield of oil, coal, and natural gas has to be put right back into extracting and processing oil, coal, and natural gas—and this leaves less and less for all other uses.

That's the vise that's tightening around the American economy these days. The great fracking boom, to the extent that it wasn't simply one more speculative gimmick aimed at the pocketbooks of chumps, was an attempt to make up for the ongoing decline of America's conventional oilfields by going after oil that was far more expensive to extract. The fact that none of the companies at the heart of the fracking boom ever turned a profit, even when oil brought more than $100 a barrel, gives some sense of just how costly shale oil is to get out of the ground. The financial cost of extraction, though, is a proxy for the energy cost of extraction—the amount of energy, and of the products of energy, that had to be thrown into the task of getting a little extra oil out of marginal source rock.

Energy needed to extract energy, again, can't be used for any other purpose. It doesn't contribute to the energy surplus that makes economic development possible. As the energy industry itself takes a bigger bite out of each year's energy production, every other economic activity loses part of the fuel that makes it run. That, in turn, is the core reason why the American economy is on the ropes, America's infrastructure is falling to bits— and Americans in Detroit and Baltimore are facing a transition to Third World conditions, without electricity or running water.

I suspect, for what it's worth, that the shutoff notices being mailed to tens of thousands of poor families in those two cities are a good working model for the way that industrial civilization itself will wind down. It won't be sudden; for decades to come, there will still be people who have access to what Americans today consider the ordinary necessities and comforts of every-day life; there will just be fewer of them each year. Outside that narrowing circle, the number of economic nonpersons will grow steadily, one shutoff notice at a time.

As I've pointed out in previous posts, the line of fracture be-tween the senile elite and what Arnold Toynbee called the inter-nal proletariat—the people who live within a failing civilization's borders but receive essentially none of its benefits—eventually opens into a chasm that swallows what's left of the civilization. Sometimes the tectonic processes that pull the chasm open are hard to miss, but there are times when they're a good deal more difficult to sense in action, and this is one of these latter times. Listen to the whisper of the shutoff valve, and you'll hear tens of thousands of Americans being cut off from basic services the rest of us, for the time being, still take for granted.

414: THE ERA OF PRETENSE

(Originally published 13 May 2015)

I've mentioned in previous posts here on *The Archdruid Report* the educational value of the comments I receive from readers in the wake of each week's essay. My post two weeks ago on the death of the internet was unusually productive along those lines. One of the comments I got in response to that post gave me the theme for last week's essay, but there was at least one other comment calling for the same treatment. Like the one that sparked last week's post, it appeared on one of the many other internet forums on which *The Archdruid Report*, and it unintentionally pointed up a common and crucial failure of imagination that shapes, or rather misshapes, the conventional wisdom about our future.

Curiously enough, the point that set off the commenter in question was the same one that incensed the author of the denunciation mentioned in last week's post: my suggestion in passing that fifty years from now, most Americans may not have access to electricity or running water. The commenter pointed out angrily that I'd claimed that the twilight of industrial civilization would be a ragged arc of decline over one to three centuries. Now, he claimed, I was saying that it was going to take place in the next fifty years, and this apparently convinced him that everything I said ought to be dismissed out of hand.

I run into this sort of confusion all the time. If I suggest that the decline and fall of a civilization usually takes several centuries, I get accused of inconsistency if I then note that one of the sharper downturns included in that process may be imminent. If I point out that the United States is likely within a decade or two of serious economic and political turmoil, driven partly by the implosion of its faltering global hegemony and partly by a massive crisis of legitimacy that's all but dissolved the tacit contract between the existing order of US society and the masses who passively support it, I get accused once again of inconsistency if I then say that whatever comes out the far side of that crisis — whether it's a battered and bruised United States or a patchwork of successor states — will then face a couple of centuries of further decline and disintegration before the deindustrial dark age bottoms out.

Now of course there's nothing inconsistent about any of these statements. The decline and fall of a civilization isn't a single event, or even a single linear process; it's a complex fractal reality composed of many different events on many different scales in space and time. If it takes one to three centuries, as usual, those centuries are going to be taken up by an uneven drumbeat of wars, crises, natural disasters, and assorted breakdowns on a variety of time frames with an assortment of local, regional, national, or global effects. The collapse of US global hegemony is one of those events; the unraveling of the economic and technological framework that currently provides most Americans with electricity and running water is another, but neither of those is anything like the whole picture.

It's probably also necessary to point out that any of my readers who think that being deprived of electricity and running water is the most drastic kind of collapse imaginable have, as the saying goes, another think coming. Right now, in our oh-so-modern world, there are billions of people who get by without regular access to electricity and running water, and most of them aren't living under dark age conditions. A century and a half ago, when railroads, telegraphs, steamships, and mechanical printing presses were driving one of history's great transformations of transport and information technology, next to nobody had electricity or running water in their homes. The technologies of 1865 are not dark age technologies; in fact, the gap between 1865 technologies and dark age technologies is considerably greater, by most metrics, than the gap between 1865 technologies and the ones we use today.

Furthermore, whether or not Americans have access to running water and electricity may not have as much to say about the future of industrial society everywhere in the world as the conventional wisdom would suggest. I know that some of my American readers will be shocked out of their socks to hear this, but the United States is not the whole world. It's not even the center of the world. If the United States implodes over the next two decades, leaving behind a series of bankrupt failed states to squabble over its territory and the little that remains of its once-lavish resource base, that process will be a great source of gaudy and gruesome stories for the news media of the world's other continents, but it won't affect the lives of the readers of those stories much more than equivalent events in Africa and the Middle East affect the lives of Americans today.

As it happens, over the next one to three centuries, the benefits of industrial civilization are going to go away for everyone. (The costs will be around a good deal longer—in the case of the nuclear wastes we're so casually heaping up for our descendants, a good quarter of a million years, but those and their effects are rather more localized than some of today's apocalyptic rhetoric likes to suggest.) The reasoning here is straightforward. White's Law, one of the fundamental principles of human ecology, states that economic development is a function of energy per capita; the immense treasure trove of concentrated energy embodied in fossil fuels, and that alone, made possible the sky-high levels of energy per capita that gave the world's industrial nations their brief era of exuberance; as fossil fuels deplete, and remaining reserves require higher and higher energy inputs to extract, the levels of energy per capita the industrial nations are used to having will go away forever.

It's important to be clear about this. Fossil fuels aren't simply one energy source among others; in terms of concentration, usefulness, and fungibility—that is, the ability to be turned into any other form of energy that might be required—they're in a category all by themselves. Repeated claims that fossil fuels can be replaced with nuclear power, renewable energy resources, or what have you sound very good on paper, but every attempt to put those claims to the test so far has either gone belly up in short order, or become a classic subsidy dumpster surviving purely on a diet of government funds and mandates.

Three centuries ago, the earth's fossil fuel reserves were the largest single deposit of concentrated energy in this part of the universe; now we've burnt through nearly all the easily accessible reserves, and we're scrambling to keep the tottering edifice of industrial society going by burning through the dregs that remain. As those run out, the remaining energy resources—almost all of them renewables—will certainly sustain a variety of human societies, and some of those will be able to achieve a fairly high level of complexity and maintain some kinds of advanced technologies. The kind of absurd extravagance that passes for a normal standard of living among the more privileged inmates of the industrial nations is another matter, and as the fossil fuel age sunsets out, it will end forever.

The fractal trajectory of decline and fall mentioned earlier in this post is simply the way this equation works out on the day-to-day scale of ordinary history. Still, those of us who happen to be living through a part of that trajectory might reasonably be curious about how it's likely to unfold in our lifetimes. I've discussed in a previous series of posts, and in my book *Decline and Fall: The End of Empire and the Future of Democracy in 21st Century America*, how the end of US global hegemony is likely to unfold, but as already noted, that's only a small portion of the broader picture. Is a broader view possible?

Fortunately history, the core resource I've been using to try to make sense of our future, has plenty to say about the broad patterns that unfold when civilizations decline and fall. Now of course I know all I have to do is mention that history might be relevant to our present predicament, and a vast chorus of voices across the North American continent and around the world will bellow at rooftop volume, "But it's different this time!" With apologies to my regular readers, who've heard this before, it's probably necessary to confront that weary thoughtstopper again before we proceed.

As I've noted before, claims that it's different this time are right where it doesn't matter and wrong where it counts. Predictions made on the basis of history—and not just by me—have consistently predicted events over the last decade or so far more accurately than predictions based on the assumption that history doesn't matter. How many times, dear reader, have you heard someone insist that industrial civilization is going to crash to ruin in the next six months, and then watched those six months roll merrily by without any sign of the predicted crash? For that matter, how many times have you heard someone insist that this or that policy that's never worked any other time that it's been tried, or this or that piece of technological vaporware that's been the subject of failed promises for decades, will inevitably put industrial society back on its alleged trajectory to the stars—and how many times has the policy or the vaporware been quietly shelved, and something else promoted using the identical rhetoric, when it turned out not to perform as advertised?

It's been a source of wry amusement to me to watch the same weary, dreary, repeatedly failed claims of imminent apocalypse and inevitable progress being rehashed year after year, varying only in the fine details of the cataclysm du jour and the techno-savior du jour, while the future nobody wants to talk about is busily taking shape around us. Decline and fall isn't something that will happen sometime in the conveniently distant future; it's happening right now in the United States and around the world. The amusement, though, is tempered with a sense of familiarity, because the period in which decline is under way but nobody wants to admit that fact is one of the recurring features of the history of decline.

There are, very generally speaking, five broad phases in the decline and fall of a civilization. I know it's customary in historical literature to find nice dull labels for such things, but I'm in a contrary mood as I write this, so I'll give them unfashionably colorful names: the eras of pretense, impact, response, breakdown, and dissolution. Each of these is complex enough that it'll need a discussion of its own; this week, we'll talk about the era of pretense, which is the one we're in right now.

Eras of pretense are by no means limited to the decline and fall of civilizations. They occur whenever political, economic, or social arrangements no longer work, but the immediate costs of admitting that those arrangements don't work loom considerably larger in the collective imagination than the future costs of leaving those arrangements in place. It's a curious but consistent wrinkle of human psychology that this happens even if those future costs soar right off the scale of frightfulness and lethality; if the people who would have to pay the immediate costs don't want to do so, in fact, they will reliably and cheerfully pursue policies that lead straight to their own total bankruptcy or violent extermination, and never let themselves notice where they're headed.

Speculative bubbles are a great setting in which to watch eras of pretense in full flower. In the late phases of a bubble, when it's clear to anyone who has two spare neurons to rub together that the boom du jour is cobbled together of equal parts delusion and chicanery, the people who are most likely to lose their shirts in the crash are the first to insist at the top of their lungs that the bubble isn't a bubble and their investments are guaranteed to keep on increasing in value forever. Those of my readers who got the chance to watch some of their acquaintances go broke in the real estate bust of 2008-9, as I did, will have heard this sort of self-deception at full roar; those who missed the opportunity can make up for the omission by checking out the ongoing torrent of claims that the soon-to-be-late fracking bubble is really a massive energy revolution that will make America wealthy and strong again.

The history of revolutions offers another helpful glimpse at eras of pretense. France in the decades before 1789, to cite a conveniently well-documented example, was full of people who had every reason to realize that the current state of affairs was hopelessly unsustainable and would have to change. The things about French politics and economics that had to change, though, were precisely those things that the French monarchy and aristocracy were unwilling to change, because any such reforms would have cost them privileges they'd had since time out of mind and were unwilling to relinquish.

Louis XIV, who finished up his long and troubled reign a supreme realist, is said to have muttered "Après moi, le déluge" — "Once I'm gone, this sucker's going down" may not be a literal translation, but it catches the flavor of the utterance — but that degree of clarity was rare in his generation, and all but absent in those of his increasingly feckless successors. Thus the courtiers and aristocrats of the Old Regime amused themselves at the nation's expense, dabbled in avant-garde thought, and kept their eyes tightly closed to the consequences of their evasions of looming reality, while the last opportunities to excuse themselves from a one-way trip to visit the guillotine and spare France the cataclysms of the Terror and the Napoleonic wars slipped silently away.

That's the bitter irony of eras of pretense. Under most circumstances, they're the last period when it would be possible to do anything constructive on the large scale about the crisis looming immediately ahead, but the mass evasion of reality that frames the collective thinking of the time stands squarely in the way of any such constructive action. In the era of pretense before a speculative bust, people who could have quietly cashed in their positions and pocketed their gains double down on their investments, and guarantee that they'll be ruined once the market stops being liquid. In the era of pretense before a revolution, in the same way, those people and classes that have the most to lose reliably take exactly those actions that ensure that they will in fact lose everything. If history has a sense of humor, this is one of the places that it appears in its most savage form.

The same points are true, in turn, of the eras of pretense that precede the downfall of a civilization. In a good many cases, where too few original sources survive, the age of pretense has to be inferred from archeological remains. We don't know what motives inspired the ancient Mayans to build their biggest pyramids in the years immediately before the Terminal Classic period toppled over into a savage political and demographic collapse, but it's hard to imagine any such project being set in motion without the usual evasions of an era of pretense being involved Where detailed records of dead civilizations survive, though, the sort of rhetorical handwaving common to bubbles before the bust and decaying regimes on the brink of revolution shows up with knobs on. Thus the panegyrics of the Roman imperial court waxed ever more lyrical and bombastic about Rome's invincibility and her civilizing mission to the nations as the Empire stumbled deeper into its terminal crisis, echoing any number of other court poets in any number of civilizations in their final hours.

For that matter, a glance through classical Rome's literary remains turns up the remarkable fact that those of her essayists and philosophers who expressed worries about her survival wrote, almost without exception, during the Republic and the early Empire; the closer the fall of Rome actually came, the more certainty Roman authors expressed that the Empire was eternal and the latest round of troubles was just one more temporary bump on the road to peace and prosperity. It took the outsider's vision of Augustine of Hippo to proclaim that Rome really was falling — and even that could only be heard once the Visigoths sacked Rome and the era of pretense gave way to the age of impact.

The present case is simply one more example to add to an already lengthy list. In the last years of the nineteenth century, it was common for politicians, pundits, and mass media in the United States, the British empire, and other industrial nations to discuss the possibility that the advanced civilization of the time might be headed for the common fate of nations in due time. The intellectual history of the twentieth century is, among other things, a chronicle of how that discussion was shoved to the margins of our collective discourse, just as the ecological history of the same century is among other things a chronicle of how the worries of the previous era became the realities of the one we're in today. The closer we've moved toward the era of impact, that is, the more unacceptable it has become for anyone in public life to point out that the problems of the age are not just superficial.

Listen to the pablum that passes for political discussion in Washington DC or the mainstream US media these days, or the even more vacuous noises being made by party flacks as the country stumbles wearily toward yet another presidential election. That the American dream of upward mobility has become an American nightmare of accelerating impoverishment outside the narrowing circle of the kleptocratic rich, that corruption and casual disregard for the rule of law are commonplace in political institutions from local to Federal levels, that our medical industry charges more than any other nation's and still provides the worst health care in the industrial world, that our schools no longer teach anything but contempt for learning, that the national infrastructure and built environment are plunging toward Third World conditions at an ever-quickening pace, that a brutal and feckless foreign policy embraced by both major parties is alienating our allies while forcing our enemies to set aside their mutual rivalries and make common cause against us: these are among the issues that matter, but they're not the issues you'll hear discussed as the latest gaggle of carefully airbrushed candidates go through their carefully scripted elect-me routines on their way to the 2016 election.

If history teaches anything, though, it's that eras of pretense eventually give way to eras of impact. That doesn't mean that the pretense will go away—long after Alaric the Visigoth sacked Rome, for example, there were still plenty of rhetors trotting out the same tired clichés about Roman invincibility—but it does mean that a significant number of people will stop finding the pretense relevant to their own lives. How that happens in other historical examples, and how it might happen in our own time, will be the theme of next week's post.

415: THE ERA OF IMPACT

(Originally published 20 May 2015)

Of all the wistful superstitions that cluster around the concept of the future in contemporary popular culture, the most enduring has to be the notion that somehow, sooner or later, something will happen to shake the majority out of its complacency and get it to take seriously the crisis of our age. Week after week, I field comments and emails that presuppose that belief. People want to know how soon I think the shock of awakening will finally hit, or wonder whether this or that event will do the trick, or simply insist that the moment has to come sooner or later.

To all such inquiries and expostulations I have no scrap of comfort to offer. Quite the contrary, what history shows is that a sudden awakening to the realities of a difficult situation is far and away the least likely result of what I've called the era of impact, the second of the five stages of collapse. (The first, for those who missed last week's post, is the era of pretense; the remaining three, which will be covered in the coming weeks, are the eras of response, breakdown, and dissolution.)

The era of impact is the point at which it becomes clear to most people that something has gone wrong with the most basic narratives of a society—not just a little bit wrong, in the sort of way that requires a little tinkering here and there, but really, massively, spectacularly wrong. It arrives when an asset class that was supposed to keep rising in price forever stops rising, does its Wile E. Coyote moment of hang time, and then drops like a stone. It shows up when an apparently entrenched political system, bristling with soldiers and secret police, implodes in a matter of days or weeks and is replaced by a provisional government whose leaders look just as stunned as everyone else. It comes whenever a state of affairs that was assumed to be permanent runs into serious trouble — but somehow it never seems to succeed in getting people to notice just how temporary that state of affairs always was.

Since history is the best guide we've got to how such events work out in the real world, I want to take a couple of examples of the kind just outlined and explore them in a little more detail. The stock market bubble of the 1920s makes a good case study on a relatively small scale. In the years leading up to the crash of 1929, stock values in the US stock market quietly disconnected themselves from the economic fundamentals and began what was, for the time, an epic climb into la-la land. There were important if unmentionable reasons for that airy detachment from reality; the most significant was the increasingly distorted distribution of income in 1920s America, which put more and more of the national wealth in the hands of fewer and fewer people and thus gutted the national economy.

It's one of the repeated lessons of economic history that money in the hands of the rich does much less good for the economy as a whole than money in the hands of the working classes and the poor. The reasoning here is as simple as it is inescapable. Industrial economies survive and thrive on consumer expenditures, but consumer expenditures are limited by the ability of consumers to buy the things they want and need. As money is diverted away from the lower end of the economic pyramid, you get demand destruction — the process by which those who can't afford to buy things stop buying them — and consumer expenditures fall off. The rich, by contrast, divert a large share of their income out of the consumer economy into investments; the richer they get, the more of the national wealth ends up in investments rather than consumer expenditures; and as consumer expenditures falter, and investments linked to the consumer economy falter in turn, more and more money ends up in illiquid speculative vehicles that are disconnected from the productive economy and do nothing to stimulate demand.

That's what happened in the 1920s. All through the decade in the US, the rich got richer and the poor got screwed, speculation took the place of productive investment throughout the US economy, and the well-to-do wallowed in the wretched excess chronicled in F. Scott Fitzgerald's *The Great Gatsby* while most other people struggled to get by. The whole decade was a classic era of pretense, crowned by the delusional insistence — splashed all over the media of the time—that everyone in the US could invest in the stock market and, since the market was of course going to keep on rising forever, everyone in the US would thus inevitably become rich.

It's interesting to note that there were people who saw straight through the nonsense and tried to warn their fellow Americans about the inevitable consequences. They were denounced six ways from Sunday by all right-thinking people, in language identical to that used more recently on those of us who've had the effrontery to point out that an infinite supply of oil can't be extracted from a finite planet. The people who insisted that the soaring stock values of the late 1920s were the product of one of history's great speculative bubbles were dead right; they had all the facts and figures on their side, not to mention plain common sense; but nobody wanted to hear it.

When the stock market peaked just before the Labor Day weekend in 1929 and started trending down, therefore, the immediate response of all right-thinking people was to insist at the top of their lungs that nothing of the sort was happening, that the market was simply catching its breath before its next great upward leap, and so on. Each new downward lurch was met by a new round of claims along these lines, louder, more dogmatic, and more strident than the one that preceded it, and nasty personal attacks on anyone who didn't support the delusional consensus filled the media of the time.

People were still saying those things when the bottom dropped out of the market.

Tuesday, October 29, 1929 can reasonably be taken as the point at which the era of pretense gave way once and for all to the era of impact. That's not because it was the first day of the crash—there had been ghastly slumps on the previous Thursday and Monday, on the heels of two months of less drastic but still seriously ugly declines—but because, after that day, the pundits and the media pretty much stopped pretending that nothing was wrong. Mind you, next to nobody was willing to talk about what exactly had gone wrong, or why it had gone wrong, but the pretense that the good fairy of capitalism had promised Americans happy days forever was out the window once and for all.

It's crucial to note, though, that what followed this realization was the immediate and all but universal insistence that happy days would soon be back if only everyone did the right thing. It's even more crucial to note that what nearly everyone identified as "the right thing" — running right out and buying lots of stocks — was a really bad idea that bankrupted many of those who did it, and didn't help the imploding US economy at all.

It's probably necessary to talk about this in a little more detail, since it's been an article of blind faith in the United States for many decades now that it's always a good idea to buy and hold stocks. (I suspect that stockbrokers have had a good deal to do with the promulgation of this notion.) It's been claimed that someone who bought stocks in 1929 at the peak of the bubble, and then held onto them, would have ended up in the black eventually, and for certain values of "eventually," this is quite true — but it took the Dow Jones industrial average until the mid-1950s to return to its 1929 high, and so for a quarter of a century our investor would have been underwater on his stock purchases.

What's more, the Dow isn't necessarily a good measure of stocks generally; many of the darlings of the market in the 1920s either went bankrupt in the Depression or never again returned to their 1929 valuations. Nor did the surge of money into stocks in the wake of the 1929 crash stave off the Great Depression, or do much of anything else other than provide a great example of the folly of throwing good money after bad. The moral to this story? In an era of impact, the advice you hear from everyone around you may not be in your best interest.

That same moral can be shown just as clearly in the second example I have in mind, the French Revolution. We talked briefly in last week's post about the way that the French monarchy and aristocracy blinded themselves to the convulsive social and economic changes that were pushing France closer and closer to a collective explosion on the grand scale, and pursued business as usual long past the point at which business as usual was anything but a recipe for disaster. Even when the struggle between the Crown and the aristocracy forced Louis XVI to convene the États-Généraux — the rarely-held national parliament of France, which had powers more or less equivalent to a constitutional convention in the US — next to nobody expected anything but long rounds of political horse-trading from which some modest shifts in the balance of power might result.

That was before the summer of 1789. On June 17, the deputies of the Third Estate—the representatives of the commoners—declared themselves a National Assembly and staged what amounted to a coup d'etat; on July 14, faced with the threat of a military response from the monarchy, the Parisian mob stormed the Bastille, kickstarting a wave of revolt across the country that put government and military facilities in the hands of the revolutionary National Guard and broke the back of the feudal system; on August 4, the National Assembly abolished all feudal rights and legal distinctions between the classes. Over less than two months, a political and social system that had been welded firmly in place for a thousand years all came crashing to the ground.

Those two months marked the end of the era of pretense and the arrival of the era of impact. The immediate response, with a modest number of exceptions among the aristocracy and the inner circles of the monarchy's supporters, was frantic cheering and an insistence that everything would soon settle into a wonderful new age of peace, prosperity, and liberty. All the overblown dreams of the *philosophes* about a future age governed by reason were trotted out and treated as self-evident fact. Of course that's not what happened; once it was firmly in power, the National Assembly used its unchecked authority as abusively as the monarchy had once done; factional struggles spun out of control, and before long mob rule and the guillotine were among the basic facts of life in Revolutionary France.

Among the most common symptoms of an era of impact, in other words, is the rise of what we may as well call "crackpot optimism"—the enthusiastic and all but universal insistence, in the teeth of the evidence, that the end of business as usual will turn out to be the door to a wonderful new future. In the wake of the 1929 stock market crash, people were urged to pile back into the market in the belief that this would cause the economy to boom again even more spectacularly than before, and most of the people who followed this advice proceeded to lose their shirts. In the wake of the revolution of 1789, likewise, people across France were encouraged to join with their fellow citizens in building the shining new utopia of reason, and a great many of those who followed that advice ended up decapitated or, a little later, dying of gunshot or disease in the brutal era of pan-European warfare that extended almost without a break from the cannonade of Valmy in 1792 to the battle of Waterloo in 1815.

And the present example? That's a question worth exploring, if only for the utterly pragmatic reason that most of my readers are going to get to see it up close and personal.

That the United States and the industrial world generally are deep in an era of pretense is, I think, pretty much beyond question at this point. We've got political authorities, global bankers, and a galaxy of pundits insisting at the top of their lungs that nothing is wrong, everything is fine, and we'll be on our way to the next great era of prosperity if we just keep pursuing a set of boneheaded policies that have never — not once in the entire span of human history — brought prosperity to the countries that pursued them. We've got shelves full of books for sale in upscale bookstores insisting, in the strident language usual to such times, that life is wonderful in this best of all possible worlds, and it's going to get better forever because, like, we have technology, dude! Across the landscape of the cultural mainstream, you'll find no shortage of cheerleaders insisting at the top of their lungs that everything's going to be fine, that even though they said ten years ago that we only have ten years to do something before disaster hits, why, we still have ten years before disaster hits, and when ten more years pass by, why, you can be sure that the same people will be insisting that we have ten more.

This is the classic rhetoric of an era of pretense. Over the last few years, though, it's seemed to me that the voices of crackpot optimism have gotten more shrill, the diatribes more fact-free, and the logic even shoddier than it was in Bjorn Lomborg's day, which is saying something. We've reached the point that state governments are making it a crime to report on water quality and forbidding officials from using such unwelcome phrases as "climate change." That's not the action of people who are confident in their beliefs; it's the action of a bunch of overgrown children frantically clenching their eyes shut, stuffing their fingers in their ears, and shouting "La, la, la, I can't hear you."

That, in turn, suggests that the transition to the era of impact may be fairly close. Exactly when it's likely to arrive is a complex question, and exactly what's going to land the blow that will crack the crackpot optimism and make it impossible to ignore the arrival of real trouble is an even more complex one. In 1929, those who hadn't bought into the bubble could be perfectly sure — and in fact, a good many of them were perfectly sure — that the usual mechanism that brings bubbles to a catastrophic end was about to terminate the boom of the 1920s with extreme prejudice, as indeed it did. In the last decades of the French monarchy, it was by no means clear exactly what sequence of events would bring the Ancien Régime crashing down, but such thoughtful observers as Talleyrand knew that something of the sort was likely to follow the crisis of legitimacy then under way.

The problem with trying to predict the trigger that will bring our current situation to a sudden stop is that we're in such a target-rich environment. Looking over the potential candidates for the sudden shock that will stick a fork in the well-roasted corpse of business as usual, I'm reminded of the old board game *Clue*. Will Mr. Boddy's killer turn out to be Colonel Mustard in the library with a lead pipe, Professor Plum in the conservatory with a candlestick, or Miss Scarlet in the dining room with a rope?

In much the same sense, we've got a global economy burdened to the breaking point with more than a quadrillion dollars of unpayable debt; we've got a global political system coming apart at the seams as the United States slips toward the usual fate of empires and its rivals circle warily, waiting for the kill; we've got a domestic political system here in the US entering a classic prerevolutionary condition under the impact of a textbook crisis of legitimacy; we've got a global climate that's hammered by our rank stupidity in treating the atmosphere as a gaseous sewer for our wastes; we've got a global fossil fuel industry that's frantically trying to pretend that scraping the bottom of the barrel means that the barrel is full, and the list goes on. It's as though Colonel Mustard, Professor Plum, Miss Scarlet, and the rest of them all ganged up on Mr. Boddy at once, and only the most careful autopsy will be able to determine which of them actually dealt the fatal blow.

In the midst of all this uncertainty, there are three things that can, I think, be said for certain about the end of the current era of pretense and the coming of the era of impact. The first is that it's going to happen. When something is unsustainable, it's a pretty safe bet that it won't be sustained indefinitely, and a society that keeps on embracing policies that swap short-term gains for long-term problems will sooner or later end up awash in the consequences of those policies. Timing such transitions is difficult at best; it's an old adage among stock traders that the market can stay irrational longer than you can stay solvent. Still, points made above—especially the increasingly shrill tone of the defenders of the existing order—suggest to me that the era of impact may be here within a decade or so at the outside.

The second thing that can be said for certain about the coming era of impact is that it's not the end of the world. Apocalyptic fantasies are common and popular in eras of pretense, and for good reason; fixating on the supposed imminence of the Second Coming, human extinction, or what have you, is a great way to distract yourself from the real crisis that's breathing down your neck. If the real crisis in question is partly or wholly a result of your own actions, while the apocalyptic fantasy can be blamed on someone or something else, that adds a further attraction to the fantasy.

The end of industrial civilization will be a long, bitter, painful cascade of conflicts, disasters, and accelerating decline in which a vast number of people are going to die before they otherwise would, and a great many things of value will be lost forever. That's true of any falling civilization, and the misguided decisions of the last forty years have pretty much guaranteed that the current example is going to have an extra helping of all these unwelcome things. I've discussed at length, in earlier posts in the Dark Age America sequence here and in other sequences as well, why the sort of apocalyptic sudden stop beloved of Hollywood scriptwriters is the least likely outcome of the predicament of our time; still, insisting on the imminence and inevitability of some such game-ending event will no doubt be as popular as usual in the years immediately ahead.

The third thing that I think can be said for certain about the coming era of impact, though, is the one that counts. If it follows the usual pattern, as I expect it to do, once the crisis hits there will be serious, authoritative, respectable figures telling everyone exactly what they need to do to bring an end to the troubles and get the United States and the world back on track to renewed peace and prosperity. Taking these pronouncements seriously and following their directions will be extremely popular, and it will almost certainly also be a recipe for unmitigated disaster. If forewarned is forearmed, as the saying has it, this is a piece of firepower to keep handy as the era of pretense winds down. In next week's post, we'll talk about comparable weaponry relating to the third stage of collapse—the era of response.

416: THE ERA OF RESPONSE

(Originally published 27 May 2015)

The third stage of the process of collapse, following what I've called the eras of pretense and impact, is the era of response. It's easy to misunderstand what this involves, because both of the previous eras have their own kinds of response to whatever is driving the collapse; it's just that those kinds of response are more precisely nonresponses, attempts to make the crisis go away without addressing any of the things that are making it happen.

If you want a first-rate example of the standard nonresponse of the era of pretense, you'll find one in the sunny streets of Miami Beach, Florida right now. As a result of global climate change, sea level has gone up and the Gulf Stream has slowed down. One consequence is that these days, whenever Miami Beach gets a high tide combined with a stiff onshore wind, salt water comes boiling up through the storm sewers of the city all over the low-lying parts of town. The response of the Florida state government has been to issue an order to all state employees that they're not allowed to utter the phrase "climate change."

That sort of thing is standard practice in an astonishing range of subjects in America these days. Consider the roles that the essentially nonexistent recovery from the housing-bubble crash of 2008-9 has played in political rhetoric since that time. The current inmate of the White House has been insisting through most of two terms that happy days are here again, and the usual reams of doctored statistics have been churned out in an effort to convince people who know better that they're just imagining that something is wrong with the economy. We can expect to hear that same claim made in increasingly loud and confident tones right up until the day the bottom finally drops out.

With the end of the era of pretense and the arrival of the era of impact comes a distinct shift in the standard mode of nonresponse, which can be used quite neatly to time the transition from one era to another. Where the nonresponses of the era of pretense insist that there's nothing wrong and nobody has to do anything outside the realm of business as usual, the nonresponses of the era of impact claim just as forcefully that whatever's gone wrong is a temporary difficulty and everything will be fine if we all unite to do even more of whatever activity defines business as usual. That this normally amounts to doing more of whatever made the crisis happen in the first place, and thus reliably makes things worse, is just one of the little ironies history has to offer.

What unites the era of pretense with the era of impact is the unshaken belief that in the final analysis, there's nothing essentially wrong with the existing order of things. Whatever little difficulties may show up from time to time may be ignored as irrelevant or talked out of existence, or they may have to be shoved aside by some concerted effort, but it's inconceivable to most people in these two eras that the existing order of things is itself the source of society's problems, and has to be changed in some way that goes beyond the cosmetic dimension. When the inconceivable becomes inescapable, in turn, the second phase gives way to the third, and the era of response has arrived.

This doesn't mean that everyone comes to grips with the real issues, and buckles down to the hard work that will be needed to rebuild society on a sounder footing. Winston Churchill once noted with his customary wry humor that the American people can be counted on to do the right thing, once they have exhausted every other possibility. He was of course quite correct, but the same rule can be applied with equal validity to every other nation this side of Utopia, too. The era of response, in practice, generally consists of a desperate attempt to find something that will solve the crisis du jour, other than the one thing that everyone knows will solve the crisis du jour but nobody wants to do.

Let's return to the two examples we've been following so far, the outbreak of the Great Depression and the coming of the French Revolution. In the aftermath of the 1929 stock market crash, once the initial impact was over and the "sucker's rally" of early 1930 had come and gone, the federal government and the various power centers and pressure groups that struggled for influence within its capacious frame were united in pursuit of a single goal: finding a way to restore prosperity without doing either of the things that had to be done in order to restore prosperity. That task occupied the best minds in the US elite from the summer of 1930 straight through until April of 1933, and the mere fact that their attempts to accomplish this impossibility proved to be a wretched failure shouldn't blind anyone to the Herculean efforts that were involved in the attempt.

The first of the two things that had to be tackled in order to restore prosperity was to do something about the drastic imbalance in the distribution of income in the United States. As noted in previous posts, an economy dependent on consumer expenditures can't thrive unless consumers have plenty of money to spend, and in the United States in the late 1920s, they didn't—well, except for the very modest number of those who belonged to the narrow circles of the well-to-do. It's not often recalled these days just how ghastly the slums of urban America were in 1929, or how many rural Americans lived in squalid one-room shacks of the sort you pretty much have to travel to the Third World to see these days. Labor unions and strikes were illegal in 1920s America; concepts such as a minimum wage, sick pay, and health benefits didn't exist, and the legal system was slanted savagely against the poor.

You can't build prosperity in a consumer society when a good half of your citizenry can't afford more than the basic necessities of life. That's the predicament that America found clamped to the tender parts of its economic anatomy at the end of the 1920s. In that decade, as in our time, the temporary solution was to inflate a vast speculative bubble, under the endearing delusion that this would flood the economy with enough unearned cash to make the lack of earned income moot. That worked over the short term and then blew up spectacularly, since a speculative bubble is simply a Ponzi scheme that the legal authorities refuse to prosecute as such, and inevitably ends the same way.

There were, of course, effective solutions to the problem of inadequate consumer income. They were exactly those measures that were taken once the era of response gave way to the era of breakdown; everyone knew what they were, and nobody with access to political or economic power was willing to see them put into effect, because those measures would require a modest decline in the relative wealth and political dominance of the rich as compared to everyone else. Thus, as usually happens, they were postponed until the arrival of the era of breakdown made it impossible to avoid them any longer.

The second thing that had to be changed in order to restore prosperity was even more explosive, and I'm quite certain that some of my readers will screech like banshees the moment I mention it. The United States in 1929 had a precious metal-backed currency in the most literal sense of the term. Paper bills in those days were quite literally receipts for a certain quantity of gold – 1.5 grams, for much of the time the US spent on the gold standard. That sort of arrangement was standard in most of the world's industrial nations; it was backed by a dogmatic orthodoxy all but universal among respectable economists; and it was strangling the US economy.

It's fashionable among certain sects on the economic fringes these days to look back on the era of the gold standard as a kind of economic Utopia in which there were no booms and busts, just a warm sunny landscape of stability and prosperity until the wicked witches of the Federal Reserve came along and spoiled it all. That claim flies in the face of economic history. During the entire period that the United States was on the gold standard, from 1873 to 1933, the US economy was a moonscape cratered by more than a dozen significant depressions. There's a reason for that, and it's relevant to our current situation – in a backhanded manner, admittedly.

Money, let us please remember, is not wealth. It's a system of arbitrary tokens that represent real wealth – that is, actual, nonfinancial goods and services. Every society produces a certain amount of real wealth each year, and those societies that use money thus need to have enough money in circulation to more or less correspond to the annual supply of real wealth. That sounds simple; in practice, though, it's anything but. Nowadays, for example, the amount of real wealth being produced in the United States each year is contracting steadily as more and more of the nation's economic output has to be diverted into the task of keeping it supplied with fossil fuels. That's happening, in turn, because of the limits to growth – the awkward but inescapable reality that you can't extract infinite resources, or dump limitless wastes, on a finite planet.

The gimmick currently being used to keep fossil fuel extraction funded and cover the costs of the rising impact of environmental disruptions, without cutting into a culture of extravagance that only cheap abundant fossil fuel and a mostly intact biosphere can support, is to increase the money supply ad infinitum. That's become the bedrock of US economic policy since the 2008-9 crash. It's not a gimmick with a long shelf life; as the mismatch between real wealth and the money supply balloons, distortions and discontinuities are surging out through the crawlspaces of our economic life, and crisis is the most likely outcome.

In the United States in the first half or so of the twentieth century, by contrast, the amount of real wealth being produced each year soared, largely because of the steady increases in fossil fuel energy being applied to every sphere of life. While the nation was on the gold standard, though, the total supply of money could only grow as fast as gold could be mined out of the ground, which wasn't even close to fast enough. So you had more goods and services being produced than there was money to pay for them; people who wanted goods and services couldn't buy them because there wasn't enough money to go around; business that wanted to expand and hire workers were unable to do so for the same reason. The result was that moonscape of economic disasters I mentioned a moment ago.

The necessary response at that time was to go off the gold standard. Nobody in power wanted to do this, partly because of the dogmatic economic orthodoxy noted earlier, and partly because a money shortage paid substantial benefits to those who had guaranteed access to money. The rentier class — those people who lived off income from their investments — could count on stable or falling prices as long as the gold standard stayed in place, and the mere fact that the same stable or falling prices meant low wages, massive unemployment, and widespread destitution troubled them not at all. Since the rentier class included the vast majority of the US economic and political elite, in turn, going off the gold standard was unthinkable until it became unavoidable.

The period of the French revolution from the fall of the Bastille in 1789 to the election of the National Convention in 1792 was a period of the same kind, though driven by different forces. Here the great problem was how to replace the Old Regime — not just the French monarchy, but the entire lumbering mass of political, economic, and social laws, customs, forms, and institutions that France had inherited from the Middle Ages and never quite gotten around to adapting to drastically changed conditions — with something that would actually work. It's among the more interesting features of the resulting era of response that nearly every detail differed from the American example just outlined, and yet the results were remarkably similar.

Thus the leaders of the National Assembly who suddenly became the new rulers of France in the summer of 1789 had no desire whatsoever to retain the traditional economic arrangements that gave France's former elites their stranglehold on an oversized share of the nation's wealth. The abolition of manorial rights that summer, together with the explosive rural uprisings against feudal landlords and their chateaux in the wake of the Bastille's fall, gutted the feudal system and left most of its former beneficiaries the choice between fleeing into exile and trying to find some way to make ends meet in a society that had no particular market for used aristocrats. The problem faced by the National Assembly wasn't that of prying the dead fingers of a failed system off the nation's throat; it was that of trying to find some other basis for national unity and effective government.

It's a surprisingly difficult challenge. Those of my readers who know their way around current events will already have guessed that an attempt was made to establish a copy of whatever system was most fashionable among liberals at the time, and that this attempt turned out to be an abject failure. What's more, they'll have been quite correct. The National Assembly moved to establish a constitutional monarchy along British lines, bring in British economic institutions, and the like; it was all very popular among liberal circles in France and, naturally, in Britain as well, and it flopped. Those who recall the outcome of the attempt to turn Iraq into a nice pseudo-American democracy in the wake of the US invasion will have a tolerably good sense of how the project unraveled.

One of the unwelcome but reliable facts of history is that democracy doesn't transplant well. It thrives only where it grows up naturally, out of the civil institutions and social habits of a people; when liberal intellectuals try to impose it on a nation that hasn't evolved the necessary foundations for it, the results are pretty much always a disaster. That latter was the situation in France at the time of the Revolution. What happened thereafter is what almost always happens to a failed democratic experiment: a period of chaos, followed by the rise of a talented despot who's smart and ruthless enough to impose order on a chaotic situation and allow new, pragmatic institutions to emerge to replace those destroyed by clueless democratic idealists. In many cases, though by no means all, those pragmatic institutions have ended up providing a bridge to a future democracy, but that's another matter.

Here again, those of my readers who have been paying attention to current events already know this; the collapse of the Soviet Union was followed in classic form by a failed democracy, a period of chaos, and the rise of a talented despot. It's a curious detail of history that the despots in question are often rather short. Russia has had the great good fortune to find, as its despot du jour, a canny realist who has successfully brought it back from the brink of collapse and reestablished it as a major power with a body count considerably smaller than usual.. France was rather less fortunate; the despot it found, Napoleon Bonaparte, turned out to be a megalomaniac with an Alexander the Great complex who proceeded to plunge Europe into a quarter century of cataclysmic war. Mind you, things could have been even worse; when Germany ended up in a similar situation, what it got was Adolf Hitler.

Charismatic strongmen are a standard endpoint for the era of response, but they properly belong to the era that follows, the era of breakdown, which will be discussed next week. What I want to explore here is how an era of response might work out in the future immediately before us, as the United States topples from its increasingly unsteady imperial perch and industrial civilization as a whole slams facefirst into the limits to growth. The examples just cited outline the two most common patterns by which the era of response works itself out. In the first pattern, the old elite retains its grip on power, and fumbles around with increasing desperation for a response to the crisis. In the second, the old elite is shoved aside, and the new holders of power are left floundering in a political vacuum.

We could see either pattern in the United States. For what it's worth, I suspect the latter is the more likely option; the spreading crisis of legitimacy that grips the country these days is exactly the sort of thing you saw in France before the Revolution, and in any number of other countries in the few decades just prior to revolutionary political and social change. Every time a government tries to cope with a crisis by claiming that it doesn't exist, every time some member of the well-to-do tries to dismiss the collective burdens its culture of executive kleptocracy imposes on the country by flinging abuse at critics, every time institutions that claim to uphold the rule of law defend the rule of entrenched privilege instead, the United States takes another step closer to the revolutionary abyss.

I use that last word advisedly. It's a common superstition in every troubled age that any change must be for the better—that the overthrow of a bad system must by definition lead to the establishment of a better one. This simply isn't true. The vast majority of revolutions have established governments that were far more abusive than the ones they replaced. The exceptions have generally been those that brought about a social upheaval without wrecking the political system: where, for example, an election rather than a coup d'etat or a mass rising put the revolutionaries in power, and the political institutions of an earlier time remained in place with only such reshaping as new necessities required.

We could still see that sort of transformation as the United States sees the end of its age of empire and has to find its way back to a less arrogant and extravagant way of functioning in the world. I don't think it's likely, but I think it's possible, and it would probably be a good deal less destructive than the other alternative. It's worth remembering, though, that history is under no obligation to give us the future we think we want.

417: THE ERA OF BREAKDOWN

(Originally published 3 June 2015)

The fourth of the stages in the sequence of collapse we've been discussing is the era of breakdown. (For those who haven't been keeping track, the first three phases are the eras of pretense, impact, and response; the final phase, which we'll be discussing next week, is the era of dissolution.) The era of breakdown is the phase that gets most of the press, and thus inevitably no other stage has attracted anything like the crop of misperceptions, misunderstandings, and flat-out hokum as this one.

The era of breakdown is the point along the curve of collapse at which business as usual finally comes to an end. That's where the confusion comes in. It's one of the central articles of faith in pretty much every human society that business as usual functions as a bulwark against chaos, a defense against whatever problems the society might face. That's exactly where the difficulty slips in, because in pretty much every human society, what counts as business as usual — the established institutions and familiar activities on which everyone relies day by day — is the most important cause of the problems the society faces, and the primary cause of collapse is thus quite simply that societies inevitably attempt to solve their problems by doing all the things that make their problems worse.

The phase of breakdown is the point at which this exercise in futility finally grinds to a halt. The three previous phases are all attempts to avoid breakdown: in the phase of pretense, by making believe that the problems don't exist; in the phase of impact, by making believe that the problems will go away if only everyone doubles down on whatever's causing them; and in the phase of response, by making believe that changing something other than the things that are causing the problems will fix the problems. Finally, after everything else has been tried, the institutions and activities that define business as usual either fall apart or are forcibly torn down, and then—and only then—it becomes possible for a society to do something about its problems.

It's important not to mistake the possibility of constructive action for the inevitability of a solution. The collapse of business as usual in the breakdown phase doesn't solve a society's problems; it doesn't even prevent those problems from being made worse by bad choices. It merely removes the primary obstacle to a solution, which is the wholly fictitious aura of inevitability that surrounds the core institutions and activities that are responsible for the problems. Once people in a society realize that no law of God or nature requires them to maintain a failed status quo, they can then choose to dismantle whatever fragments of business as usual haven't yet fallen down of their own weight.

That's a more important action than it might seem at first glance. It doesn't just put an end to the principal cause of the society's problems. It also frees up resources that have been locked up in the struggle to keep business as usual going at all costs, and those newly freed resources very often make it possible for a society in crisis to transform itself drastically in a remarkably short period of time. Whether those transformations are for good or ill, or as usually happens, a mixture of the two, is another matter, and one I'll address a little further on.

Stories in the media, some recent, some recently reprinted, happen to have brought up a couple of first-rate examples of the way that resources get locked up in unproductive activities during the twilight years of a failing society. A California newspaper, for example, recently mentioned that Elon Musk's large and much-ballyhooed fortune is almost entirely a product of government subsidies. Musk is a smart guy; he obviously realized a good long time ago that federal and state subsidies for technology was where the money was at, and he's constructed an industrial empire funded by US taxpayers to the tune of many billions of dollars. None of his publicly traded firms has ever made a profit, and as long as the subsidies keep flowing, none of them ever has to; between an overflowing feed trough of government largesse and the longstanding eagerness of fools to be parted from their money by way of the stock market, he's pretty much set for life.

This is business as usual in today's America. An article from

2013 pointed out, along the same lines, that the profits made by the five largest US banks were almost exactly equal to the amount of taxpayer money those same five banks got from the government. Like Elon Musk, the banks in question have figured out where the money is, and have gone after it with their usual verve; the revolving door that allows men in suits to shuttle back and forth between those same banks and the financial end of the US government doesn't exactly hinder that process. It's lucrative, it's legal, and the mere fact that it's bankrupting the real economy of goods and services in order to further enrich an already glutted minority of kleptocrats is nothing anyone in the citadels of power worries about.

A useful light on a different side of the same process comes from an editorial which claims that something like half of all current scientific papers are unreliable junk. Is this the utterance of an archdruid, or some other wild-eyed critic of science? No, it comes from the editor of *Lancet*, one of the two or three most reputable medical journals on the planet. The managing editor of *The New England Journal of Medicine*, which has a comparable ranking to *Lancet*, expressed much the same opinion of the shoddy experimental design, dubious analysis, and blatant conflicts of interest that pervade contemporary scientific research.

Notice that what's happening here affects the flow of information in the same way that misplaced government subsidies affect the flow of investment. The functioning of the scientific process, like that of the market, depends on the presupposition that everyone who takes part abides by certain rules. When those rules are flouted, individual actors profit, but they do so at the expense of the whole system: the results of scientific research are distorted so that (for example) pharmaceutical firms can profit from drugs that don't actually have the benefits claimed for them, just as the behavior of the market is distorted so that (for example) banks that would otherwise struggle for survival, and would certainly not be able to pay their CEOs gargantuan bonuses, can continue on their merry way.

The costs imposed by these actions are real, and they fall on all other participants in science and the economy respectively. Scientists these days, especially but not only in such blatantly corrupt fields as pharmaceutical research, face a lose-lose choice between basing their own investigations on invalid studies, on the one hand, or having to distrust any experimental results they don't replicate themselves, on the other. Meanwhile the consumers of the products of scientific research — yes, that would be all of us — have to contend with the fact that we have no way of knowing whether any given claim about the result of research is the product of valid science or not. Similarly, the federal subsidies that direct investment toward politically savvy entrepreneurs like Elon Musk, and politically well-connected banks such as Goldman Sachs, and away from less parasitic and more productive options distort the entire economic system by preventing the normal workings of the market from weeding out nonviable projects and firms, and rewarding the more viable ones.

Turn to the historical examples we've been following for the last three weeks, and distortions of the same kind are impossible to miss. In the US economy before and during the stock market crash of 1929 and its long and brutal aftermath, a legal and financial system dominated by a handful of very rich men saw to it that the bulk of the nation's wealth flowed uphill, out of productive economic activities and into speculative ventures increasingly detached from the productive economy. When the markets imploded, in turn, the same people did their level best to see to it that their lifestyles weren't affected even though everyone else's was. The resulting collapse in consumer expenditures played a huge role in driving the cascading collapse of the US economy that, by the spring of 1933, had shuttered every consumer bank in the nation and driven joblessness and impoverishment to record highs.

That's what Franklin Roosevelt fixed. It's always amused me that the people who criticize FDR — and of course there's plenty to criticize in a figure who, aside from his far greater success as a wartime head of state, can best be characterized as America's answer to Mussolini — always talk about the very mixed record of the economic policies of his second term. They rarely bother to mention the Hundred Days, in which FDR stopped a massive credit collapse in its tracks. The Hundred Days and their aftermath are the part of FDR's presidency that mattered most; it was in that brief period that he slapped shock paddles on an economy in cardiac arrest and got a pulse going, by violating most of the rules that had guided the economy up to that time. That's one of the two things his critics have never been able to forgive; the other is that it worked.

In the same way, France before, during, and immediately after the Revolution was for all practical purposes a medieval state that had somehow staggered its way to the brink of the nineteenth century. The various revolutionary governments that succeeded one another in quick succession after 1789 made some badly needed changes, but it was left to Napoléon Bonaparte to drag France by the scruff of its collective neck out of the late Middle Ages. Napoléon has plenty of critics—and of course there's plenty to criticize in a figure who was basically what Mussolini wanted to be when he grew up—but the man's domestic policies were by and large inspired. To name only one of his most important changes, he abolished the entire body of existing French law in favor of a newly created legal system, the Code Napoléon. When he was overthrown, that stayed; in fact, a great many other countries in Europe and elsewhere proceeded to adopt the Code Napoléon in place of their existing legal systems. There were several reasons for this, but one of the most important was that the new Code simply made that much more sense.

Both men were able to accomplish what they did, in turn, because abolishing the political, economic, and cultural distortions imposed on their respective countries by a fossilized status quo freed up all the resources that had bene locked up in maintaining those distortions. Slapping a range of legal barriers and taxes on the more egregious forms of speculative excess—another of the major achievements of the Roosevelt era—drove enough wealth back into the productive economy to lay the foundations of America's postwar boom; in the same way, tipping a galaxy of feudal customs into history's compost bin transformed France from the economic basket case it was in 1789 to the conqueror of Europe twenty years later, and the succesful and innovative economic and cultural powerhouse it became during most of the nineteenth century thereafter.

That's one of the advantages of revolutionary change. By breaking down existing institutions and the encrusted layers of economic parasitism that inevitably build up around them over time, it reliably breaks loose an abundance of resources that were not available in the prerevolutionary period. Here again, it's crucial to remember that the availability of resources doesn't guarantee that they'll be used wisely; they may be thrown away on absurdities of one kind or another. Nor, even more critically, does it mean that the same abundance of resources will be available indefinitely. The surge of additional resources made available by catabolizing old and corrupt systems is a temporary jackpot, not a permanent state of affairs. That said, when you combine the collapse of fossilized institutions that stand in the way of change, and a sudden rush of previously unavailable resources of various kinds, quite a range of possibilities previously closed to a society suddenly come open.

Applying this same pattern to the crisis of modern industrial civilization, though, requires attention to certain inescapable but highly unwelcome realities. In 1789, the problem faced by France was the need to get rid of a thousand years of fossilized political, economic, and social institutions at a time when the coming of the industrial age had made them hopelessly dysfunctional. In 1929, the problem faced by the United States was the need to pry the dead hand of an equally dysfunctional economic orthodoxy off the throat of the nation so that its economy would actually function again. In both cases, the era of breakdown was catalyzed by a talented despot, and was followed, after an interval of chaos and war, by a period of relative prosperity.

We may well get the despot this time around, too, not to mention the chaos and war, but the period of prosperity is probably quite another matter. The problem we face today, in the United States and more broadly throughout the world's industrial societies, is that all the institutions of industrial civilization presuppose limitless economic growth, but the conditions that provided the basis for continued economic growth simply aren't there any more. The 300-year joyride of industrialism was made possible by vast and cheaply extractable reserves of highly concentrated fossil fuels and other natural resources, on the one hand, and a biosphere sufficiently undamaged that it could soak up the wastes of human industry without imposing burdens on the economy, on the other. We no longer have either of those requirements.

With every passing year, more and more of the world's total economic output has to be diverted from other activities to keep fossil fuels and other resources flowing into the industrial world's power plants, factories, and fuel tanks; with every passing year, in turn, more and more of the world's total economic output has to be diverted from other activities to deal with the rising costs of climate change and other ecological disruptions.

These are the two jaws of the trap sketched out more than forty years ago in the pages of *The Limits to Growth*, still the most accurate (and thus inevitably the most savagely denounced) map of the predicament we face. The consequences of that trap can be summed up neatly: on a finite planet, after a certain point—the point of diminishing returns, which we've already passed—the costs of growth rise faster than the benefits, and finally force the global economy to its knees.

The task ahead of us is thus in some ways the opposite of the one that France faced in the aftermath of 1789. Instead of replacing a sclerotic and failing medieval economy with one better suited to a new era of industrial expansion, we need to replace a sclerotic and failing industrial economy with one better suited to a new era of deindustrial contraction. That's a tall order, no question, and it's not something that can be achieved easily, or in a single leap. In all probability, the industrial world will have to pass through the whole sequence of phases we've been discussing several times before things finally bottom out in the deindustrial dark ages to come.

Still, I'm going to shock my fans and critics alike here by pointing out that there's actually some reason to think that positive change on more than an individual level will be possible as the industrial world slams facefirst into the limits to growth. Two things give me that measured sense of hope. The first is the sheer scale of the resources locked up in today's spectacularly dysfunctional political, economic, and social institutions, which will become available for other uses when those institutions come apart. The $83 billion a year currently being poured down the oversized rathole of the five biggest US banks, just for starters, could pay for a lot of solar water heaters, training programs for organic farmers, and other things that could actually do some good.

Throw in the resources currently being chucked into all of the other attempts currently under way to prop up a failing system, and you've got quite the jackpot that could, in an era of breakdown, be put to work doing things worth while. It's by no means certain, as already noted, that these resources will go to the best possible use, but it's all but certain that they'll go to something less stunningly pointless than, say, handing Elon Musk his next billion dollars.

The second thing that gives me a measured sense of hope is at once subtler and far more profound. These days, despite a practically endless barrage of rhetoric to the contrary, the great majority of Americans are getting fewer and fewer benefits from the industrial system, and are being forced to pay more and more of its costs, so that a relatively small fraction of the population can monopolize an ever-increasing fraction of the national wealth and contribute less and less in exchange. What's more, a growing number of Americans are aware of this fact. The traditional schism of a collapsing society into a dominant minority and an internal proletariat, to use Arnold Toynbee's terms, is a massive and accelerating social reality in the United States today.

As that schism widens, and more and more Americans are forced into the Third World poverty that's among the unmentionable realities of public life in today's United States, several changes of great importance are taking place. The first, of course, is precisely that a great many Americans are perforce learning to live with less—not in the playacting style popular just now on the faux-green end of the privileged classes, but really, seriously living with much less, because that's all there is. That's a huge shift and a necessary one, since the absurd extravagance many Americans consider to be a normal lifestyle is among the most important things that will be landing in history's compost heap in the not too distant future.

At the same time, the collective consensus that keeps the hopelessly dysfunctional institutions of today's status quo glued in place is already coming apart, and can be expected to dissolve completely in the years ahead. What sort of consensus will replace it, after the inevitable interval of chaos and struggle, is anybody's guess at this point—though it's vanishingly unlikely to have anything to do with the current political fantasies of left and right. It's just possible, given luck and a great deal of hard work, that whatever new system gets cobbled together during the breakdown phase of our present crisis will embody at least some of the values that will be needed to get our species back into some kind of balance with the biosphere on which our lives depend. A future post will discuss how that might be accomplished—after, that is, we explore the last phase of the collapse process: the era of dissolution, which will be the theme of next week's post.

418: THE ERA OF DISSOLUTION

(Originally published 10 June 2015)

The last of the five phases of the collapse process we've been discussing here in recent posts is the era of dissolution. (For those
that haven't been keeping track, the first four are the eras of pretense, impact, response, and breakdown). I suppose you could
call the era of dissolution the Rodney Dangerfield of collapse,
though it's not so much that it gets no respect; it generally doesn't
even get discussed.

To some extent, of course, that's because a great many of the
people who talk about collapse don't actually believe that it's
going to happen. That lack of belief stands out most clearly in
the rhetorical roles assigned to collapse in so much of modern
thinking. People who actually believe that a disaster is imminent
generally put a lot of time and effort into getting out of its way in
one way or another; it's those who treat it as a scarecrow to elicit
predictable emotional reactions from other people, or from themselves, who never quite manage to walk their talk.

Interestingly, the factor that determines the target of scare-
crow-tactics of this sort seems to be political in nature. Groups
that think they have a chance of manipulating the public into following their notion of good behavior tend to use the scarecrow of
collapse to affect other people; for them, collapse is the horrible
fate that's sure to gobble us up if we don't do whatever it is they
want us to do. Those who've given up any hope of getting a response from the public, by contrast, turn the scarecrow around
and use it on themselves; for them, collapse is a combination of
Dante's Inferno and the Big Rock Candy Mountain, the fantasy
setting where the wicked get the walloping they deserve while
they themselves get whatever goodies they've been unsuccessful
at getting in the here and now.

Then, of course, you get the people for whom collapse is less scarecrow than teddy bear, the thing that allows them to drift off comfortably to sleep in the face of an unwelcome future. It's been my repeated observation that many of those who insist that humanity will become totally extinct in the very near future fall into this category. Most people, faced with a serious threat to their own lives, will take drastic action to save themselves; faced with a threat to the survival of their family or community, a good many people will take actions so drastic as to put their own lives at risk in an effort to save others they care about. The fact that so many people who insist that the human race is doomed go on to claim that the proper reaction is to sit around feeling very, very sad about it all does not inspire confidence in the seriousness of that prediction — especially when feeling very, very sad seems mostly to function as an excuse to keep enjoying privileged lifestyles for just a little bit longer.

So we have the people for whom collapse is a means of claiming unearned power, the people for whom it's a blank screen on which to project an assortment of self-regarding fantasies, and the people for whom it's an excuse to do nothing in the face of a challenging future. All three of those are popular gimmicks with an extremely long track record, and they'll doubtless all see plenty of use millennia after industrial civilization has taken its place in the list of failed civilizations. The only problem with them is that they don't happen to provide any useful guidance for those of us who have noticed that collapse isn't merely a rhetorical gimmick meant to get emotional reactions — that it's something that actually happens, to actual civilizations, and that it's already happening to ours.

From the three perspectives already discussed, after all, realistic questions about what will come after the rubble stops bouncing are entirely irrelevant. If you're trying to use collapse as a boogeyman to scare other people into doing what you tell them, your best option is to combine a vague sense of dread with an assortment of cherrypicked factoids intended to make a worst-case scenario look not nearly bad enough; if you're trying to use collapse as a source of revenge fantasies where you get what you want and the people you don't like get what's coming to them, daydreams of various levels and modes of dampness are far more useful to you than sober assessments; while if you're trying to use collapse as an excuse to maintain an unsustainable and planet-damaging SUV lifestyle, your best bet is to insist that everyone and everything dies all at once, so nothing will ever matter again to anybody.

On the other hand, there are also those who recognize that collapse happens, that we're heading toward one, and that it might be useful to talk about what the world might look like on the far side of that long and difficult process. I've tried to sketch out a portrait of the postcollapse world in last year's series of posts here on Dark Age America, and I haven't yet seen any reason to abandon that portrait of a harsh but livable future, in which a sharply reduced global population returns to agrarian or nomadic lives in those areas of the planet not poisoned by nuclear or chemical wastes or rendered uninhabitable by prolonged drought or the other impacts of climate change, and in which much or most of today's scientific and technological knowledge is irretrievably lost.

The five phases of collapse discussed in this latest sequence of posts is simply a description of how we get there—or, more precisely, of one of the steps by which we get there. That latter point's a detail that a good many of my readers, and an even larger fraction of my critics, seem to have misplaced. The five-stage model is a map of how human societies shake off an unsustainable version of business as usual and replace it with something better suited to the realities of the time. It applies to a very wide range of social transformations, reaching in scale from the local to the global and in intensity from the relatively modest to the cataclysmic. To insist that it's irrelevant because the current example of the species covers more geographical area than any previous example, or has further to fall than most, is like insisting that a law of physics that governs the behavior of marbles and billiards must somehow stop working just because you're trying to do the same thing with bowling balls.

A difference of scale is not a difference of kind. Differences of scale have their own implications, which we'll discuss a little later on in this post, but the complex curve of decline is recognizably the same in small things as in big ones, in the most as in the least catastrophic examples. That's why I've used a relatively modest example—the collapse of the economic system of 1920s America and the resulting Great Depression—and an example from the midrange — the collapse of the French monarchy and the descent of 18th-century Europe into the maelstrom of the Napoleonic Wars — to provide convenient outlines for something toward the upper end of the scale — the decline and fall of modern industrial civilization and the coming of a deindustrial dark age. Let's return to those examples, and see how the thread of collapse winds to its end.

As we saw in last week's thrilling episode, the breakdown stage of the Great Depression came when the newly inaugurated Roosevelt administration completely redefined the US currency system. Up to that time, US dollar bills were in effect receipts for gold held in banks; after that time, those receipts could no longer be exchanged for gold, and the gold held by the US government became little more than a public relations gimmick. That action succeeded in stopping the ghastly credit crunch that shuttered every bank and most businesses in the US in the spring of 1933.

Roosevelt's policies didn't get rid of the broader economic dysfunction the 1929 crash had kickstarted. That was inherent in the industrial system itself, and remains a massive issue today, though its effects were papered over for a while by a series of temporary military, political, and economic factors that briefly enabled the United States to prosper at the expense of the rest of the world. The basic issue is simply that replacing human labor with machines powered by fossil fuel results in unemployment, and no law of nature or economics requires that new jobs can be found or created to replace the ones that are eliminated by mechanization. The history of the industrial age has been powerfully shaped by a whole series of attempts to ignore, evade, or paper over that relentless arithmetic.

Until 1940, the Roosevelt administration had no more luck with that project than the governments of most other nations. It wasn't until the Second World War made the lesson inescapable that anyone realized that the only way to provide full employment in an industrial society was to produce far more goods than consumers could consume, and let the military and a variety of other gimmicks take up the slack. That was a temporary gimmick, due to stark limitations in the resource base needed to support the mass production of useless goods, but in 1940, and even more so in 1950, few people recognized that and fewer cared. It's our bad luck to be living at the time when that particular bill is coming due.

The first lesson to learn from the history of collapse, then, is that the breakdown phase doesn't necessarily solve all the problems that brought it about. It doesn't even necessarily take away every dysfunctional feature of the status quo. What it does with fair reliability is eliminate enough of the existing order of things that the problems being caused by that order decline to a manageable level. The more deeply rooted the problematic features of the status quo are in the structure of society and daily life, the harder it will be to change them, and the more likely other features are to be changed: in the example just given, it was much easier to break the effective link between the US currency and gold, and expand the money supply enough to get the economy out of cardiac arrest, than it was to break a link between mechanization and unemployment that's hardwired into the basic logic of industrialism.

What this implies in turn is that it's entirely possible for one collapse to cycle through the five stages we've explored, and then to have the era of dissolution morph straight into a new era of pretense in which the fact that all society's problems haven't been solved is one of the central things nobody in any relation to the centers of power wants to discuss. If the Second World War, the massive expansion of the petroleum economy, the invention of suburbia, the Cold War, and a flurry of other events hadn't ushered in the immensely wasteful but temporarily prosperous boomtime of late 20th century America, there might well have been another vast speculative bubble in the mid- to late 1940s, resulting in another crash, another depression, and so on. This is after all what we've seen over the last twenty years: the tech stock bubble and bust, the housing bubble and bust, the fracking bubble and bust, each one hammering the economy further down the slope of decline.

With that in mind, let's turn to our second example, the French Revolution. This is particularly fascinating since the aftermath of that particular era of breakdown saw a nominal return to the conditions of the era of pretense. After Napoleon's final defeat in 1815, the Allied powers found an heir to the French throne and plopped him into the throne of the Bourbons as Louis XVIII to well-coached shouts of "Vive le Roi!" On paper, nothing had changed.

In reality, everything had changed, and the monarchy of post-Napoleonic France had roots about as deep and sturdy as the democracy of post-Saddam Iraq. Louis XVIII was clever enough to recognize this, and so managed to end his reign in the traditional fashion, feet first from natural causes. His heir Charles X was nothing like so clever, and got chucked off the throne after six years on it by another revolution in 1830. King Louis-Philippe went the same way in 1848 — the French people were getting very good at revolution by that point. There followed a Republic, an Empire headed by Napoleon's nephew, and finally another Republic which lasted out the century. All in all, French politics in the 19th century was the sort of thing you'd expect to see in an unusually excitable banana republic.

The lesson to learn from this example is that it's very easy, and very common, for a society in the dissolution phase of collapse to insist that nothing has changed and pretend to turn back the clock. Depending on just how traumatic the collapse has been, everybody involved may play along with the charade, the way everyone in Rome nodded and smiled when Augustus Caesar pretended to uphold the legal forms of the defunct Roman Republic, and their descendants did exactly the same thing centuries later when Theodoric the Ostrogoth pretended to uphold the legal forms of the defunct Roman Empire. Those who recognize the charade as charade and play along without losing track of the realities, like Louis XVIII, can quite often navigate such times successfully; those who mistake charade for reality, like Charles X, are cruising for a bruising and normally get it in short order.

Combine these two lessons and you'll get what I suspect will turn out to be a tolerably good sketch of the American future. Whatever comes out of the impact, response, and breakdown phases of the crisis looming ahead of the United States just now — whether it's a fragmentary mess of successor states, a redefined nation beginning to recover from a period of personal rule by some successful demagogue or, just possibly, a battered and weary republic facing a long trudge back to its foundational principles, it seems very likely that everyone involved will do their level best to insist that nothing has really changed. If the current constitution has been abolished, it may be officially reinstated with much fanfare; there may be new elections, and some shuffling semblance of the two-party system may well come lurching out of the crypts for one or two more turns on the stage.

None of that will matter. The nation will have changed decisively in ways we can only begin to envision at this point, and the forms of twentieth-century American politics will cover a reality that has undergone drastic transformations, just as the forms of nineteenth-century French monarchy did. In due time, by some combination of legal and extralegal means, the forms will be changed to reflect the new realities, and the territory we now call the United States of America — which will almost certainly have a different name, and may well be divided into several different and competing nations by then — will be as prepared to face the next round of turmoil as it's going to get.

Yes, there will be a next round of turmoil. That's the thing that most people miss when thinking about the decline and fall of a civilization: it's not a single event, or even a single linear process. It's a whole series of cascading events that vary drastically in their importance, geographical scope, and body count. That's true of every process of historic change.

It was true even of so simple an event as the 1929 crash and Great Depression: 1929 saw the crash, 1930 the suckers' rally, 1931 the first wave of European bank failures, 1932 the unraveling of the US banking system, and so on until bombs falling on Pearl Harbor ushered in a different era. It was even more true of the French Revolution: between 1789 and 1815 France basically didn't have a single year without dramatic events and drastic changes of one kind or another, and the echoes of the Revolution kept things stirred up for decades to come. Check out the fall of civilizations and you'll see the same thing unfolding on a truly vast scale, with crisis after crisis along an arc centuries in length.

The process that's going on around us is the decline and fall of industrial civilization. Everything we think of as normal and natural, modern and progressive, solid and inescapable is going to melt away into nothingness in the years, decades, and centuries ahead, to be replaced first by the very different but predictable institutions of a dark age, and then by the new and wholly unfamiliar forms of the successor societies of the far future. There's nothing inevitable about the way we do things in today's industrial world; our political arrangements, our economic practices, our social instutions, our cultural habits, our sciences and our technologies all unfold from industrial civilization's distinctive and profoundly idiosyncratic worldview. So does the central flaw in the entire baroque edifice, our lethally muddleheaded inability to understand our inescapable dependence on the biosphere that supports our lives. All that is going away in the time before us—but it won't go away suddenly, or all at once.

Here in the United States, we're facing one of the larger downward jolts in that prolonged process, the end of American global empire and of the robust economic benefits that the machinery of empire pumps from the periphery to the imperial center. Until recently, the five per cent of us who lived here got to enjoy a quarter of the world's energy supply and raw materials and a third of its manufactured products. Those figures have already decreased noticeably, with consequences that are ringing through every corner of our society; in the years to come they're going to decrease much further still, most likely to something like a five per cent share of the world's wealth or even a little less. That's going to impact every aspect of our lives in ways that very few Americans have even begun to think about.

All of that is taking place in a broader context, to be sure. Other countries will have their own trajectories through the arc of industrial civilization's decline and fall, and some of those trajectories will be considerably less harsh in the short term than ours. In the long run, the human population of the globe is going to decline sharply; the population bubble that's causing so many destructive effects just now will be followed in due time by a population bust, in which those four guys on horseback will doubtless play their usual roles. In the long run, furthermore, the vast majority of today's technologies are going to go away as the resource base needed to support them gets used up, or stops being available due to other bottlenecks. Those are givens—but the long run is not the only scale that matters.

It's not at all surprising that the foreshocks of that immense change are driving the kind of flight to fantasy criticized in the opening paragraphs of this essay. That's business as usual when empires go down; pick up a good cultural history of the decline and fall of any empire in the last two millennia or so and you'll find plenty of colorful prophecies of universal destruction. I'd like to encourage my readers, though, to step back from those fantasies—entertaining as they are—and try to orient themselves instead to the actual shape of the future ahead of us. That shape's not only a good deal less gaseous than the current offerings of the Apocalypse of the Month Club (internet edition), it also offers an opportunity to do something about the future—a point we'll be discussing further in posts to come.

419: AN AFFIRMING FLAME

(Originally published 17 June 2015)

According to an assortment of recent news stories, this Thursday, June 18, is the make-or-break date by which a compromise has to be reached between Greece and the EU if a Greek default, with the ensuing risk of a potential Greek exit from the Eurozone, is to be avoided. If that's more than just media hype, there's a tremendous historical irony in the fact. June 18 is after all the 200th anniversary of the Battle of Waterloo, where a previous attempt at European political and economic integration came to grief.

Now of course there are plenty of differences between the two events. In 1815 the preferred instrument of integration was raw military force; in 2015, for a variety of reasons, a variety of less overt forms of political and economic pressure have taken the place of Napoleon's Grande Armée. The events of 1815 were also much further along the curve of defeat than those of 2015. Waterloo was the end of the road for France's dream of pan-European empire, while the current struggles over the Greek debt represent a noticeably earlier milepost along the same road, so the faceless bureaucrats who are filling Napoleon's role this time around won't be on their way to St. Helena for some time yet.

"What discords will drive Europe into that artificial unity — only dry or drying sticks can be tied into a bundle — which is the decadence of every civilization?" William Butler Yeats wrote that in 1936. It was a poignant question but also a highly relevant one, since the discords in question were moving rapidly toward explosion as he penned the last pages of *A Vision*, where those words appear. Like most of those who see history in cyclical terms, Yeats recognized that the patterns that recur from age to age are trends and motifs rather than exact narratives. The part played by a conqueror in one era can end up in the hands of a heroic failure in the next, for circumstances can define a historical role but not the irreducibly human strengths and foibles of the person who happens to fill it.

Thus it's not too hard to look at the rising spiral of stresses in the European Union just now and foresee the eventual descent of the continent into some blend of domestic insurgency and local authoritarian nationalism, with the oncoming tide of mass migration from Africa and the Middle East adding further pressure to an already explosive mix. Exactly how that will play out over the next century, though, is an extraordinarily difficult question to answer. A century from now, for reasons of basic demography, many countries that are now European in culture and heritage will be majority-Muslim nations that look to Mecca for the roots of their faith, culture and history — but which countries, and how brutal or otherwise will the transition be? That's impossible to know in advance.

There are plenty of similar examples just now; for the student of historical cycles, 2015 practically defines the phrase "target-rich environment." Still, I want to focus on something a little different here. Partly, this is because the example I have in mind makes a good opportunity to point out the the way that what philosophers call the contingent nature of events — in less high-flown language, the sheer cussedness of things — keeps history's dice constantly rolling. Partly, though, it's because this particular example is likely to have a substantial impact on the future of everyone reading this blog.

Last year saw a great deal of talk in the media about possible parallels between the current international situation and that of the world precisely a century ago, in the weeks leading up to the outbreak of the First World War. Mind you, since I contributed to that discussion, I'm hardly in a position to reject the parallels out of hand. Still, the more I've observed the current situation, the more I've come to think that a different date makes a considerably better match to present conditions. To be precise, instead of a replay of 1914, I think we're about to see an equivalent of 1939 — but not quite the 1939 we know.

Two entirely contingent factors, added to all the other pressures driving toward that conflict, made the Second World War what it was. The first, of course, was the personality of Adolf Hitler. It was probably a safe bet that somebody in Weimar Germany would figure out how to build a bridge between the politically active but fragmented nationalist Right and the massive but politically inert German middle classes, restore Germany to great-power status, and gear up for a second attempt to elbow aside the British Empire. That the man who happened to do these things was an eccentric anti-Semite ideologue who combined shrewd political instincts, utter military incompetence, and a frankly psychotic faith in his own infallibility, though, was in no way required by the logic of history.

Had Corporal Hitler taken an extra lungful of gas on the Western Front, someone else would likely have filled the same role in the politics of the time. We don't even have to discuss the results if the nation that birthed Frederick the Great and Otto von Bismarck had managed to come up with a statesman of the same caliber. If the German head of state in 1939 had been merely a competent pragmatist with government experience and connections to the imperial German military, and guided Germany's actions in the final crises of the 1930s by a logic less topsy-turvy than Hitler's, the trajectory of those years would have been considerably different.

The second contingent factor that defined the outcome of the great wars of the twentieth century is broader in focus than the quirks of a single personality, but it was just as subject to those vagaries that make hash out of attempts at precise historical prediction. As discussed in an earlier post on this blog, it was by no means certain that America would be Britain's ally when war finally came. From the Revolution onward, Britain was in many Americans' eyes the national enemy; as late as the 1930s, when the US Army held its summer exercises, the standard scenario involved a British invasion of US territory.

All along, there was an Anglophile party in American cultural life, and its ascendancy in the years after 1900 played a major role in bringing the United States into two world wars on Britain's side. Still, there was a considerably more important factor in play, which was a systematic British policy of conciliating the United States. From the American Civil War on, Britain allowed the United States liberties it would never have given any other power. When the United States expanded its influence in Latin America and the Carribbean, Britain allowed itself to be upstaged there; when the United States shook off its isolationism and built a massive blue-water navy, the British even allowed US naval vessels to refuel at British coaling stations during the global voyage of the "Great White Fleet" in 1907-9.

This was partly a reflection of the common cultural heritage that made many British politicians think of the United States as a sort of boisterous younger brother of theirs, and partly a cold-eyed recognition, in the wake of the Civil War, that war between Britain and the United States would almost certainly lead to a US invasion of Canada that Britain was very poorly positioned to counter. Still, there was another issue of major importance. To an extent few people realized at the time, the architecture of European peace after Waterloo depended on political arrangements that kept the German-speaking lands of the European core splintered into a diffuse cloud of statelets too small to threaten any of the major powers.

The great geopolitical fact of the 1860s was the collapse of that cloud into the nation of Germany, under the leadership of the dour northeastern kingdom of Prussia. In 1866, the Prussians pounded the stuffing out of Austria and brought the rest of the German states into a federation; in 1870-1871, the Prussians and their allies did the same thing to France, which was a considerably tougher proposition—this was the same French nation, remember, which brought Europe to its knees in Napoleon's day—and the federation became the German Empire. The Austro-Hungarian Empire was widely considered the third most powerful nation in Europe until 1866; until 1870, France was the second; everybody knew that sooner or later the Germans were going to take on nation number one.

British policy toward the United States from 1871 onward was thus tempered by the harsh awareness that Britain could not afford to alienate any major power who might become an ally, or even a friendly neutral, when the inevitable war with Germany arrived. Above all, an alliance between Germany and the United States would have been Britain's death warrant, and everyone in the Foreign Office and the Admiralty in London had to know that. The thought of German submarines operating out of US ports, German and American fleets combining to take on the Royal Navy, and American armies surging into Canada and depriving Britain of a critical source of raw materials while the British Army was pinned down on the killing fields of France, must have given British planners many sleepless nights.

After 1918, that recognition must have been even more sharply pointed, because US loans and munition shipments played a massive role in saving the western Allies from collapse in the face of the final German offensive in the autumn of 1917, and turned the tide in a war that, until then, had largely gone Germany's way. During the two decades leading up to 1939, as Germany recovered and rearmed, British governments did everything they could to keep the United States on their side, with results that paid off handsomely when the Second World War finally came.

Let's imagine, though, an alternative timeline in which the Foreign Office and the Admiralty from 1918 on are staffed by idiots. Let's further imagine that Parliament is packed with clueless ideologues whose sole conception of foreign policy is that everyone, everywhere, ought to be bludgeoned into compliance with Britain's edicts. Let's say that one British government after another conducts its policy toward the United States on the basis of arrogant smugness, and any move the United States makes to assert itself on the international stage can count on an angry response from London. The United States launches an aircraft carrier? A threat to world peace, the London *Times* roars. The United States exerts diplomatic pressure on Mexico, and builds military airfields in Panama? British diplomats head for the Carribbean and Latin America to stir up as much opposition to America's agenda as possible.

Let's say, furthermore, that in this alternative timeline, Adolf Hitler did indeed take one too many deep breaths on the Western Front, and lies in a military cemetery, one more forgotten casualty of the Great War. In his absence, the German Workers Party remains a fringe group, and the alliance between the nationalist Right and the middle classes is built instead by the Deutsche Volksfreiheitspartei (DVFP), which seizes power in 1934. Ulrich von Hassel, the new Chancellor, is a Prussian insider who knows how to listen to his diplomats and General Staff, and German foreign and military policy under his leadership pursues the goal of restoring Germany to world-power status using considerably less erratic means than those used by von Hassel's equivalent in our timeline.

Come 1939, finally, as rising tensions between Germany and the Anglo-French alliance over Poland's status move toward war,

Chancellor von Hassel welcomes US President Charles Lindbergh to Berlin, where the two heads of state sign a galaxy of agreements and talk earnestly about the need to establish a multipolar world order to replace Britain's global hegemony. A second world war is in the offing, but the shape of that war will be very different from the one that broke out in our 1939, and while the United States certainly will be among the victors, Britain just as certainly will not.

Does all this sound absurd? Let's change the names around and see.

Just as the great rivalry of the first half of the twentieth century was fought out between Britain and Germany, the great rivalry of the century's second half was between the United States and Russia. If nuclear weapons hadn't been invented, it's probably a safe bet that at some point the rivalry would have ended in a third world war. As it was, the threat of mutually assured destruction meant that the struggle for global power had to be fought out less directly, in a flurry of proxy wars, manufactured insurgencies, economic warfare, subversion, sabotage, and bare-knuckle diplomacy. In that war, the United States came out on top, and Soviet Russia went the way of Imperial Germany, plunging into the same sort of political and economic chaos that beset the Weimar Republic in its day.

The supreme strategic imperative of the United States in that war was finding ways to drive as deep a wedge as possible between Russia and China. That wasn't actually that difficult a task, since the two nations have very little in common and many conflicting interests. Nixon's 1972 trip to China was arguably the defining moment in the Cold War, the point at which China's separation from the Soviet bloc became total and Chinese integration with the American economic order began. From that point on, for Russia, it was basically all downhill.

In the aftermath of Russia's defeat, the same strategic imperative remained, but the conditions of the post-Cold War world made it almost absurdly easy to carry out. All that would have been needed were American policies that gave Russia and China meaningful, concrete reasons to think that their national interests and aspirations would be easier to achieve in cooperation with a US-led global order than in opposition to it. Granting Russia and China the same position of regional influence that the US accords to Germany and Japan as a matter of course probably would have been enough. A little forbearance, a little foreign aid, a little adroit diplomacy, and the United States would have been in the catbird's seat, with Russia and China glaring suspiciously at each other across their long and problematic mutual border, and bidding against each other for US support in their various disagreements.

But that's not what happened, of course.

What happened instead was that the US embraced a foreign policy so astonishingly stupid that I'm honestly not sure the English language has adequate words to describe it. Since 1990, one US administration after another, with the enthusiastic bipartisan support of Congress and the capable assistance of bureaucrats across official Washington from the Pentagon and the State Department on down, has pursued policies guaranteed to force Russia and China to set aside their serious mutual differences and make common cause against us. Every time the US faced a choice between competing policies, it's consistently chosen the option most likely to convince Russia, China, or both nations at once that they had nothing to gain from further cooperation with American agendas.

What's more, the US has more recently managed the really quite impressive feat of bringing Iran into rapprochement with the emerging Russo-Chinese alliance. It's hard to think of another nation on Earth that has fewer grounds for constructive engagement with Russia or China than the Islamic Republic of Iran, and it took several decades of hamfisted American blundering and bullying to accomplish so difficult a job. My American readers can now take pride in the state-of-the-art Russian air defense systems defending Tehran, the bustling highways carrying Russian and Iranian products to each other's markets, and the Russian and Chinese intelligence officers who are doubtless settling into comfortable digs on the north shore of the Persian Gulf, where they can snoop on the daisy chain of US bases along the southern shore; a quarter century of US foreign policy made those things happen.

It's one thing to engage in this kind of serene disregard for reality when you've got the political unity, the economic abundance, and the military superiority to back it up. The United States today, like the British Empire in 1939, no longer has those.

We've got an impressive fleet of aircraft carriers, sure, but Britain had an equally impressive fleet of battleships in 1939, and you'll notice how much good those did them. Like Britain in 1939, the United States today is perfectly prepared for a kind of war that nobody fights any more, while rival nations less constrained by the psychology of previous investment and less riddled with graft are fielding novel weapons systems designed to do end runs around our strengths and focus with surgical precision on our weaknesses.

Meanwhile, inside the baroque carapace of carriers, drones, and all the other high-tech claptrap of an obsolete way of war, the United States is a society in freefall, far worse off than Britain was during its comparatively mild 1930s downturn. Its leaders have forfeited the respect of a growing majority of its citizens; its economy has morphed into a Potemkin-village capitalism in which the manipulation of an absurd volume of unpayable IOUs has all but replaced the actual production of goods and services; its infrastructure is so far fallen into decay that many US counties no longer pave their roads; outside the narrowing circle of wealth and privilege, most of its own people now treat its political institutions as the enemy and its loudly proclaimed ideals as some kind of sick joke. The national unity that made victory in the two world wars and the Cold War possible went by the boards a long time ago, drowned in a tub jointly by Tea Party conservatives who thought they were getting rid of government and limousine liberals who were going through the motions of sticking it to the Man.

I could go on tracing parallels for some time — in particular, despite a common rhetorical trope of US Russophobes, Vladimir Putin is not an Adolf Hitler but a fair equivalent of the Ulrich von Hassel of my alternate-history narrative — but here again, my readers can do the math themselves. The point I want to make is that all the signs suggest we are entering an era of international conflict in which the United States has thrown away nearly all its potential strengths, and handed its enemies advantages they would never have had if our leaders had the brains the gods gave geese. Since nuclear weapons still foreclose the option of major wars between the great powers, the conflict in question will doubtless be fought using the same indirect methods as the Cold War; in fact, it's already being fought by those means, as the victims of proxy wars in Ukraine, Syria, and Yemen already know. The question in my mind is simply how soon those same methods get applied on American soil.

We thus stand at the beginning of a long, brutal epoch, as unforgiving as the one that dawned in 1939. Those who pin Utopian hopes on the end of American hegemony will get to add disappointment to the mix, since hegemony remains what it is no matter who happens to be perched temporarily in the saddle. (I also wonder how many of the people who think they'll rejoice at the end of American hegemony have thought through the impact on their hopes of collective betterment, not to mention their own lifestyles, once the 5% of the world's population who live in the US can no longer claim a quarter or so of the world's resources and wealth.) If there's any hope possible at such a time, to my mind, it's the one W.H. Auden proposed as the conclusion of his bleak and brilliant poem "September 1, 1939":

> Defenceless under the night,
> Our world in stupor lies;
> Yet, dotted everywhere,
> Ironic points of light
> Flash out wherever the just
> Exchange their messages:
> May I, composed like them
> Of Eros and of dust,
> Beleaguered by the same
> Negation and despair,
> Show an affirming flame.

420: THE DELUSION OF CONTROL
(Originally published 24 June 2015)

I'm sure most of my readers have heard at least a little of the hullaballoo surrounding the release of Pope Francis' encyclical on the environment, Laudato Si. It's been entertaining to watch, not least because so many politicians in the United States who like to use Vatican pronouncements as window dressing for their own agendas have been left scrambling for cover now that the wind from Rome is blowing out of a noticeably different quarter.

Take Rick Santorum, a loudly Catholic Republican who used to be in the US Senate and now spends his time entertaining an assortment of faux-conservative venues with his own flavor of hate speech. Santorum loves to denounce fellow Catholics who disagree with Vatican edicts as "cafeteria Catholics," and announced a while back that John F. Kennedy's famous defense of the separation of church and state made him sick to his stomach. In the wake of Laudato Si, care to guess who's elbowing his way to the head of the cafeteria line? Yes, that would be Santorum, who's been insisting since the encyclical came out that the Pope is wrong and American Catholics shouldn't be obliged to listen to him.

What makes all the yelling about Laudato Si a source of wry amusement to me is that it's not actually a radical document at all. It's a statement of plain common sense. It should have been obvious all along that treating the air as a gaseous sewer was a really dumb idea, and in particular, that dumping billions upon billions of tons of infrared-reflecting gases into the atmosphere would change its capacity for heat retention in unwelcome ways. It should have been just as obvious that all the other ways we maltreat the only habitable planet we've got were guaranteed to end just as badly. That this wasn't obvious — that huge numbers of people find it impossible to realize that you can only wet your bed so many times before you have to sleep in a damp spot—deserves much more attention than it's received so far.

It's really a curious blindness, when you think about it. Since our distant ancestors climbed unsteadily down from the trees of late Pliocene Africa, the capacity to anticipate threats and do something about them has been central to the success of our species. A rustle in the grass might indicate the approach of a leopard, a series of unusually dry seasons might turn the local water hole into undrinkable mud: those of our ancestors who paid attention to such things, and took constructive action in response to them, were more likely to survive and leave offspring than those who shrugged and went on with business as usual. That's why traditional societies around the world are hedged about with a dizzying assortment of taboos and customs meant to guard against every conceivable source of danger.

Somehow, though, we got from that to our present situation, where substantial majorities across the world's industrial nations seem unable to notice that something bad can actually happen to them, where thoughtstoppers of the "I'm sure they'll think of something" variety take the place of thinking about the future, and where, when something bad does happen to someone, the immediate response is to find some way to blame the victim for what happened, so that everyone else can continue to believe that the same thing can't happen to them. A world where Laudato Si is controversial, not to mention necessary, is a world that's become dangerously detached from the most basic requirements of collective survival.

For quite some time now, I've been wondering just what lies behind the bizarre paralogic with which most people these days turn blank and uncomprehending eyes on their onrushing fate. The process of writing last week's blog post on the astonishing stupidity of US foreign policy, though, seems to have helped me push through to clarity on the subject. I may be wrong, but I think I've figured it out.

Let's begin with the issue at the center of last week's post, the realy remarkable cluelessness with which US policy toward Russia and China has convinced both nations they have nothing to gain from cooperating with a US-led global order, and are better off allying with each other and opposing the US instead. US politicians and diplomats made that happen, and the way they did it was set out in detail in a recent and thoughtful article by Paul R. Pillar in the online edition of *The National Interest*.

Pillar's article pointed out that the United States has evolved a uniquely counterproductive notion of how negotiation works. Elsewhere on the planet, people understand that when you negotiate, you're seeking a compromise where you get whatever you most need out of the situation, while the other side gets enough of its own agenda met to be willing to cooperate. To the US, by contrast, negotiation means that the other side complies with US demands, and that's the end of it. The idea that other countries might have their own interests, and might expect to receive some substantive benefit in exchange for cooperation with the US, has apparently never entered the heads of official Washington — and the absence of that idea has resulted in the cascading failures of US foreign policy in recent years.

It's only fair to point out that the United States isn't the only practitioner of this kind of self-defeating behavior. A first-rate example has been unfolding in Europe in recent months — yes, that would be the ongoing non-negotiations between the Greek government and the so-called troika, the coalition of unelected bureaucrats who are trying to force Greece to keep pursuing a failed economic policy at all costs. The attitude of the troika is simple: the only outcome they're willing to accept is capitulation on the part of the Greek government, and they're not willing to give anything in return. Every time the Greek government has tried to point out to the troika that negotiation usually involves some degree of give and take, the bureaucrats simply give them a blank look and reiterate their previous demands.

That attitude has had drastic political consequences. It's already convinced Greeks to elect a radical leftist government in place of the compliant centrists who ruled the country in the recent past. If the leftists fold, the neofascist Golden Dawn party is waiting in the wings. The problem with the troika's stance is simple: the policies they're insisting that Greece must accept have never — not once in the history of market economies — produced anything but mass impoverishment and national bankruptcy. The Greeks, among many other people, know this; they know that Greece will not return to prosperity until it defaults on its foreign debts the way Russia did in 1998, and scores of other countries have done as well.

If the troika won't settle for a negotiated debt-relief program, and the current Greek government won't default, the Greeks will elect someone else who will, no matter who that someone else happens to be; it's that, after all, or continue along a course that's already caused the Greek economy to lose a quarter of its precrisis GDP, and shows no sign of stopping anywhere this side of failed-state status. That this could quite easily hand Greece over to a fascist despot is just one of the potential problems with the troika's strategy. It's astonishing that so few people in Europe seem to be able to remember what happened the last time an international political establishment committed itself to the preservation of a failed economic orthodoxy no matter what; those of my readers who don't know what I'm talking about may want to pick up any good book on the rise of fascism in Europe between the wars.

Let's step back from specifics, though, and notice the thinking that underlies the dysfunctional behavior in Washington and Brussels alike. In both cases, the people who think they're in charge have lost track of the fact that Russia, China, and Greece have needs, concerns, and interests of their own, and aren't simply dolls that the US or EU can pose at will. These other nations can, perhaps, be bullied by threats over the short term, but that's a strategy with a short shelf life. Successful diplomacy depends on giving the other guy reasons to want to cooperate with you, while demanding cooperation at gunpoint guarantees that the other guy is going to look for ways to shoot back.

The same sort of thinking in a different context underlies the brutal stupidity of American drone attacks in the Middle East. Some wag in the media pointed out a while back that the US went to war against an enemy 5,000 strong, we've killed 10,000 of them, and now there are only 20,000 left. That's a good summary of the situation; the US drone campaign has been a total failure by every objective measure, having worked out consistently to the benefit of the Muslim extremist groups against which it's aimed, and yet nobody in official Washington seems capable of noticing this fact.

It's hard to miss the conclusion, in fact, that the Obama administration thinks that in pursuing its drone-strike program, it's playing some kind of video game, which the United States can win if it can rack up enough points. Notice the way that every report that a drone has taken out some al-Qaeda leader gets hailed in the media: hey, we nailed a commander, doesn't that boost our score by five hundred? In the real world, meanwhile the indiscriminate slaughter of civilians by US drone strikes has become a core factor convincing Muslims around the world that the United States is just as evil as the jihadis claim, and thus sending young men by the thousands to join the jihadi ranks. Has anyone in the Obama administration caught on to this straightforward arithmetic of failure? Surely you jest.

For that matter, I wonder how many of my readers recall the much-ballyhooed "surge" in Afghanistan several years back. The "surge" was discussed at great length in the US media before it was enacted on Afghan soil; talking heads of every persuasion babbled learnedly about how many troops would be sent, how long they'd stay, and so on. It apparently never occurred to anybody in the Pentagon or the White House that the Taliban could visit websites, read newspapers, and get a pretty good idea of what the US forces in Afghanistan were about to do. That's exactly what happened, too; the Taliban simply hunkered down for the duration, and popped back up the moment the extra troops went home.

Both these examples of US military failure are driven by the same problem discussed earlier in the context of diplomacy: an inability to recognize that the other side has its own agenda, and will respond to US actions in ways that further its own agenda, rather than playing along with the US. More broadly, it's the same failure of thought that leads so many people to assume that the biosphere is somehow obligated to give us all the resources we want and take all the abuse we choose to dump on it, without ever responding in ways that might inconvenience us.

We can sum up all these forms of acquired stupidity in a single sentence: most people these days seem to have lost the ability to grasp that the other side can learn.

The entire concept of learning has been so poisoned by certain bad habits of contemporary thought that it's probably necessary to pause here. Learning, in particular, isn't the same thing as rote imitation. If you memorize a set of phrases in a foreign language, for example, that doesn't mean you've learned that language. To learn the language means to grasp the underlying structure, so that you can come up with your own phrases and say whatever you want, not just what you've been taught to say.

In the same way, if you memorize a set of disconnected factoids about history, you haven't learned history. This is something of a loaded topic right now in the US, because recent "reforms" in the American public school system have replaced learning with rote memorization of disconnected factoids that are then regurgitated for multiple choice tests. This way of handling education penalizes those children who figure out how to learn, since they might well come up with answers that differ from the ones the test expects. That's one of many ways that US education these days actively discourages learning — but that's a subject for another post.

To learn is to grasp the underlying structure of a given subject of knowledge, so that the learner can come up with original responses to it. That's what Russia and China did; they grasped the underlying structure of US diplomacy, figured out that they had nothing to gain by cooperating with that structure, and came up with a creative response, which was to ally against the United States. That's what Greece is doing, too. Bit by bit, the Greeks seem to be figuring out the underlying structure of troika policy, which amounts to the systematic looting of southern Europe for the benefit of Germany and a few of its allies, and are trying to come up with a response that doesn't simply amount to unilateral submission.

That's also what the jihadis and the Taliban are doing in the face of US military activity. If life hands you lemons, as the saying goes, make lemonade; if the US hands you drone strikes that routinely slaughter noncombatants, you can make very successful propaganda out of it — and if the US hands you a surge, you roll your eyes, hole up in your mountain fastnesses, and wait for the Americans to get bored or distracted, knowing that this won't take long. That's how learning works, but that's something that US planners seem congenitally unable to take into account.

The same analysis, interestingly enough, makes just as much sense when applied to nonhuman nature. As Ervin Laszlo pointed out a long time ago in *Introduction to Systems Philosophy*, any sufficiently complex system behaves in ways that approximate intelligence. Consider the way that bacteria respond to antibiotics. Individually, bacteria are as dumb as politicians, but their behavior on the species level shows an eerie similarity to learning;

faced with antibiotics, a species of bacteria "tries out" different biochemical approaches until it finds one that sidesteps the antibiotic. In the same way, insects and weeds "try out" different responses to pesticides and herbicides until they find whatever allows them to munch on crops or flourish in the fields no matter how much poison the farmer sprays on them.

We can even apply the same logic to the environmental crisis as a whole. Complex systems tend to seek equilibrium, and will respond to anything that pushes them away from equilibrium by pushing back the other way. Any field biologist can show you plenty of examples: if conditions allow more rabbits to be born in a season, for instance, the population of hawks and foxes rises accordingly, reducing the rabbit surplus to a level the ecosystem can support. As humanity has put increasing pressure on the biosphere, the biosphere has begun to push back with increasing force, in an increasing number of ways; is it too much to think of this as a kind of learning, in which the biosphere "tries out" different ways to balance out the abusive behavior of humanity, and will eventually find one that works?

Now of course it's long been a commonplace of modern thought that natural systems can't possibly learn. The notion that nature is static, timeless, and unresponsive, a passive stage on which human beings alone play active roles, is welded into modern thought, unshaken even by the realities of biological evolution or the rising tide of evidence that natural systems are in fact quite able to adapt their way around human meddling. There's a long and complex history to the notion of passive nature, but that's a subject for another day; what interests me just now is that since 1990 or so, the governing classes of the United States, and some other Western nations as well, have applied the same frankly delusional logic to everything in the world other than themselves.

"We're an empire now, and when we act, we create our own reality," neoconservative guru Karl Rove is credited as saying to reporter Ron Suskind. "We're history's actors, and you, all of you, will be left to just study what we do." That seems to be the thinking that governs the US government these days, on both sides of the supposed partisan divide. Obama says we're in a recovery, and if the economy fails to act accordingly, why, rooms full of industrious flacks churn out elaborately fudged statistics to erase that unwelcome reality. That history's self-proclaimed actors might turn out to be just one more set of flotsam awash on history's vast tides has never entered their darkest dream.

Let's step back from specifics again, though. What's the source of this bizarre paralogic—the delusion that leads politicians to think that they create reality, and that everyone and everything else can only fill the roles they've been assigned by history's actors? I think I know. I think it comes from a simple but remarkably powerful fact, which is that the people in question, along with most people in the privileged classes of the industrial world, spend most of their time, from childhood on, dealing with machines.

We can define a machine as a subset of the universe that's been deprived of the capacity to learn. The whole point of building a machine is that it does what you want, when you want it, and nothing else. Flip the switch on, and it turns on and goes through whatever rigidly defined set of behaviors it's been designed to do, flip the switch off, and it stops. It may be fitted with controls, so you can manipulate its behavior in various tightly limited ways; nowadays, especially, the set of behaviors assigned to it may be extremely complex. There's no inner life behind the facade, though. It can't learn, and to the extent that it pretends to learn, all that comes out of it is the product of the sort of rote memorization described above as the antithesis of learning.

A machine that learned would be capable of making its own decisions and coming up with a creative response to your actions—and that's the opposite of what machines are meant to do, because that response might well involve frustrating your intentions so the machine can get what it wants instead. That's why the trope of machines going to war against human beings has so large a presence in popular culture: it's exactly because we expect machines not to act like people, not to pursue their own needs and interests, that the thought of machines acting the way we do gets so reliable a frisson of horror.

The habit of thought that treats other people as passive machines, existing only to fulfill whatever purpose they might be assigned by their operators, is another matter entirely. Its origins can be traced back to the dawning of the scientific revolution in the seventeenth century, when a handful of thinkers first began to suggest that the universe might not be a vast organism—as everybody in the western world had presupposed for millennia before then — but might instead be a vast machine. It's indicative that one immediate and popular response to this idea was to insist that other living things were simply "meat machines" who didn't actually suffer pain under the vivisector's knife, but had been designed by God to imitate sounds of pain in order to inspire feelings of pity in human beings.

The delusion of control — the conviction, apparently immune to correction by mere facts, that the world is a machine incapable of doing anything but the things we want it to do — pervades contemporary life in the world's industrial societies. People in those societies spend so much more time dealing with machines than they do interacting with other people and other living things without a machine interface getting in the way, that it's no wonder that this delusion is so widespread. As long as it retains its grip, though, we can expect the industrial world, and especially its privileged classes, to stumble onward from one preventable disaster to another. That's the inner secret of the delusion of control, after all: those who insist on seeing the world in mechanical terms end up behaving mechanically themselves; those who deny all other things the ability to learn lose the ability to learn from their own mistakes, and lurch robotically onward along a trajectory that leads straight to the scrapheap of the future.

421: THE DREAM OF THE MACHINE

(Originally published 1 July 2015)

As I type these words, it looks as though the wheels are coming off the global economy. Greece and Puerto Rico have both defaulted on their debts, and China's stock market, which spent the last year in a classic speculative bubble, is now seeing a classic speculative bust. Those of my readers who know their way around John Kenneth Galbraith's lively history *The Great Crash 1929* already know all about the Chinese situation, including the outcome—and since vast amounts of money from all over the world went into Chinese stocks, and most of that money is in the process of turning into twinkle dust, the impact of the crash will inevitably proliferate through the global economy.

So, in all probability, will the Greek and Puerto Rican defaults. In today's bizarre financial world, the kind of bad debts that used to send investors backing away in a hurry attract speculators in droves, and so it turns out that some big New York hedge funds are in trouble as a result of the Greek default, and some of the same firms that got into trouble with mortgage-backed securities in the recent housing bubble are in the same kind of trouble over Puerto Rico's unpayable debts. How far will the contagion spread? It's anybody's guess.

Oh, and nearly half a million acres of Alaska burned up in a single day during the past week, while glaciers in Greenland are collapsing so frequently and forcefully that the resulting earthquakes are rattling seismographs thousands of miles away. These and plenty of other signals of a biosphere in crisis make good reminders of the fact that the current economic mess isn't happening in a vacuum. As peak oil blogger Ugo Bardi pointed out in a thoughtful article, finance is the flotsam on the surface of the ocean of real exchanges of real goods and services, and the current drumbeat of financial crises may be symptomatic of the real crisis — the arrival of the limits to growth that so many people have been discussing, and so many more have been trying to ignore, for the last half century or so.

A great many people in the doomward end of the blogosphere are talking about what's going on in the global economy and what's likely to blow up next. Around the time the next round of financial explosions start shaking the world's windows, a great many of those same people will likely be talking about what to do about it all. I don't plan on joining them in that discussion. As blog posts here have pointed out more than once, time has to be considered when getting ready for a crisis. The industrial world would have had to start backpedaling away from the abyss decades ago in order to forestall the crisis we're now in, and the same principle applies to individuals; the slogan "collapse now and avoid the rush!" loses most of its point, after all, when the rush is already under way.

Any of my readers who are still pinning their hopes on survival ecovillages and rural doomsteads they haven't gotten around to buying or building yet, in other words, are very likely out of luck. They, like the rest of us, will be meeting this where they are, with what they have right now. This is ironic, in that ideas that might have been worth adopting three or four years ago are just starting to get traction now. I'm thinking here particularly of a recent article on how to use permaculture to prepare for a difficult future. There's enough common ground between that article and the themes of my book Green Wizardry that I'm left wondering just how widely that book has penetrated into permaculture circles. The awkward fact remains that when the global banking industry shows signs of grinding to a full stop, putting credit for land purchases out of reach of most people for years to come, the article's advice may have come rather too late.

That doesn't mean, of course, that my readers ought to crawl under their beds and wait for death. What we're facing, after all, isn't the end of the world — though it may feel like that for those who are too deeply invested, in any sense of that last word you care to use, in the existing order of industrial society. As Visigoth mothers used to remind their impatient sons, Rome wasn't sacked in a day. The crisis ahead of us marks the end of what I've called abundance industrialism and the transition to scarcity

204 | *The Archdruid Report: The Twilight of Progress*

industrialism, as well as the end of America's global hegemony and the emergence of a new international order whose main beneficiary hasn't been settled yet. Those paired transformations will most likely unfold across several decades of economic chaos, political turmoil, environmental disasters, and widespread warfare. Plenty of people got through the equivalent cataclysms of the first half of the twentieth century with their skins intact, even if the crisis caught them unawares, and no doubt plenty of people will get through the mess that's approaching us in much the same condition.

Thus I don't have any additional practical advice to offer my readers just now. Those who've already collapsed and gotten ahead of the rush can break out the popcorn and watch what promises to be a truly gaudy show. Those who didn't — well, you might as well get some popcorn going and try to enjoy the show anyway. If you come out the other side of it all, schoolchildren who aren't even born yet may eventually ask you awed questions about what happened when the markets crashed in '15.

In the meantime, while the popcorn is popping and the sidewalks of Wall Street wait to receive their traditional tithe of plummeting stockbrokers, I'd like to return to the theme of last week's post and talk about the way that the myth of the machine — if you prefer, the widespread mental habit of thinking about the world in mechanistic terms — pervades and cripples the modern mind.

Of all the responses that last week's post fielded, those I found most amusing, and also most revealing, were the ones that insisted that of course the universe is a machine, and so is everything and everybody in it. That's amusing because most of the authors of these comments made it very clear that they embraced the sort of scientific-materialist atheism that rejects any suggestion that the universe has a creator or a purpose. A machine, though, is a purposive artifact; by definition, it's made by someone to accomplish something. If the universe is a machine, then, it has a creator and a purpose, and if it doesn't have a creator and a purpose, logically speaking, it can't be a machine.

That sort of unintentional comedy inevitably comes into play whenever people don't think through the implications of their favorite metaphors. Still, chase that habit further along its giddy path and you'll find a deeper absurdity at work. When people say "the universe is a machine," unless they mean that statement as a poetic simile, they're engaging in a very dubious sort of logic. As Alfred Korzybski pointed out a good many years ago, pretty much any time you say "this is that," unless you take the time to qualify what you mean in very careful terms indeed, you've just uttered nonsense.

The difficulty lies in that seemingly innocuous word "is." What Korzybski called the "is of identity"—the use of the word "is" to represent =, the sign of equality—makes sense only in a very narrow range of uses. You can use the "is of identity" with good results in categorical definitions; when I commented above that a machine is a purposive artifact, that's what I was doing. Here is a concept, "machine;" here are two other concepts, "purposive" and "artifact;" the concept "machine" logically includes the concepts "purposive" and "artifact," so anything that can be described by the words "a machine" can also be described as "purposive" and "an artifact." That's how categorical definitions work.

Let's consider a second example, though: "a machine is a purple dinosaur." That utterance uses the same structure as the one we've just considered. I hope I don't have to prove to my readers, though, that the concept "machine" doesn't include the concepts "purple" and "dinosaur" in any but the most whimsical of senses. There are plenty of things that can be described by the label "machine," in other words, that can't be described by the labels "purple" or "dinosaur." The mere fact that some machines can accurately be described as purple dinosaurs, by the way—an electronic Barney doll comes to mind here—doesn't make the definition any less silly; it simply means that the statement "no machine is a purple dinosaur" can't be justified either.

With that in mind, let's take a closer look at the statement "the universe is a machine." As pointed out earlier, the concept "machine" implies the concepts "purposive" and "artifact," so if the universe is a machine, somebody made it for some purpose. Those of my readers who happen to belong to Christianity, Islam, or another religion that envisions the universe as the creation of one or more deities—not all religions make this claim, by the way—will find this conclusion wholly unproblematic. My atheist readers will disagree, of course, and their reaction is the one I want to discuss here. (Notice how "is" functions in the previous sentence: "the reaction of the atheists" equals "the reaction

I want to discuss." This is one of the few other uses of "is" that doesn't reliably generate nonsense.)

In my experience, at least, atheists faced with the argument about the meaning of the word "machine" I've presented here pretty reliably respond with something like "It's not a machine in *that* sense." That response takes us straight to the heart of the logical problems with the "is of identity." In what sense is the universe a machine? Pursue the argument far enough, and unless the atheist storms off in a huff—which tends to happen more often than not, admittedly—what you'll get amounts to "the universe and a machine share certain characteristics in common," which packs considerably less of a punch. Go further still—and at this point the atheist will almost certainly storm off in a huff—and you'll discover that the characteristics that the universe is supposed to share with a machine are all things we can't actually prove one way or another about the universe, such as whether it has a creator or a purpose.

The statement "the universe is a machine," in other words, doesn't do what it appears to do. It appears to state a categorical identity; it actually makes an unsupported generalization in absolute terms. It takes a mental model abstracted from one corner of human experience and applies it to something else. In this case, for polemic reasons, it does so in a predictably one-sided way: deductions approved by the person making the statement ("the universe is a machine, therefore it lacks life and consciousness") are acceptable, while deductions the person making the statement doesn't like ("the universe is a machine, therefore it was made by someone for some purpose") get the dismissive response noted above.

This sort of Orwellian doublethink appears all through the landscape of contemporary nonconversation and nondebate, to be sure, but the problems with the "is of identity" don't stop with its polemic abuse. Any time you say "this is that," and mean something other than "this has some features in common with that," you've just fallen victim to one of the central boobytraps hardwired into the structure of human thought.

Human beings think in categories. That's what made ancient Greek logic, which takes categories as its basic element, so massive a revolution in the history of human thinking: by watching the way that one category includes or excludes another, which is what the Greek logicians did, you can catch a very large fraction of human stupidities in the making. What Alfred Korzybski pointed out, in effect, is that there's a metalogic that the ancient Greeks didn't get to, and logical theorists since their time haven't really tackled either: the extremely murky relationship between the categories we think with and the things we experience, which don't come with category labels spraypainted on them.

Here is a green plant with a woody stem. Is it a tree or a shrub? That depends on exactly where you draw the line between those two categories, and as any botanist can tell you, that isn't an easy or an obvious thing. As long as you remember that categories exist within the human mind as conveniences for us to think with, you can navigate around the difficulties, but when you slip into thinking that the categories are more real than the unique and diverse things they describe, you're in deep, deep trouble.

It's not at all surprising that human thought should have such problems built into it. If, as I do, you accept the Darwinian thesis that human beings evolved out of prehuman primates by the normal workings of the laws of evolution, it follows logically that our nervous systems and cognitive structures didn't evolve for the purpose of understanding the truth about the cosmos; they evolved to assist us in getting food, attracting mates, fending off predators, and a range of similar, intellectually undemanding tasks. If, as many of my theist readers do, you believe that human beings were created by a deity, the yawning chasm between creator and created, between an infinite and a finite intelligence, stands in the way of any claim that human beings can know the unvarnished truth about the cosmos. Neither viewpoint supports the claim that a category created by the human mind is anything but a convenience to help our very modest mental powers grapple with an ultimately incomprehensible cosmos.

Any time human beings try to make sense of the universe or any part of it, in turn, they have to choose from among the available categories in an attempt to make the object of inquiry fit the capacities of their minds. That's what the founders of the scientific revolution did in the seventeenth century, by taking the category of "machine" and applying it to the universe to see how well it would fit. That was a perfectly rational choice from within their cultural and intellectual standpoint. The founders of the scientific revolution were Christians to a man, and some of them (for example, Isaac Newton) were devout even by the standards of the time; the idea that the universe had been made by someone for some purpose, after all, wasn't problematic in the least to people who took it as given that the universe was made by God for the purpose of human salvation. It was also a useful choice in practical terms, because it allowed certain features of the universe — specifically, the behavior of masses in motion — to be accounted for and modeled with a clarity that previous categories hadn't managed to achieve.

The fact that one narrowly defined aspect of the universe seems to behave like a machine, though, does not prove that the universe is a machine, any more than the fact that one machine happens to look like a purple dinosaur proves that all machines are purple dinosaurs. The success of mechanistic models in explaining the behavior of masses in motion proved that mechanical metaphors are good at fitting some of the observed phenomena of physics into a shape that's simple enough for human cognition to grasp, and that's all it proves. To get from that modest fact to the claim that the universe and everything in it are machines takes an intellectual leap of pretty spectacular dimensions. Part of the reason that leap was taken in the seventeenth century was the religious frame of scientific inquiry at that time, as already mentioned, but there was another factor, too.

It's a curious fact that mechanistic models of the universe appeared in western European cultures, and become wildly popular there, well before the machines did. In the early seventeenth century, machines played a very modest role in the life of most Europeans; most tasks were done using hand tools powered by human and animal muscle, the way they had been done since the dawn of the agricultural revolution eight millennia or so before. The most complex devices available at the time were pendulum clocks, printing presses, handlooms, and the like — you know, the sort of thing that people who want to get away from technology these days like to use instead of machines.

For reasons that historians of ideas are still trying to puzzle out, though, western European thinkers during these same years were obsessed with machines, and with mechanical explanations for the universe. Those latter ranged from the plausible to the frankly preposterous — René Descartes, for example, proposed a theory of gravity in which little corkscrew-shaped particles went zooming up from the earth to screw themselves into pieces of matter and yank them down. Until Isaac Newton, furthermore, theories of nature based on mechanical models didn't actually explain that much. Until the cascade of inventive adaptations of steam power that ended with James Watt's epochal steam engine nearly a century after Newton, the idea that machines could elbow aside craftspeople with hand tools and animals pulling carts was an unproven hypothesis, and yet a great many people in western Europe believed in the power of the machine as devoutly as their ancestors had believed in the power of the bones of the local saints.

A habit of thought very widespread in today's culture assumes that technological change happens first and the world of ideas changes in response to it. The facts simply won't support that claim, though. As the history of mechanistic ideas in science shows clearly, the ideas come first and the technologies follow— and there's good reason why this should be so. Technologies don't invent themselves, after all. Somebody has to put in the work to invent them, and then other people have to invest the resources to take them out of the laboratory and give them a role in everyday life. The decisions that drive invention and investment, in turn, are powerfully shaped by cultural forces, and these in turn are by no means as rational as the people influenced by them generally like to think.

People in western Europe and a few of its colonies dreamed of machines, and then created them. They dreamed of a universe reduced to the status of a machine, a universe made totally transparent to the human mind and totally subservient to the human will, and then set out to create it. That latter attempt hasn't worked out so well, for a variety of reasons, and the rising tide of disasters sketched out in the first part of this week's post unfold from the failure of the dream. In the next few posts, I want to talk about why that failure was inevitable, and where we might go from here.

422: THE LIMITS OF HUMAN INTELLIGENCE

(Originally published 8 July 2015)

Our age has no shortage of curious features, but for me, at least, one of the oddest is the way that so many people these days don't seem to be able to think through the consequences of their own beliefs. Pick an ideology, any ideology, straight across the spectrum from the most devoutly religious to the most stridently secular, and you can count on finding a bumper crop of people who claim to hold that set of beliefs and recite them with all the uncomprehending enthusiasm of a well-trained mynah bird, but haven't noticed that those beliefs contradict other beliefs they claim to hold with equal devotion.

I'm not talking here about ordinary hypocrisy. The hypocrites we have with us always; our species being what it is, plenty of people have always seen the advantages of saying one thing and doing another. No, what I have in mind is saying one thing and saying another, without ever noticing that if one of those statements is true, the other is by definition false. My readers may recall the way that cowboy-hatted heavies in old Westerns used to say to each other, "This town ain't big enough for the two of us;" there are plenty of ideas and beliefs that are like that, but too many modern minds resemble nothing so much as an OK Corral where the gunfight never happens.

An example that I've satirized in an earlier post is the bizarre way that so many people on the rightward end of the US political landscape these days claim to be, at one and the same time, devout Christians and fervid adherents of Ayn Rand's violently atheist and anti-Christian ideology. The difficulty here, of course, is that Jesus tells his followers to humble themselves before God and help the poor, while Rand tells hers to despise God, wallow in their own self-proclaimed superiority, and kick the poor into the nearest available gutter. There's quite precisely no common ground between the two belief systems, and yet self-proclaimed Christians who spout Rand's turgid drivel at every opportunity make up a significant fraction of the Republican Party just now.

Still, it's only fair to point out that this sort of weird disconnect is far from unique to religious people, or for that matter to Republicans. One of the places it crops up most often nowadays is the remarkable unwillingness of people who say they accept Darwin's theory of evolution to think through what that theory implies about the nature and power of human intelligence.

If Darwin's right, as I've had occasion to point out here several times already, human intelligence isn't the world-shaking superpower our collective egotism likes to suppose. It's simply a somewhat more sophisticated version of the sort of mental activity found in many other animals these days. The thing that supposedly sets it apart from all other forms of mentation, the use of abstract language, isn't all that unique; several species of cetaceans and an assortment of the brainier birds communicate with their kin using vocalizations that show all the signs of being languages in the full sense of the word — that is, structured patterns of abstract vocal signs that take their meaning from convention rather than instinct.

What differentiates human beings from bottlenosed porpoises, African gray parrots, and other talking species is the mere fact that in our case, language and abstract thinking happened to evolve in a species that also had the sort of grasping limbs, fine motor control, and instinctive drive to pick things up and fiddle with them, that primates have and most other animals don't. There's no reason why sentience should be associated with the sort of neurological bias that leads to manipulating the environment, and thence to technology. For all we know, bottlenosed porpoises have a rich philosophical, scientific, and literary culture dating back twenty million years; they just don't have hands, so they don't have technology. All things considered, this may be an advantage, since it means they won't have had to face the kind of self-induced disasters our species is so busy preparing for itself through its frankly idiotic misuse of the inveterate primate tendency to, ahem, monkey around with things.

I've long suspected that one of the reasons why human beings haven't yet figured out how to carry on a conversation with bottlenosed porpoises, African gray parrots, et al. in their own language is quite simply that we're terrified of what they might say to us—not least because it's entirely possible that they'd be right. Another reason for the lack of communication, though, leads straight back to the limits of human intelligence. If our minds have emerged out of the ordinary processes of evolution, what we've got between our ears is simply an unusually complex variation on the standard social primate brain, adapted over millions of years to the mental tasks that are important to social primates—that is, staying fed, attracting mates, competing for status, and staying out of the jaws of hungry leopards.

Notice that "discovering the objective truth about the nature of the universe" isn't part of this list, and if Darwin's theory of evolution is correct—as I believe it to be—there's no conceivable way it could be. Now of course the mental activities of social primates, and all other living things, have to take the rest of the world into account in certain specific ways; our perceptions of food, mates, rivals, and leopards, for example, have to correspond to what's there in the environment; but it's actually an advantage to a social primate to screen out anything that doesn't relate to such immediate benefits or threats, so that adequate attention can be paid to the things that matter. We perceive colors, which most mammals don't, because primates need to be able to judge the ripeness of fruit from a distance; we don't perceive the polarization of light, as bees do, because primates don't need to navigate by the angle of the sun.

What's more, the basic mental categories we use to make sense of the tiny fraction of our surroundings that we perceive are just as much a product of our primate ancestry as the set of senses we have and don't have. That includes the basic structures of human language, which most research suggests are inborn in our species, such derivations from language as logic, and such concepts as the relation between cause and effect—this latter simply takes the grammatical relation between subjects, verbs, and objects, and projects it onto the nonlinguistic world. In the real world, every phenomenon is part of an ongoing cascade of interactions so hypercomplex that labels like "cause" and "effect" are hopelessly simplistic; what's more, a great many things—for example, the decay of radioactive nuclei—just up and happen randomly without being triggered by any specific cause at all. We simplify all this into cause and effect because just enough things seem to work that way to make the habit useful to us.

Another thing that has much more to do with our cognitive apparatus than with the world we perceive is number. Does one apple plus one apple equal two apples? In our number-using minds, yes; in the real world, it depends entirely on the size of the apples in question. We convert qualities into quantities because quantities are easier for us to think with. That was one of the core discoveries that kickstarted the scientific revolution; when Galileo became the first human being in history to think of speed as a quantity, he made it possible for everyone after him to get their minds around the concept of velocity in a way that people before him had never quite been able to do.

In physics, converting qualities to quantities works very, very well. In some other sciences, the same thing is true, though the further you go away from the exquisite simplicity of masses in motion, the harder it is to translate everything that matters into quantitative terms, and the more inevitably gets left out of the resulting theories. By and large, the more complex the phenomena under discussion, the less useful quantitative models are. Not coincidentally, the more complex the phenomena under discussion, the harder it is to control all the variables in play—the essential step in using the scientific method—and the more tentative, fragile, and dubious the models that result.

So when we try to figure out what bottlenosed porpoises are saying to each other, we're facing what's probably an insuperable barrier. All our notions of language are social-primate notions, shaped by the peculiar mix of neurology and hardwired psychology that proved most useful to bipedal apes on the East African savannah over the last few million years. The structures that shape porpoise speech, in turn, are social-cetacean notions, shaped by the utterly different mix of neurology and hardwired psychology that's most useful if you happen to be a bottlenosed porpoise or one of its ancestors.

Mind you, porpoises and humans are at least fellow-mammals, and likely have common ancestors only a couple of hundred million years ago. If you want to talk to a gray parrot, you're trying to cross a much vaster evolutionary distance, since the ancestors of our therapsid forebears and the ancestors of the parrot's archosaurian progenitors have been following divergent tracks since way back in the Paleozoic. Since language evolved independently in each of the lineages we're discussing, the logic of convergent evolution comes into play: as with the eyes of vertebrates and cephalopods — another classic case of the same thing appearing in very different evolutionary lineages — the functions are similar but the underlying structure is very different. Thus it's no surprise that it's taken exhaustive computer analyses of porpoise and parrot vocalizations just to give us a clue that they're using language too.

The takeaway point I hope my readers have grasped from this is that the human mind doesn't know universal, objective truths. Our thoughts are simply the way that our species of social primate happens to like to sort out the universe into chunks simple enough for us to think with. Does that make human thought useless or irrelevant? Of course not; it simply means that its uses and relevance are as limited as everything else about our species — and, of course, every other species as well. If any of my readers see this as belittling humanity, I'd like to suggest that fatuous delusions of omnipotence aren't a useful habit for any species, least of all ours, and those delusions have played a huge role in landing us in the rising spiral of crises we're in today.

Human beings are one species among many; we've got remarkable gifts, but then so does every other living thing. We're not the masters of the planet, and our attempt to play that role with the help of a lot of fossil carbon hasn't exactly turned out well, you must admit. I know some people find it unbearable to see our species denied its supposed place as the precious darlings of the cosmos, but that's just one of life's little learning experiences, isn't it? Most of us make a comparable discovery on the individual scale in the course of growing up, and from my perspective, it's high time that humanity do a little growing up of its own, ditch the delusions of cosmic importance and interstellar destiny, and get to work making the most of the undeniable talents we do possess over the course of however much time we happen to have on this beautiful and fragile planet.

The recognition that there's a middle ground between omnipotence and uselessness seems to be very hard for a lot of people to grasp just now. I don't know if other bloggers in the doomosphere have this happen to them, but every few months or so I field a flurry of attempted comments by people who want to insist that human beings don't have free will. I don't put them through, and not just because they're inevitably off topic; that frankly poisonous ideology is based on shopworn Victorian determinism that got chucked by working scientists rather more than a century ago, but it's still being recycled by too many people who haven't noticed that it belongs in the trash can of dead theories.

It used to be a commonplace of popular scientific ideology that cause and effect ruled everything, and the whole universe was fated to rumble along a rigidly invariant sequence of events from the get-go. The claim was that a sufficiently vast intelligence, provided with a sufficiently complete data set about the position and velocity of every particle in the cosmos at one point in time, could literally predict everything that would ever happen after that time. All that sort of thinking went out the window, or should have, once experiments in the early 20th century showed conclusively that quantum phenomena are random in the strictest sense of the world. They're not caused by some hidden variable, in other words; they just happen when they happen, without any triggering cause.

What determines when a given atom of an unstable isotope will throw off an alpha particle or some gamma rays and turn into a different element? Pure dumb luck. Since radiation discharges from single atoms of unstable isotopes are among the main causes of genetic mutations, in turn, this is much more important than it looks. Genetic variation is the raw material on which evolution works—that is to say, a major driving force behind the evolutionary process is completely random. The stray alpha particles and gamma rays that gave you your eye color, gave an otherwise uninteresting species of lobefin fish the adaptations that made it the ancestor of all land vertebrates, and provided the raw material for countless other evolutionary transformations were random events, and would have happened differently if certain unstable atoms had decayed at a different time—as they very well could have. So it doesn't matter how vast the intelligence or complete the data set you've got, the course of life on earth, and a great many other things that unfold from it, are inherently impossible to predict.

With the phantom of determinism laid to rest, we can proceed to the question of free will. We can define free will operationally as the ability to produce genuine novelty in behavior—that is, to do things that can't be predicted in advance. Human beings do this all the time, and there are very good evolutionary reasons why this should be so. Any of my readers who know game theory will recall that the best strategy in any competitive game includes an element of randomness, which prevents the other side from anticipating and forestalling your side's actions. Food gathering, in game theory terms, is a competitive game; so are trying to attract a mate, competing for social prestige, staying out of the jaws of hungry leopards, and most of the other activities that keep social primates busy.

Unpredictability is so highly valued by our species, in fact, that every human culture ever recorded has had formal ways to increase the total amount of sheer randomness guiding human action. Yes, we're talking about divination—for those who don't know the jargon, this term refers to what you do with Tarot cards, the I Ching, tea leaves, horoscopes, and all the myriad other ways human cultures have worked out to get a quick glimpse of the nonrational. Aside from whatever else may be involved in divination—a point that isn't relevant to this blog—it does a great job of generating unpredictability. So does flipping a coin, for that matter, but fully developed divination systems like those just named provide a much richer palette of choices than the simple coin toss, and thus enable people to introduce a much richer range of novelty into their actions.

Still, human beings also have their own onboard novelty generators. The process involved here was understood by philosophers a long time ago, and no doubt the neurologists will get around to figuring it out one of these days too. The core of it is that humans don't respond directly to stimuli, external or internal; instead, they respond to their own mental representations of stimuli, which are constructed by the act of cognition and are laced with extraneous material garnered from memory and linked to the stimulus in uniquely personal, irrational, even whimsical ways, following loose processes of association and contiguity that have nothing to do with logic—much less cause and effect—and everything to do with the roots of creativity.

Each human society tries to load its children with some approximation of its own culturally defined set of representations—that's what's going on when children learn language, pick up the customs of their community, ask for the same story to be read to them for the umpteen hundredth time, and so on. Those culturally defined representations proceed to get tangled up with the inborn, genetically defined representations that each of us get for free with each brand new human nervous system. The existence of these biologically and culturally defined representations, and of various ways that they can be manipulated to some extent by other people with or without the benefit of the media, make up the ostensible reason why the people mentioned above insist that free will doesn't exist.

Here again, though, the fact that human thinking isn't omnipotent doesn't make it a rigidly mechanical process. Think about what happens, say, when a straight stick is thrust into water at an angle, and the stick seems to pick up a sudden bend at the water's surface, due to differential refraction in water and air. The illusion is as clear as anything, but if you show this to a child and let the child experiment with it, you can watch the representation "the stick is bent" give way to "the stick *looks* bent." Notice what's happening here: the stimulus remains the same, but the representation changes, and so do the actions that result from it. That's a simple example of how representations create the possibility of freedom.

In the same way, when the media spouts some absurd bit of manipulative nonsense, if you take the time to think about it, you can watch your own representation shift from "that guy's having an orgasm from slurping that fizzy brown sugar water" to "that guy's being paid to pretend to have an orgasm, so somebody can try to get me to buy fizzy brown sugar water." If you're really paying attention, it may shift again to "why am I wasting my time watching this guy pretend to have an orgasm from fizzy brown sugar water?" and may even lead you to chuck your television out a second story window into an open dumpster, as I did to the last one I ever owned. (The flash and bang when the picture tube imploded, by the way, was far more entertaining than anything that had ever appeared on the screen.)

Human beings have finite intelligence. Our capacities for thinking exist within fairly hard limits—but then so do our capacities for the perception of color, a fact that hasn't stopped artists from the Paleolithic to the present from putting those colors to work in a galaxy of dizzyingly original ways. A clear awareness of the possibilities and the limits of the human mind makes it easier to play the hand we've been dealt in Darwin's casino—and it also points toward a generally unsuspected reason why civilizations come apart, which we'll discuss next week.

423: THE CIMMERIAN HYPOTHESIS
PART ONE: CIVILIZATION AND BARBARISM

(Originally published 15 July 2015)

One of the oddities of the writer's life is the utter unpredictability of inspiration. There are times when I sit down at the keyboard knowing what I have to write, and plod my way though the day's allotment of prose in much the same spirit that a gardener turns the earth in the beds of a big garden; there are times when a project sits there grumbling to itself and has to be coaxed or prodded into taking shape on the page; but there are also times when something grabs hold of me, drags me kicking and screaming to the keyboard, and holds me there with a squamous paw clamped on my shoulder until I've finished whatever it is that I've suddenly found out that I have to write.

Over the last two months, I've had that last experience on a considerably larger scale than usual; to be precise, I've just completed the first draft of a 70,000-word novel in eight weeks. Those of my readers and correspondents who've been wondering why I've been slower than usual to respond to them now know the reason. The working title is *Moon Path to Innsmouth*; it deals, in the sidelong way for which fiction is so well suited, with quite a number of the issues discussed on this blog; I'm pleased to say that I've lined up a publisher, and so in due time the novel will be available to delight the rugose hearts of the Great Old Ones and their eldritch minions everywhere.

None of that would be relevant to the theme of the current series of posts on *The Archdruid Report*, except that getting the thing written required quite a bit of reference to the weird tales of an earlier era—the writings of H.P. Lovecraft, of course, but also those of Clark Ashton Smith and Robert E. Howard, who both contributed mightily to the fictive mythos that took its name from Lovecraft's iconic squid-faced devil-god Cthulhu. One Howard story leads to another — or at least it does if you spent your impressionable youth stewing your imagination in a bubbling cauldron of classic fantasy fiction, as I did — and that's how it happened that I ended up revisiting the final lines of "Beyond the Black River," part of the saga of Conan of Cimmeria, Howard's brawny hero:

"'Barbarism is the natural state of mankind,' the borderer said, still staring somberly at the Cimmerian. 'Civilization is unnatural. It is a whim of circumstance. And barbarism must always ultimately triumph.'"

It's easy to take that as nothing more than a bit of bluster meant to add color to an adventure story — easy but, I'd suggest, inaccurate. Science fiction has made much of its claim to be a "literature of ideas," but a strong case can be made that the weird tale as developed by Lovecraft, Smith, Howard, and their peers has at least as much claim to the same label, and the ideas that feature in a classic weird tale are often a good deal more challenging than those that are the stock in trade of most science fiction: "gee, what happens if I extrapolate this technological trend a little further?" and the like. The authors who published with *Weird Tales* back in the day, in particular, liked to pose edgy questions about the way that the posturings of our species and its contemporary cultures appeared in the cold light of a cosmos that's wholly uninterested in our overblown opinion of ourselves.

Thus I think it's worth giving Conan and his fellow barbarians their due, and treating what we may as well call the Cimmerian hypothesis as a serious proposal about the underlying structure of human history. Let's start with some basics. What is civilization? What is barbarism? What exactly does it mean to describe one state of human society as natural and another unnatural, and how does that relate to the repeated triumph of barbarism at the end of every civilization?

The word "civilization" has a galaxy of meanings, most of them irrelevant to the present purpose. We can take the original meaning of the word — in late Latin, *civilisatio* — as a workable starting point; it means "being or becoming a member of a settled community." A people known to the Romans was civilized if its members lived in *civitates*, cities or towns. We can generalize this a little further, and say that a civilization is a form of human society in which people live in artificial environments. Is there more to civilization than that? Of course there is, but as I hope to show, most of it unfolds from the distinction just traced out.

A city, after all, is a human environment from which the ordinary workings of nature have been excluded, to as great an extent as the available technology permits. When you go outdoors in a city, nearly all the things you encounter have been put there by human beings; even the trees are where they are because someone decided to put them there, not by way of the normal processes by which trees reproduce their kind and disperse their seeds. Those natural phenomena that do manage to elbow their way into an urban environment — rats, pigeons, and the like — are interlopers, and treated as such. The gradient between urban and rural settlements can be measured precisely by what fraction of the things that residents encounter is put there by human action, as compared to the fraction that was put there by ordinary natural processes.

What is barbarism? The root meaning here is a good deal less helpful. The Greek word βαρβαροι, *barbaroi*, originally meant "people who say 'bar bar bar'" instead of talking intelligibly in Greek. In Roman times that usage got bent around to mean "people outside the Empire," and thus in due time to "tribes who are too savage to speak Latin, live in cities, or give up without a fight when we decide to steal their land." Fast forward a century or two, and that definition morphed uncomfortably into "tribes who are too savage to speak Latin, live in cities, or stay peacefully on their side of the border" — enter Alaric's Visigoths, Genseric's Vandals, and the ebullient multiethnic horde that marched westwards under the banners of Attila the Hun.

This is also where Conan enters the picture. In crafting his fictional Hyborian Age, which was vaguely located in time between the sinking of Atlantis and the beginning of recorded history, Howard borrowed freely from various eras of the past, but the Roman experience was an important ingredient — the story cited above, framed by a struggle between the kingdom of Aquilonia and the wild Pictish tribes beyond the Black River, drew noticeably on Roman Britain in the fourth century, though it also took elements from the Old West and elsewhere. The entire concept of a barbarian hero swaggering his way south into the lands of civilization, which Howard introduced to fantasy fiction (and which has been so freely and ineptly plagiarized since his time), has its roots in the late Roman and post-Roman experience, a time when a great many enterprising warriors did just that, and when some, like Conan, became kings.

What sets barbarian societies apart from civilized ones is precisely that a much smaller fraction of the environment barbarians encounter results from human action. When you go outdoors in Cimmeria—if you're not outdoors to start with, which you probably are—nearly everything you encounter has been put there by nature. There are no towns of any size, just scattered clusters of dwellings in the midst of a mostly unaltered environment. Where your Aquilonian town dweller who steps outside may have to look hard to see anything that was put there by nature, your Cimmerian who shoulders his battle-ax and goes for a stroll may have to look hard to see anything that was put there by human beings.

What's more, there's a difference in what we might usefully call the transparency of human constructions. In Cimmeria, if you do manage to get in out of the weather, the stones and timbers of the hovel where you've taken shelter are recognizable lumps of rock and pieces of tree; your hosts smell like the pheromone-laden social primates they are; and when their barbarian generosity inspires them to serve you a feast, they send someone out to shoot a deer, hack it into gobbets, and cook the result in some relatively simple manner that leaves no doubt in anyone's mind that you're all chewing on parts of a dead animal. Follow Conan's route down into the cities of Aquilonia, and you're in a different world, where paint and plaster, soap and perfume, and fancy cookery, among many other things, obscure nature's contributions to the human world.

So that's our first set of distinctions. What makes human societies natural or unnatural? It's all too easy to sink into a festering swamp of unsubstantiated presuppositions here, since people in every human society think of their own ways of doing things as natural and normal, and everyone else's ways of doing the same things as unnatural and abnormal. Worse, there's the pervasive bad habit in industrial Western cultures of lumping all non-Western cultures with relatively simple technologies together as "primitive man"—as though there's only one of him, sitting there in a feathered war bonnet and a lionskin kilt playing the didgeridoo—in order to flatten out human history into an imaginary straight line of progress that leads from the caves to the stars.

In point of anthropological fact, the notion of "primitive man" as an allegedly unspoiled child of nature is pure hokum, and generally racist hokum at that. "Primitive" cultures — that is to say, human societies that rely on relatively simple technological suites — differ from one another just as dramatically as they differ from modern Western industrial societies; nor do simpler technological suites correlate with simpler cultural forms. Traditional Australian aboriginal societies, which have extremely simple material technologies, are considered by many anthropologists to have among the most intricate cultures known anywhere, embracing stunningly elaborate systems of knowledge in which cosmology, myth, environmental knowledge, social custom, and scores of other fields normally kept separate in our society are woven together into dizzyingly complex tapestries of knowledge.

What's more, those tapestries of knowledge have changed and evolved over time. The hokum that underlies that label "primitive man" presupposes, among other things, that societies that use relatively simple technological suites have all been stuck in some kind of time warp since the Neolithic — think of the common habit of speech that claims that hunter-gatherer tribes are "still in the Stone Age" and so forth. Back of that habit of speech is the industrial world's irrational conviction that all human history is an inevitable march of progress that leads straight to our kind of society, technology, and so forth. That other human societies might evolve in different directions and find their own wholly valid ways of making a home in the universe is anathema to most people in the industrial world these days — even though all the evidence suggests that this way of looking at the history of human culture makes far more sense of the data than does the fantasy of inevitable linear progress toward us.

Thus traditional tribal societies are no more natural than civilizations are, in one important sense of the word "natural;" that is, tribal societies are as complex, abstract, unique, and historically contingent as civilizations are. There is, however, one kind of human society that doesn't share these characteristics — a kind of society that tends to be intellectually and culturally as well as technologically simpler than most, and that recurs in astonishingly similar forms around the world and across time. We've talked about it at quite some length in this blog; it's the distinctive dark age society that emerges in the ruins of every fallen civilization after the barbarian war leaders settle down to become petty kings, the survivors of the civilization's once-vast population get to work eking out a bare subsistence from the depleted topsoil, and most of the heritage of the wrecked past goes into history's dumpster.

If there's such a thing as a natural human society, the basic dark age society is probably it, since it emerges when the complex, abstract, unique, and historically contingent cultures of the former civilization and its hostile neighbors have both imploded, and the survivors of the collapse have to put something together in a hurry with nothing but raw human relationships and the constraints of the natural world to guide them. Of course once things settle down the new society begins moving off in its own complex, abstract, unique, and historically contingent direction; the dark age societies of post-Mycenean Greece, post-Roman Britain, post-Heian Japan, and their many equivalents have massive similarities, but the new societies that emerged from those cauldrons of cultural rebirth had much less in common with one another than their dark age forbears did.

In Howard's fictive history, the era of Conan came well before the collapse of Hyborian civilization; he was not himself a dark age warlord, though he doubtless would have done well in that setting. The Pictish tribes whose activities on the Aquilonian frontier inspired the quotation cited earlier in this post weren't a dark age society, either, though if they'd actually existed, they'd have been well along the arc of transformation that turns the hostile neighbors of a declining civilization into the breeding ground of the warbands that show up on cue to finish things off. The Picts of Howard's tale, though, were certainly barbarians—that is, they didn't speak Aquilonian, live in cities, or stay peaceably on their side of the Black River—and they were still around long after the Hyborian civilizations were gone.

That's one of the details Howard borrowed from history. By and large, human societies that don't have urban centers tend to last much longer than those that do. In particular, human societies that don't have urban centers don't tend to go through the distinctive cycle of decline and fall ending in a dark age that urbanized societies undergo so predictably. As we've seen, a core difference between civilizations and other human societies is that people in civilizations tend to cut themselves off from the immediate experience of nature nature to a much greater extent than the uncivilized do. Does this help explain why civilizations crash and burn so reliably, leaving the barbarians to play drinking games with mead while perched unsteadily on the ruins?

As it happens, I think it does.

As we've discussed at length in the last three weekly posts here, human intelligence is not the sort of protean, world-transforming superpower with limitless potential it's been labeled by the more overenthusiastic partisans of human exceptionalism. Rather, it's an interesting capacity possessed by one species of social primates, and quite possibly shared by some other animal species as well. Like every other biological capacity, it evolved through a process of adaptation to the environment—not, please note, to some abstract concept of the environment, but to the specific stimuli and responses that a social primate gets from the African savanna and its inhabitants, including but not limited to other social primates of the same species. It's indicative that when our species originally spread out of Africa, it seems to have settled first in those parts of the Old World that had roughly savanna-like ecosystems, and only later worked out the bugs of living in such radically different environments as boreal forests, tropical jungles, and the like.

The interplay between the human brain and the natural environment is considerably more significant than has often been realized. For the last forty years or so, a scholarly discipline called ecopsychology has explored some of the ways that interactions with nature shape the human mind. More recently, in response to the frantic attempts of American parents to isolate their children from a galaxy of largely imaginary risks, psychologists have begun to talk about "nature deficit disorder," the set of emotional and intellectual dysfunctions that show up reliably in children who have been deprived of the normal human experience of growing up in intimate contact with the natural world.

All of this should have been obvious from first principles. Studies of human and animal behavior alike have shown repeatedly that psychological health depends on receiving certain highly specific stimuli at certain stages in the maturation process. The famous experiments by Henry Harlow, who showed that monkeys raised with a mother-substitute wrapped in terrycloth grew up more or less normal, while those raised with a bare metal mother-substitute turned out psychotic even when all their other needs were met, are among the more famous of these, but there have been many more, and many of them can be shown to affect human capacities in direct and demonstrable ways. Children learn language, for example, only if they're exposed to speech during a certain age window; lacking the right stimulus at the right time, the capacity to use language shuts down and apparently can't be restarted again.

In this latter example, exposure to speech is what's known as a triggering stimulus — something from outside the organism that kickstarts a process that's already hardwired into the organism, but will not get under way until and unless the trigger appears. There are other kinds of stimuli that play different roles in human and animal development. The maturation of the human mind, in fact, might best be seen as a process in which inputs from the environment play a galaxy of roles, some of them of critical importance. What happens when the natural inputs that were around when human intelligence evolved get shut out, and replaced by very different inputs put there by human beings? We'll discuss that next week, in the second part of this post.

PART TWO: A LANDSCAPE OF HALLUCINATIONS
(Originally published 22 July 2015)

Last week's post covered a great deal of ground — not surprising, really, for an essay that started from a quotation from a *Weird Tales* story about Conan the Barbarian — and it may be useful to recap the core argument here. Civilizations — meaning here human societies that concentrate power, wealth, and population in urban centers — have a distinctive historical trajectory of rise and fall that isn't shared by societies that lack urban centers. There are plenty of good reasons why this should be so, from the ecological costs of urbanization to the buildup of maintenance costs that drives catabolic collapse, but there's also a cognitive dimension.

Look over the histories of fallen civilizations, and far more often than not, societies don't have to be dragged down the slope of decline and fall. Rather, they go that way at a run, convinced that the road to ruin must inevitably lead them to heaven on earth. Arnold Toynbee, whose voluminous study of the rise and fall of civilizations has been one of the main sources for this blog since its inception, wrote at length about the way that the elite classes of falling civilizations lose the capacity to come up with new responses for new situations, or even to learn from their mistakes; thus they keep on trying to use the same failed policies over and over again until the whole system crashes to ruin. That's an important factor, no question, but it's not just the elites who seem to lose track of the real world as civilizations go sliding down toward history's compost heap, it's the masses as well.

Those of my readers who want to see a fine example of this sort of blindness to the obvious need only check the latest headlines. Within the next decade or so, for example, the entire southern half of Florida will become unfit for human habitation due to rising sea levels, driven by our dumping of greenhouse gases into an already overloaded atmosphere. Low-lying neighborhoods in Miami already flood with sea water whenever a high tide and a strong onshore wind hit at the same time; one more foot of sea level rise and salt water will pour over barriers into the remaining freshwater sources, turning southern Florida into a vast brackish swamp and forcing the evacuation of most of the millions who live there.

That's only the most dramatic of a constellation of climatic catastrophes that are already tightening their grip on much of the United States. Out west, the rain forests of western Washington are burning in the wake of years of increasingly severe drought, California's vast agricultural acreage is reverting to desert, and the entire city of Las Vegas will probably be out of water—as in, you turn on the tap and nothing but dust comes out—in less than a decade. As waterfalls cascade down the seaward faces of Antarctic and Greenland glaciers, leaking methane blows craters in the Siberian permafrost, and sea level rises at rates considerably faster than the worst case scenarios scientists were considering a few years ago, these threats are hardly abstract issues; is anyone in America taking them seriously enough to, say, take any concrete steps to stop using the atmosphere as a gaseous sewer, starting with their own personal behavior? Surely you jest.

No, the Republicans are still out there insisting at the top of their lungs that any scientific discovery that threatens their rich friends' profits must be fraudulent, the Democrats are still out there proclaiming just as loudly that there must be some way to deal with anthropogenic climate change that won't cost them their frequent-flyer miles, and nearly everyone outside the political sphere is making whatever noises they think will allow them to keep on pursuing exactly those lifestyle choices that are bringing on planetary catastrophe. Every possible excuse to insist that what's already happening won't happen gets instantly pounced on as one more justification for inertia — the claim currently being splashed around the media that the Sun might go through a cycle of slight cooling in the decades ahead is the latest example. (For the record, even if we get a grand solar minimum, its effects will be canceled out in short order by the impact of ongoing atmospheric pollution.)

Business as usual is very nearly the only option anybody is willing to discuss, even though the long-predicted climate catastrophes are already happening and the days of business as usual in any form are obviously numbered. The one alternative that gets air time, of course, is the popular fantasy of instant planetary dieoff, which gets plenty of attention because it's just as effective an excuse for inaction as faith in business as usual. What next to nobody wants to talk about is the future that's actually arriving exactly as predicted: a future in which low-lying coastal regions around the country and the world have to be abandoned to the rising seas, while the Southwest and large portions of the mountain west become more inhospitable than the eastern Sahara or Arabia's Empty Quarter.

If the ice melt keeps accelerating at its present pace, we could be only a few decades form the point at which it's Manhattan Island's turn to be abandoned, because everything below ground level is permanently flooded with seawater and every winter storm sends waves rolling right across the island and flings driftwood logs against second story windows. A few decades more, and waves will roll over the low-lying neighborhoods of Houston, Boston, Seattle, and Washington DC, while the ruined buildings that used to be New Orleans rise out of the still waters of a brackish estuary and the ruined buildings that used to be Las Vegas are half buried by the drifting sand. Take a moment to consider the economic consequences of that much infrastructure loss, that much destruction of built capital, that many people who somehow have to be evacuated and resettled, and think about what kind of body blow that will deliver to an industrial society that is already in bad shape for other reasons.

None of this had to happen. Half a century ago, policy makers and the public alike had already been presented with a tolerably clear outline of what was going to happen if we proceeded along the trajectory we were on, and those same warnings have been repeated with increasing force year by year, as the evidence to support them has mounted up implacably—and yet nearly all of us nodded and smiled and kept going. Nor has this changed in the least as the long-predicted catastrophes have begun to show up right on schedule. Quite the contrary: faced with a rising spiral of massive crises, people across the industrial world are, with majestic consistency, doing exactly those things that are guaranteed to make those crises worse.

So the question that needs to be asked, and if possible answered, is why civilizations—human societies that concentrate population, power, and wealth in urban centers—so reliably lose the capacity to learn from their mistakes and recognize that a failed policy has in fact failed. It's also worth asking why they so reliably do this within a finite and predictable timespan: civilizations last on average around a millennium before they crash into a dark age, while uncivilized societies routinely go on for many times that period. Doubtless any number of factors drive civilizations to their messy ends, but I'd like to suggest a factor that, to my knowledge, hasn't been discussed in this context before.

Let's start with what may well seem like an irrelevancy. There's been a great deal of discussion down through the years in environmental circles about the way that the survival and health of the human body depends on inputs from nonhuman nature. There's been a much more modest amount of talk about the human psychological and emotional needs that can only be met through interaction with natural systems. One question I've never seen discussed, though, is whether the human intellect has needs that are only fulfilled by a natural environment.

As I consider that question, one obvious answer comes to mind: negative feedback.

The human intellect is the part of each of us that thinks, that tries to make sense of the universe of our experience. It does this by creating models. By "models" I don't just mean those tightly formalized and quantified models we call scientific theories; a poem is also a model of part of the universe of human experience, so is a myth, so is a painting, and so is a vague hunch about how something will work out. When a twelve-year-old girl pulls the petals off a daisy while saying "he loves me, he loves me not," she's using a randomization technique to decide between two models of one small but, to her, very important portion of the universe, the emotional state of whatever boy she has in mind.

With any kind of model, it's critical to remember Alfred Korzybski's famous rule: "the map is not the territory." A model, to put the same point another way, is a representation; it represents the way some part of the universe looks when viewed from the perspective of one or more members of our species of social primates, using the idiosyncratic and profoundly limited set of sensory equipments, neural processes, and cognitive frameworks we got handed by our evolutionary heritage. Painful though this may be to our collective egotism, it's not unfair to say that human mental models are what you get when you take the universe and dumb it down to the point that our minds can more or less grasp it.

What keeps our models from becoming completely dysfunctional is the negative feedback we get from the universe. For the benefit of readers who didn't get introduced to systems theory, I should probably take a moment to explain negative feedback. The classic example is the common household thermostat, which senses the temperature of the air inside the house and activates a switch accordingly. If the air temperature is below a certain threshold, the thermostat turns the heat on and warms things up; if the air temperature rises above a different, slightly higher threshold, the thermostat turns the heat off and lets the house cool down.

In a sense, a thermostat embodies a very simple model of one very specific part of the universe, the temperature inside the house. Like all models, this one includes a set of implicit definitions and a set of value judgments. The definitions are the two thresholds, the one that turns the furnace on and the one that turns it off, and the value judgments label temperatures below the first threshold "too cold" and those above the second "too hot." Like every human model, the thermostat model is unabashedly anthropocentric—"too cold" by the thermostat's standard would be uncomfortably warm for a polar bear, for example—and selects out certain factors of interest to human beings from a galaxy of other things we don't happen to want to take into consideration.

The models used by the human intellect to make sense of the universe are usually less simple than the one that guides a thermostat—there are unfortunately exceptions—but they work according to the same principle. They contain definitions, which may be implicit or explicit: the girl plucking petals from the daisy may have not have an explicit definition of love in mind when she says "he loves me," but there's some set of beliefs and expectations about what those words imply underlying the model. They also contain value judgments: if she's attracted to the boy in question, "he loves me" has a positive value and "he loves me not" has a negative one.

Notice, though, that there's a further dimension to the model, which is its interaction with the observed behavior of the thing it's supposed to model. Plucking petals from a daisy, all things considered, is not a very good predictor of the emotional states of twelve-year-old boys; predictions made on the basis of that method are very often disproved by other sources of evidence, which is why few girls much older than twelve rely on it as an information source. Modern western science has formalized and quantified that sort of reality testing, but it's something that most people do at least occasionally. It's when they stop doing so that we get the inability to recognize failure that helps to drive, among many other things, the fall of civilizations.

Individual facets of experienced reality thus provide negative feedback to individual models. The whole structure of experienced reality, though, is capable of providing negative feedback on another level—when it challenges the accuracy of the entire mental process of modeling.

Nature is very good at providing negative feedback of that kind. Here's a human conceptual model that draws a strict line between mammals, on the one hand, and birds and reptiles, on the other. Not much more than a century ago, it was as precise as any division in science: mammals have fur and don't lay eggs, reptiles and birds don't have fur and do lay eggs. Then some Australian settler met a platypus, which has fur and lays eggs. Scientists back in Britain flatly refused to take it seriously until some live platypuses finally made it there by ship. Plenty of platypus egg was splashed across plenty of distinguished scientific faces, and definitions had to be changed to make room for another category of mammals and the evolutionary history necessary to explain it.

Here's another human conceptual model, the one that divides trees into distinct species. Most trees in most temperate woodlands, though, actually have a mix of genetics from closely related species. There are few red oaks; what you have instead are mostly-red, partly-red, and slightly-red oaks. Go from the northern to the southern end of a species' distribution, or from wet to dry regions, and the variations within the species are quite often more extreme than those that separate trees that have been assigned to different species. Here's still another human conceptual model, the one that divides trees from shrubs — plenty of species can grow either way, and the list goes on.

The human mind likes straight lines, definite boundaries, precise verbal definitions. Nature doesn't. People who spend most of their time dealing with undomesticated natural phenomena, accordingly, have to get used to the fact that nature is under no obligation to make the kind of sense the human mind prefers. I'd suggest that this is why so many of the cultures our society calls "primitive" — that is, those that have simple material technologies and interact directly with nature much of the time — so often rely on nonlogical methods of thought: those our culture labels "mythological," "magical," or — I love this term — "prescientific." (That the "prescientific" will almost certainly turn out to be the postscientific as well is one of the lessons of history that modern industrial society is trying its level best to ignore.) Nature as we experience it isn't simple, neat, linear, and logical, and so it makes sense that the ways of thinking best suited to dealing with nature directly aren't simple, neat, linear, and logical either.

With this in mind, let's return to the distinction discussed in last week's post. I noted there that a city is a human settlement from which the direct, unmediated presence of nature has been removed as completely as the available technology permits. What replaces natural phenomena in an urban setting, though, is as important as what isn't allowed there. Nearly everything that surrounds you in a city was put there deliberately by human beings; it is the product of conscious human thinking, and it follows the habits of human thought just outlined. Compare a walk down a city street to a walk through a forest or a shortgrass prairie: in the city street, much more of what you see is simple, neat, linear, and logical. A city is an environment reshaped to reflect the habits and preferences of the human mind.

I suspect there may be a straightforwardly neurological factor in all this. The human brain, so much larger compared to body weight than the brains of most of our primate relatives, evolved because having a larger brain provided some survival advantage to those hominins who had it, in competition with those who didn't. It's probably a safe assumption that processing information inputs from the natural world played a very large role in these advantages, and this would imply, in turn, that the human brain is primarily adapted for perceiving things in natural environments—not, say, for building cities, creating technologies, and making the other common products of civilization.

Thus some significant part of the brain has to be redirected away from the things that it's adapted to do, in order to make civilizations possible. I'd like to propose that the simplified, rationalized, radically information-poor environment of the city plays a crucial role in this. (Information-poor? Of course; the amount of information that comes cascading through the five keen senses of an alert hunter-gatherer standing in an African forest is vastly greater than what a city-dweller gets from the blank walls and the monotonous sounds and scents of an urban environment.) Children raised in an environment that lacks the constant cascade of information natural environments provide, and taught to redirect their mental powers toward such other activities as reading and mathematics, grow up with cognitive habits and, in all probability, neurological arrangements focused toward the activities of civilization and away from the things to which the human brain is adapted by evolution.

One source of supporting evidence for this admittedly speculative proposal is the worldwide insistence on the part of city-dwellers that people who live in isolated rural communities, far outside the cultural ambit of urban life, are just plain stupid. What that means in practice, of course, is that people from isolated rural communities aren't used to using their brains for the particular purposes that city people value. These allegedly "stupid" countryfolk are by and large extraordinarily adept at the skills they need to survive and thrive in their own environments. They may be able to listen to the wind and know exactly where on the far side of the hill a deer waits to be shot for dinner, glance at a stream and tell which riffle the trout have chosen for a hiding place, watch the clouds pile up and read from them how many days they've got to get the hay in before the rains come and rot it in the fields — all of which tasks require sophisticated information processing, the kind of processing that human brains evolved doing.

Notice, though, how the urban environment relates to the human habit of mental modeling. Everything in a city was a mental model before it became a building, a street, an item of furniture, or what have you. Chairs look like chairs, houses like houses, and so on; it's so rare for humanmade items to break out of the habitual models of our species and the particular culture that built them that when this happens, it's a source of endless comment. Where a natural environment constantly challenges human conceptual models, an urban environment reinforces them, producing a feedback loop that's probably responsible for most of the achievements of civilization.

I suggest, though, that the same feedback loop may also play a very large role in the self-destruction of civilizations. People raised in urban environments come to treat their mental models as realities, more real than the often-unruly facts on the ground, because everything they encounter in their immediate environments reinforces those models. As the models become more elaborate and the cities become more completely insulated from the complexities of nature, the inhabitants of a civilization move deeper and deeper into a landscape of hallucinations — not least because as many of those hallucinations get built in brick and stone, or glass and steel, as the available technology permits. As a civilization approaches its end, the divergence between the world as it exists and the mental models that define the world for the civilization's inmates becomes total, and its decisions and actions become lethally detached from reality — with consequences that we'll discuss in next week's post.

PART THREE: THE END OF THE DREAM

(Originally published 29 July 2015)

Let's take a moment to recap the argument of the last two posts here on *The Archdruid Report* before we follow it through to its conclusion. There are any number of ways to sort out the diversity of human social forms, but one significant division lies between those societies that don't concentrate population, wealth, and power in urban centers, and those that do. One important difference between the societies that fall into these two categories is that urbanized societies — we may as well call these by the time-honored term "civilizations" — reliably crash and burn after a lifespan of roughly a thousand years, while societies that lack cities have no such fixed lifespans and can last for much longer without going through the cycle of rise and fall, punctuated by dark ages, that defines the history of civilizations.

It's probably necessary to pause here and clear up what seems to be a common misunderstanding. To say that societies in the first category can last for much more than a thousand years doesn't mean that all of them do this. I mention this because I fielded a flurry of comments from people who pointed to a few examples of societies without cities that collapsed in less than a millennium, and insisted that this somehow disproved my hypothesis. Not so; if everyone who takes a certain diet pill, let's say, suffers from heart damage, the fact that some people who don't take the diet pill suffer heart damagefrom other causes doesn't absolve the diet pill of responsibility. In the same way, the fact that civilizations such as Egypt and China have managed to pull themselves together after a dark age and rebuild a new version of their former civilization doesn't erase the fact of the collapse and the dark age that followed it.

The question is why civilizations crash and burn so reliably.

There are plenty of good reasons why this might happen, and it's entirely possible that several of them are responsible; the collapse of civilization could be an overdetermined process. Like the victim in the cheap mystery novel who was shot, stabbed, strangled, clubbed over the head, and then chucked out a twentieth floor window, that is, civilizations that fall may have more causes of death than were actually necessary. The ecological costs of building and maintaining cities, for example, place much greater strains on the local environment than the less costly and concentrated settlement patterns of nonurban societies, and the rising maintenance costs of capital—the driving force behind the theory of catabolic collapse I've proposed elsewhere—can spin out of control much more easily in an urban setting than elsewhere. Other examples of the vulnerability of urbanized societies can easily be worked out by those who wish to do so.

That said, there's at least one other factor at work. As noted in last week's post, civilizations by and large don't have to be dragged down the slope of decline and fall; instead, they take that route with yells of triumph, convinced that the road to ruin will infallibly lead them to heaven on earth, and attempts to turn them aside from that trajectory typically get reactions ranging from blank incomprehension to furious anger. It's not just the elites who fall into this sort of self-destructive groupthink, either: it's not hard to find, in a falling civilization, people who claim to disagree with the ideology that's driving the collapse, but people who take their disagreement to the point of making choices that differ from those of their more orthodox neighbors are much scarcer. They do exist; every civilization breeds them, but they make up a very small fraction of the population, and they generally exist on the fringes of society, despised and condemned by all those right-thinking people whose words and actions help drive the accelerating process of decline and fall.

The next question, then, is how civilizations get caught in that sort of groupthink. My proposal, as sketched out last week, is that the culprit is a rarely noticed side effect of urban life. People who live in a mostly natural environment—and by this I mean merely an environment in which most things are put there by nonhuman processes rather than by human action—have to deal constantly with the inevitable mismatches between the mental models of the universe they carry in their heads and the universe that actually surrounds them. People who live in a mostly artificial environment—an environment in which most things were made and arranged by human action—don't have to deal with this anything like so often, because an artificial environment embodies the ideas of the people who constructed and arranged it. A natural environment therefore applies negative or, as it's also called, corrective feedback to human models of the way things are, while an artificial environment applies positive feedback—the sort of thing people usually mean when they talk about a feedback loop.

This explains, incidentally, one of the other common differences between civilizations and other kinds of human society: the pace of change. Anthropologists not so long ago used to insist that what they liked to call "primitive societies"—that is, societies that have relatively simple technologies and no cities—were stuck in some kind of changeless stasis. That was nonsense, but the thin basis in fact that was used to justify the nonsense was simply that the pace of change in low-tech, non-urban societies, when they're left to their own devices, tends to be fairly sedate, and usually happens over a time scale of generations. Urban societies, on the other hand, change quickly, and the pace of change tends to accelerate over time: a dead giveaway that a positive feedback loop is at work.

Notice that what's fed back to the minds of civilized people by their artificial environment isn't simply human thinking in general. It's whatever particular set of mental models and habits of thought happen to be most popular in their civilization. Modern industrial civilization, for example, is obsessed with simplicity; our mental models and habits of thought value straight lines, simple geometrical shapes, hard boundaries, and clear distinctions. That obsession, and the models and mental habits that unfold from it, have given us an urban environment full of straight lines, simple geometrical shapes, hard boundaries, and clear distinctions—and thus reinforce our unthinking assumption that these things are normal and natural, which by and large they aren't.

Modern industrial civilization is also obsessed with the frankly rather weird belief that growth for its own sake is a good thing. (Outside of a few specific cases, that is. I've wondered at times whether the deeply neurotic American attitude toward body weight comes from the conflict between current fashions in body shape and the growth-is-good mania of the rest of our culture; if bigger is better, why isn't a big belly better than a small one?) In a modern urban American environment, it's easy to believe that growth is good, since that claim is endlessly rehashed whenever some new megawhatsit replaces something of merely human scale, and since so many of the costs of malignant growth get hauled out of sight and dumped on somebody else. In settlement patterns that haven't been pounded into their present shape by true believers in industrial society's growth-for-its-own-sake ideology, people are rather more likely to grasp the meaning of the words "too much."

I've used examples from our own civilization because they're familiar, but every civilization reshapes its urban environment in the shape of its own mental models, which then reinforce those models in the minds of the people who live in that environment. As these people in turn shape that environment, the result is positive feedback: the mental models in question become more and more deeply entrenched in the built environment and thus also the collective conversation of the culture, and in both cases, they also become more elaborate and more extreme. The history of architecture in the western world over the last few centuries is a great example of this latter: over that time, buildings became ever more completely defined by straight lines, flat surfaces, simple geometries, and hard boundaries between one space and another—and it's hardly an accident that popular culture in urban communities has simplified in much the same way over that same timespan.

One way to understand this is to see a civilization as the working out in detail of some specific set of ideas about the world. At first those ideas are as inchoate as dream-images, barely grasped even by the keenest thinkers of the time. Gradually, though, the ideas get worked out explicitly; conflicts among them are resolved or papered over in standardized ways; the original set of ideas becomes the core of a vast, ramifying architecture of thought which defines the universe to the inhabitants of that civilization. Eventually, everything in the world of human experience is assigned some place in that architecture of thought; everything that can be hammered into harmony with the core set of ideas has its place in the system, while everything that can't gets assigned the status of superstitious nonsense, or whatever other label the civilization likes to use for the realities it denies.

The further the civilization develops, though, the less it questions the validity of the basic ideas themselves, and the urban
environment is a critical factor in making this happen. By limiting, as far as possible, the experiences available to influential
members of society to those that fit the established architecture
of thought, urban living makes it much easier to confuse mental
models with the universe those models claim to describe, and
that confusion is essential if enough effort, enthusiasm, and passion are to be directed toward the process of elaborating those
models to their furthest possible extent.

A branch of knowledge that has to keep on going back to re-
visit its first principles, after all, will never get far beyond them.
This is why philosophy, which is the science of first principles,
doesn't "progress" in the simpleminded sense of that word — Ar-
istotle didn't disprove Plato, nor did Nietzsche refute Schopen-
hauer, because each of these philosophers, like all others in that
challenging field, returned to the realm of first principles from a
different starting point and so offered a different account of the
landscape. Original philosophical inquiry thus plays a very large
role in the intellectual life of every civilization early in the process of urbanization, since this helps elaborate the core ideas on
which the civilization builds its vision of reality; once that process is more or less complete, though, philosophy turns into a re-
cherché intellectual specialty or gets transformed into intellectual
dogma.

Cities are thus the Petri dishes in which civilizations ripen
their ideas to maturity — and like Petri dishes, they do this by ex-
cluding contaminating influences. It's easy, from the perspective
of a falling civilization like ours, to see this as a dreadful mistake,
a withdrawal from contact with the real world in order to pursue an abstract vision of things increasingly detached from everything else. That's certainly one way to look at the matter, but
there's another side to it as well.

Civilizations are far and away the most spectacularly creative
form of human society. Over the course of its thousand-year lifespan, the inhabitants of a civilization will create many orders of
magnitude more of the products of culture — philosophical and
religious traditions, works of art and the traditions that produce
and sustain them, and so on — than an equal number of people

living in non-urban societies and experiencing the very sedate pace of cultural change already mentioned. To borrow a metaphor from the plant world, non-urban societies are perennials, and civilizations are showy annuals that throw all their energy into the flowering process. Having flowered, civilizations then go to seed and die, while the perennial societies flower less spectacularly and remain green thereafter.

The feedback loop described above explains both the explosive creativity of civilizations and their equally explosive downfall. It's precisely because civilizations free themselves from the corrective feedback of nature, and divert an ever larger portion of their inhabitants' brainpower from the uses for which human brains were originally adapted by evolution, that they generate such torrents of creativity. Equally, it's precisely because they do these things that civilizations run off the rails into self-feeding delusion, lose the capacity to learn the lessons of failure or even notice that failure is taking place, and are destroyed by threats they've lost the capacity to notice, let alone overcome. Meanwhile, other kinds of human societies move sedately along their own life cycles, and their creativity and their craziness—and they have both of these, of course, just as civilizations do—are kept within bounds by the enduring negative feedback loops of nature.

Which of these two options is better? That's a question of value, not of fact, and so it has no one answer. Facts, to return to a point made in these posts several times, belong to the senses and the intellect, and they're objective, at least to the extent that others can say, "yes, I see it too." Values, by contrast, are a matter of the heart and the will, and they're subjective; to call something good or bad doesn't state an objective fact about the thing being discussed. It always expresses a value judgment from some individual point of view. You can't say "x is better than y," and mean anything by it, unless you're willing to field such questions as "better by what criteria?" and "better for whom?"

Myself, I'm very fond of the benefits of civilization. I like hot running water, public libraries, the rule of law, and a great many other things that you get in civilizations and generally don't get outside of them. Of course that preference is profoundly shaped by the fact that I grew up in a civilization; if I'd happened to be the son of yak herders in central Asia or tribal horticulturalists in upland Papua New Guinea, I might well have a different opinion — and I might also have a different opinion even if I'd grown up in this civilization but had different needs and predilections. Robert E. Howard, whose fiction launched the series of posts that finishes up this week, was a child of American civilization at its early twentieth century zenith, and he loathed civilization and all it stood for.

This is one of the two reasons that I think it's a waste of time to get into arguments over whether civilization is a good thing. The other reason is that neither my opinion nor yours, dear reader, nor the opinion of anybody else who might happen to want to fulminate on the internet about the virtues or vices of civilization, is worth two farts in an EF-5 tornado when it comes to the question of whether or not future civilizations will rise and fall on this planet after today's industrial civilization completes the arc of its destiny. Since the basic requirements of urban life first became available not long after the end of the last ice age, civilizations have risen wherever conditions favored them, cycled through their lifespans, and fell, and new civilizations rose again in the same places if the conditions remained favorable for that process.

Until the coming of the fossil fuel age, though, civilization was a localized thing, in a double sense. On the one hand, without the revolution in transport and military technology made possible by fossil fuels, any given civilization could only maintain control over a small portion of the planet's surface for more than a fairly short time — thus as late as 1800, when the industrial revolution was already well under way, the civilized world was still divided into separate civilizations that each pursued its own very different ideas and values. On the other hand, without the economic revolution made possible by fossil fuels, very large sections of the world were completely unsuited to civilized life, and remained outside the civilized world for all practical purposes. As late as 1800, as a result, quite a bit of the world's land surface was still inhabited by hunter-gatherers, nomadic pastoralists, and tribal horticulturalists who owed no allegiance to any urban power and had no interest in cities and their products at all — except for the nomadic pastoralists, that is, who occasionally liked to pillage one.

The world's fossil fuel reserves aren't renewable on any time scale that matters to human beings. Since we've burnt all the easily accessible coal, oil, and natural gas on the planet, and are working our way through the stuff that's difficult to get even with today's baroque and energy-intensive technologies, the world's first fossil-fueled human civilization is guaranteed to be its last as well. That means that once the deindustrial dark age ahead of us is over, and conditions favorable for the revival of civilization recur here and there on various corners of the planet, it's a safe bet that new civilizations will build atop the ruins we've left for them.

The energy resources they'll have available to them, though, will be far less abundant and concentrated than the fossil fuels that gave industrial civilization its global reach. With luck, and some hard work on the part of people living now, they may well inherit the information they need to make use of sun, wind, and other renewable energy resources in ways that the civilizations before ours didn't know how to do. As our present-day proponents of green energy are finding out the hard way just now, though, this doesn't amount to the kind of energy necessary to maintain our kind of civilization.

I've argued elsewhere, especially in my book *The Ecotechnic Future*, that modern industrial society is simply the first, clumsiest, and most wasteful form of what might be called technic society, the subset of human societies that get a significant amount of their total energy from nonbiotic sources — that is, from something other than human and animal muscles fueled by the annual product of photosynthesis. If that turns out to be correct, future civilizations that learn to use energy sparingly may be able to accomplish some of the things that we currently do by throwing energy around with wild abandon, and they may also learn how to do remarkable things that are completely beyond our grasp today. Eventually there may be other global civilizations, following out their own unique sets of ideas about the world through the usual process of dramatic creativity followed by dramatic collapse.

That's a long way off, though. As the first global civilization gives way to the first global dark age, my working guess is that civilization — that is to say, the patterns of human society necessary to support the concentration of population, wealth, and power in urban centers — is going to go away everywhere, or nearly everywhere, over the next one to three centuries. A planet hammered by climate change, strewn with chemical and radio-active poisons, and swept by mass migrations is not a safe place for cities and the other amenities of civilized life. As things calm down, say, half a millennium from now, a range of new civilizations will doubtless emerge in those parts of the planet that have suitable conditions for urban life, while human societies of other kinds will emerge everywhere else on the planet that human life is possible at all.

I realize that this is not exactly a welcome prospect for those people who've bought into industrial civilization's overblown idea of its own universal importance. Those who believe devoutly that our society is the cutting edge of humanity's future, destined to march on gloriously forever to the stars, will be as little pleased by the portrait of the future I've painted as their equal and opposite numbers, for whom our society is the end of history and must surely be annihilated, along with all seven billion of us, by some glorious cataclysm of the sort beloved by Hollywood scriptwriters. Still, the universe is under no obligation to cater to anybody's fantasies, you know. That's a lesson Robert E. Howard knew well and wove into the best of his fiction, the stories of Conan among them—and it's a lesson worth learning now, at least for those who hope to have some influence over how the future affects them, their families, and their communities, in an age of decline and fall.

424: THE SUICIDE OF THE AMERICAN LEFT
(Originally published 5 August 2015)

Regular readers of this blog know that I generally avoid partisan politics in the essays posted here. There are several reasons for that unpopular habit, but the most important of them is that we don't actually have partisan politics in today's America, except in a purely nominal sense. It's true that politicians by and large group themselves into one of two parties, which make a great show of their rivalry on a narrow range of issues. Get past the handful of culture-war hot buttons that give them their favorite opportunities for grandstanding, though, and you'll find an iron-clad consensus, especially on those issues that have the most to say about the future of the United States and the world.

It's popular on the disaffected fringes of both parties to insist that the consensus in question comes solely from the other side; dissident Democrats claim that Democratic politicians have basically adopted the GOP platform, while disgruntled Republicans claim that their politicians have capitulated to the Democratic agenda. Neither of these claims, as it happens, are true. Back when the two parties still stood for something, for example, Democrats in Congress could be counted on to back organized labor and family farmers against their corporate adversaries and to fight attempts on the part of bankers to get back into the speculation business, while their opposite numbers in the GOP were ferocious in their opposition to military adventurism overseas and government expansion at home.

Nowadays? The Democrats long ago threw their former core constituencies under the bus and ditched the Depression-era legislation that stopped kleptocratic bankers from running the economy into the ground, while the Republicans decided that they'd never met a foreign entanglement or a government handout they didn't like — unless, of course, the latter benefited the poor. An ever more intrusive and metastatic bureaucratic state funneling trillions to corrupt corporate interests, an economic policy made up primarily of dishonest statistics and money-printing operations, and a monomaniacally interventionist foreign policy: that's the bipartisan political consensus in Washington DC these days, and it's a consensus that once would have been rejected with volcanic fury by both parties if anyone had been so foolish as to suggest it.

The gap between the current Washington consensus and the former ideals of the nation's political parties, not to mention the wishes of the people on whose sovereign will the whole system is supposed to depend, has attracted an increasing amount of attention in recent years. That's driven quite a bit of debate, and no shortage of fingerpointing, about the origins and purposes of the policies that are welded into place in US politics these days. On the left, the most popular candidates just now for the position of villainous influence behind it all mostly come from the banking industry; on the right, the field is somewhat more diverse; and there's no shortage of options from further afield.

Though I know it won't satisfy those with a taste for conspiracy theory, I'd like to suggest a simpler explanation. The political consensus in Washington DC these days can best be characterized as an increasingly frantic attempt, using increasingly risky means, to maintain business as usual for the political class at a time when "business as usual" in any sense of that phrase is long past its pull date. This, in turn, is largely the product of the increasingly bleak corner into which past policies have backed this country, but it's also in part the result of a massively important but mostly unrecognized turn of events: by and large, neither the contemporary US political class nor anyone else with a significant presence in American public life seems to be able to imagine a future that differs in any meaningful way from what we've got right now.

I'd like to take a moment here to look at that last point from a different angle, with the assistance of that tawdry quadrennial three-ring circus now under way, which will sooner or later select the next inmate for the White House. For anyone who enjoys the spectacle of florid political dysfunction, the 2016 presidential race promises to be the last word in target-rich environments.

The Republican party in particular has flung itself with creditable enthusiasm into the task of taking my circus metaphor as literally as possible—what, after all, does the GOP resemble just at the moment, if not one of those little cars that roll out under the big top and fling open the doors, so that one clown after another can come tumbling out into the limelight?

They've already graced the electoral big top with a first-rate collection of clowns, too. There's Donald Trump, whose campaign is shaping up to be the loudest invocation of pure uninhibited *führerprinzip* since, oh, 1933 or so; there's Scott Walker, whose attitudes toward working Americans suggest that he'd be quite happy to sign legislation legalizing slavery if his rich friends asked him for it; there's—well, here again, "target-rich environment" is the phrase that comes forcefully to mind. The only people who have to be sweating just now, other than ordinary Americans trying to imagine any of the current round of GOP candidates as the titular leader of their country, are gag writers for satiric periodicals such as *The Onion*, who have to go to work each day and face the brutally unforgiving task of coming up with something more absurd than the press releases and public statements of the candidates in question.

Still, I'm going to leave those tempting possibilities alone for the moment, and focus on a much more dreary figure, since she and her campaign offer a useful glimpse at the yawning void beneath what's left of the American political system. Yes, that would be Hillary Clinton, the officially anointed frontrunner for the Democratic nomination. It's pretty much a foregone conclusion that she'll lose this campaign the way she lost the 2008 race, and for the same reason: neither she nor her handlers seem to grasp that she really does have to offer the American people some reason to want to vote for her.

In a way, Clinton is the most honest of the current crop of presidential candidates, though this is less a matter of personal integrity than of sheer inattention. I frankly doubt that the other candidates have a single noble motive for seeking office among them, but they have at least realized that they have to go through the motions of having convictions and pursuing policies they think are right. Clinton and her advisers apparently didn't get that memo, and as a result, the positions she's taken and the convictions she claims are a bland pastiche of carefully abstract middle-of-the-roadisms, all too obviously filtered through the same sort of marketing surveys and focus groups that big corporations use to position their newest brand of soap. That's lethal; everyone expects candidates for office in the US to pander to special interests and the voters at large, just as everyone expects candidates to have sex, but doing it right out there in public is not appreciated in either case.

Still, there's more going on here than the sheer incompetence of a campaign that hasn't noticed that a sense of entitlement isn't a qualification for office. The deeper issue that will doom the Clinton candidacy can be phrased as a simple question: does anyone actually believe for a moment that electing Hillary Clinton president will change anything that matters?

Those other candidates who are getting less tepid responses from the voters than Clinton are doing so precisely because a significant number of voters think that electing one of them will actually change something. The voters in question are wrong, of course. Barack Obama is the wave of the future here as elsewhere; after his monumentally cynical 2008 campaign, which swept him into office on a torrent of vacuous sound bites about hope and change, he proceeded to carry out exactly the same domestic and foreign policies we'd have gotten had George W. Bush served two more terms. Equally, whoever wins the 2016 election will keep those same policies in place, because those are the policies that have the unanimous support of the political class; it's just that everybody but Clinton will do their level best to pretend that they're going to do something else, as Obama did, until the day after the election.

Those policies will be kept in place, in turn, because any other choice would risk pulling the plug on a failing system. I'm not at all sure how many people outside the US have any idea just how frail and brittle the world's so-called sole hyperpower is just at this moment. To borrow a point made trenchantly some years back by my fellow blogger Dmitry Orlov, the US resembles nothing so much as the Soviet Union in the years just before the Berlin Wall came down: a grandiose international presence, backed by a baroque military arsenal and an increasingly shrill triumphalist ideology, perched uneasily atop a hollow shell of a society that has long since tipped over the brink into economic and cultural freefall.

Neither Hillary Clinton nor any of the other candidates in the running for the 2016 election will change anything that matters, in turn, because any change that isn't strictly cosmetic risks bringing the entire tumbledown, jerry-rigged structure of American political and economic power crashing down around everyone's ears. That's why, to switch examples, Barack Obama a few days ago brought out with maximum fanfare a new energy policy that consists of doing pretty much what his administration has been doing for the last six years already, as though doing what you've always done and expecting a different result wasn't a good functional definition of insanity. Any other approach to energy and climate change, or any of a hundred other issues, risks triggering a crisis that the United States can't survive in its current form—and the fact that such a crisis is going to happen sooner or later anyway just adds spice to the bubbling pot.

The one thing that can reliably bring a nation through a time of troubles of the sort we're facing is a vision of a different future, one that appeals to enough people to inspire them to unite their energies with those of the nation's official leadership, and put up with the difficulties of the transition. That's what got the United States through its three previous existential crises: the Revolutionary War, the Civil War, and the Great Depression. In each case, when an insupportable status quo finally shattered, enough of the nation united around a charismatic leader, and a vision of a future that was different from the present, to pull some semblance of a national community through the chaos.

We don't have such a vision in American politics now. To an astonishing degree, in fact, American culture has lost the ability to imagine any future that isn't simply an endless rehash of the present—other, that is, than the perennially popular fantasy of apocalyptic annihilation, with or without the salvation of a privileged minority via Rapture, Singularity, or what have you. That's a remarkable change for a society that not so long ago was brimming with visionary tomorrows that differed radically from the existing order of things. It's especially remarkable in that the leftward end of the American political spectrum, the end that's nominally tasked with the job of coming up with new visions, has spent the last forty years at the forefront of the flight from alternative futures.

I'm thinking here, as one example out of many, of an event I attended a while back, put together by one of the longtime names of the American left, and featuring an all-star cast of equally big names in what passes for environmentalism and political radicalism these days. With very few exceptions, every one of the speakers put their time on the podium into vivid descriptions of the villainy of the designated villains and all the villainous things they were going to do unless they were stopped. It was pretty grueling; at the end of the first full day, going up the stairs to the street level, I watched as a woman turned to a friend and said, "Well, that just about makes me want to go out and throw myself off a bridge" — and neither the friend nor anybody else argued.

Let's take a closer look, though, at the strategy behind the event. Was there, at this event, any real discussion of how to stop the villains in question, other than a rehash of proposals that have failed over and over again for the last four decades? Not that I heard. Did anyone offer some prospect other than maintaining the status quo endlessly against the attempts of the designated villains to make things worse? Not only was there nothing of the kind, I heard backchannel from more than one participant that the organizer had a long history of discouraging anybody at his events from offering the least shred of that sort of hope.

Dismal as it was, the event was worth attending, as it conducted an exact if unintentional autopsy of the corpse of the American left, and made the cause of death almost impossible to ignore. At the dawn of the Reagan era, to be specific, most of the movements in this country that used to push for specific goals on the leftward end of things stopped doing so, and redefined themselves in wholly reactive and negative terms: instead of trying to enact their own policies, they refocused entirely on trying to stop the enactment of opposing policies by the other side. By and large, they're still at it, even though the results have amounted to four decades of nearly unbroken failure, and the few successes — such as the legalization of same-sex marriage — were won by pressure groups unconnected to, and usually unsupported by, the professional activists of the official left.

There are at least two reasons why a strategy of pure reaction, without any coherent attempt to advance an agenda of its own or even a clear idea of what that agenda might be, has been a fruitful source of humiliation and defeat for the American left. The first is that this approach violates one of the most basic rules of strategy:

you win when you seize the initiative and force the other side to respond to your actions, and you lose by passively responding to whatever the other side comes up with. In any contest, without exception, if you surrender the initiative and let the other side set the terms of the conflict, you're begging to be beaten, and will normally get your wish in short order.

That in itself is bad enough, but there's another factor at work as well. A movement that defines itself in purely negative terms, attempting to prevent someone else's agenda from being enacted rather than pursuing a concrete agenda of its own, also suffers from another massive problem: the best such a movement can hope for is a continuation of the status quo, because the only choice it offers is the one between business as usual and something worse. That's fine if most people are satisfied with the way things are, and are willing to fling themselves into the struggle for the sake of a set of political, economic, and social arrangements that they consider worth fighting for.

I'm not sure why so many people on the leftward end of American politics haven't noticed that this is not the case today. One hypothesis that comes to mind is that by and large, the leftward end of the American political landscape is dominated by middle class and upper middle class white people from the comparatively prosperous coastal states. Many of them belong to the upper 20% by income of the American population, and the rest aren't far below that threshold. The grand bargain of the Reagan years, by which the middle classes bought a guarantee of their wealth and privilege by letting their former allies in the working classes get thrown under the bus, has profited them hugely, and holding onto what they gained by that maneuver doubtless ranks high on their unstated list of motives — much higher, certainly, than pushing for a different future that might put their privileges in jeopardy.

The other major power bloc that supports the American left these days offers an interesting lesson in the power of positive goals. That bloc is made up of certain relatively disadvantaged ethnic groups, above all the majority of the African-American community. The Democratic party has been able to hold the loyalty of most African-Americans through decades of equivocation, meaningless gestures, and outright betrayal, precisely because it can offer them a specific vision of a better future: that is, a future in which Americans of African ancestry get treated just like white folk. No doubt it'll sink in one of these days that the Democratic party has zero interest in actually seeing that future arrive—if that happened, after all, it would lose one of the most reliable of its captive constituencies—but until that day arrives, the loyalty of the African-American community to a party that offers them precious little but promises is a testimony to the power of a positive vision for the future.

That's something that the Democratic party doesn't seem to be able to offer anyone else in America, though. Even on paper, what have the last half dozen or so Democratic candidates for president offered? Setting aside crassly manipulative sound bites of the "hope and change" variety, it's all been attempts to keep things going the way they've been going, bracketed with lurid threats about the GOP's evil plans to make things so much worse. That's why, for example, the Democratic party has been eager to leap on climate change as a campaign issue, even though their performance in office on that issue is indistinguishable from that of the Republicans they claim to oppose: it's easy to frame climate change as a conflict between keeping things the way they are and making them much worse, and that's basically the only tune the American left knows how to play these days.

The difficulty, of course, is that after forty years of repeated and humiliating failure, the Democrats and the other leftward movements in American political life are caught in a brutal vise of their own making. On the one hand, very few people actually believe any more that the left is capable of preventing things from getting worse. There's good reason for that lack of faith, since a great many things have been getting steadily worse for the majority of Americans since the 1970s, and the assorted technological trinkets and distractions that have become available since then don't do much to make up for the absence of stable jobs with decent wages, functioning infrastructure, affordable health care, and all the other amenities that have gone gurgling down the nation's drain since then.

Yet there's another factor, of course, as hinted above. If the best you can offer the voters is another helping of policies that have already failed them, and show every sign of failing them more completely with every year that passes, you're not likely to get more than grudging support at most. That's the deeper issue behind the unenthusiastic popular response to Hillary Clinton's antics, and I'd like to suggest it's also what's behind Donald Trump's success in the polls—no matter how awful a president he'd be, the logic seems to run, at least he'd be *different*. When a nation reaches that degree of impatience with a status quo no one with access to power is willing to consider changing, an explosion is not far away.

425: THE WAR AGAINST CHANGE

(Originally published 12 August 2015)

Last week's post explored the way that the Democratic party over the last four decades has abandoned any claim to offer voters a better future, and has settled for offering them a future that's not quite as bad as the one the Republicans have in mind. That momentous shift can be described in many ways, but the most useful of them, to my mind, is one that I didn't bring up last week: the Democrats have become America's conservative party.

Yes, I know. That's not something you're supposed to say in today's America, where "conservative" and "liberal" have become meaningless vocal sounds linked with the greedy demands of each party's assortment of pressure groups and the plaintive cries of its own flotilla of captive constituencies. Still, back in the day when those words still meant something, "conservative" meant exactly what the word sounds like: a political stance that focuses on conserving some existing state of affairs, which liberals and radicals want to replace with some different state of affairs. Conservative politicians and parties—again, back when that word actually meant something—used to defend existing political arrangements against attempts to change them.

That's exactly what the Democratic Party has been doing for decades now. What it's trying to preserve, of course, is the welfare-state system of the New Deal of the 1930s and the Great Society programs of the 1960s—or, more precisely, the fragments of that system that still survive. That's the status quo that the Democrats are attempting to hold in place. The consequences of that conservative mission are unfolding around us in any number of ways, but the one that comes to mind just now is the current status of presidential candidate Bernard Sanders as a lightning rod for an all too familiar delusion of the wing of the Democratic party that still considers itself to be on the left.

The reason Sanders comes to mind so readily just now is that last week's post attracted an odd response from some of its readers. In the course of that post — which was not, by the way, on the subject of the American presidential race — I happened to mention three out of the twenty-odd candidates currently in the running. Somehow I didn't get taken to task by supporters of Michael O'Malley, Ted Cruz, Jesse Ventura, or any of the other candidates I didn't mention, with one exception: supporters of Sanders came out of the woodwork to denounce me for not discussing their candidate, as though he had some kind of inalienable right to air time in a blog post that, again, was not about the election.

I found the whole business a source of wry amusement, but it also made two points that are relevant to this week's post. On the one hand, what makes Sanders' talking points stand out among those of his rivals is that he isn't simply talking about maintaining the status quo; his proposals include steps that would restore a few of the elements of the welfare state that have been dismantled over the last four decades. That's the extent of his radicalism — and of course it speaks reams about the state of the Democratic party more generally that so modest, even timid, a proposal is fielding shrieks of outrage from the political establishment just now.

The second point, and to my mind the more interesting of the two, is the way that Sanders' campaign has rekindled the same messianic fantasies that clustered around Bill Clinton and Barack Obama in their first presidential runs. I remember rather too clearly the vehement proclamations by diehard liberals in 1992 that putting Bill Clinton in office would surely undo all the wrongs of the Reagan and Bush I eras; I hope none of my readers have forgotten the identical fantasies that gathered around Barack Obama in 2008. We can apparently expect another helping of them this time around, with Sanders as the beneficiary, and no doubt those of us who respond to them with anything short of blind enthusiasm will be denounced just as heatedly this time, too.

It bears remembering that despite those fantasies, Bill Clinton spent eight years in the White House following Ronald Reagan's playbook nearly to the letter, and Barack Obama has so far spent his two terms doing a really inspired imitation of the third and fourth terms of George W. Bush. If by some combination of sheer luck and hard campaigning, Bernie Sanders becomes the next president of the United States, it's a safe bet that the starry-eyed leftists who helped put him into office will once again get to spend four or eight years trying to pretend that their candidate isn't busy betraying all of the overheated expectations that helped put him into office. As Karl Marx suggested in one of his essays, if history repeats itself, the first time is tragedy but the second is generally farce; he didn't mention what the third time around was like, but we may just get to find out.

The fact that this particular fantasy has so tight a grip on the imagination of the Democratic party's leftward wing is also worth studying. There are many ways that a faction whose interests are being ignored by the rest of its party, and by the political system in general, can change that state of affairs. Unquestioning faith that this or that leader will do the job for them is not generally a useful strategy under such conditions, though, especially when that faith takes the place of any more practical activity. History has some very unwelcome things to say, for that matter, about the dream of political salvation by some great leader; so far it seems limited to certain groups on the notional left of the electorate, but if it spreads more widely, we could be looking at the first stirrings of the passions and fantasies that could bring about a new American fascism.

Meanwhile, just as the Democratic party in recent decades has morphed into America's conservative party, the Republicans have become its progressive party. That's another thing you're not supposed to say in today's America, because of the bizarre paralogic that surrounds the concept of progress in our collective discourse. What the word "progress" means, as I hope at least some of my readers happen to remember, is continuing further in the direction we're already going—and that's all it means. To most Americans today, though, the actual meaning of the word has long since been obscured behind a burden of vague emotion that treats "progressive" as a synonym for "good." Notice that this implies the very odd belief that the direction in which we're going is good, and can never be anything other than good.

For the last forty years, mind you, America has been moving steadily along an easily defined trajectory. We've moved step by step toward more political and economic inequality, more political corruption, more impoverishment for those outside the narrowing circles of wealth and privilege, more malign neglect toward the national infrastructure, and more environmental disruption, along with a steady decline in literacy and a rolling collapse in public health, among other grim trends. These are the ways in which we've been progressing, and that's the sense in which the GOP counts as America's current progressive party: the policies being proposed by GOP candidates will push those same changes even further than they've already gone, resulting in more inequality, corruption, impoverishment, and so on.

So the 2016 election is shaping up to be a contest between one set of candidates who basically want to maintain the wretchedly unsatisfactory conditions facing the American people today, and another set who want to make those conditions worse, with one outlier on the Democratic side who says he wants to turn the clock back to 1976 or so, and one outlier on the Republican side who apparently wants to fast forward things to the era of charismatic dictators we can probably expect in the not too distant future. It's not too hard to see why so many people looking at this spectacle aren't exactly seized with enthusiasm for any of the options being presented to them by the existing political order.

The question that interests me most about all this is the one I tried to raise last week—why, in the face of so many obvious dysfunctions, are so many people in and out of the political arena frozen into a set of beliefs that convince them that the only possibilities available to us involve either staying exactly where we are or going further along the route that's landed us in this mess? No doubt a good many things have contributed to that bizarre mental fixation, but there's one factor that may not have received the attention it deserves: the remarkable dominance of a particular narrative in the most imaginative fiction and mass media of our time. As far as I know, nobody's given that narrative a name yet, so I'll exercise that prerogative and call it The War Against Change.

You know that story inside and out. There's a place called Middle-Earth, or the Hogwarts School of Wizardry, or what have you—the name doesn't matter, the story's the same in every case. All of a sudden this place is threatened by an evil being named Sauron, or Voldemort, or—well, you can fill in the blanks for yourself. Did I mention that this evil being is evil? Yes, in fact, he's evilly evil out of sheer evil evilness, without any motive other than the one just named. What that evilness amounts to in practice, though, is that he wants to *change things*. Of course the change is inevitably portrayed in the worst possible light, but what it usually comes down to is that the people who currently run things will lose their positions of power, and will be replaced by the bad guy and his minions — any resemblance to the rhetoric surrounding US presidential elections is doubtless coincidental.

But wait! Before the bad guy and his evil minions can *change things*, a plucky band of heroes goes swinging into action to stop his evil scheme, and of course they succeed in the nick of time. The bad guy gets the stuffing pounded out of him, the people who are supposed to run things keep running things, everything settles down just the way it was before he showed up. Change is stopped in its tracks, and all of the characters who matter breathe a big sigh of relief and live happily ever after, or until filming starts on the sequel, take your pick.

Now of course that's a very simplified version of The War Against Change. In the hands of a really capable author — and we'll get to one of those in a minute — that story can quite readily yield great literature. Even so, it's a very curious sort of narrative to be as popular as it is, especially for a society that claims to be in love with change and novelty. The War Against Change takes place in a world in which everything's going along just the way things are supposed to be. The bad guy shows up and tries to *change things*, he gets clobbered by the good guys, and then everything goes on just the way it was. Are there, ahem, problems with the way things are run? Might *changing things* be a good idea, if the right things are changed? Does the bad guy and his evil minions possibly even have motives other than sheer evilly evil evilness for wanting to *change things*? That's not part of the narrative. At most, one or more of the individuals who are running things may be problematic, and have to be pushed aside by our plucky band of heroes so they can get on with the business of bashing the bad guy.

It happens now and then, in fact, that authors telling the story of The War Against Change go out of their way to make fun of the possibility that anyone might reasonably object to the established order of things. Did anyone else among my readers feel vaguely sick while reading the Harry Potter saga, when they encountered Rowling's rather shrill mockery of Hermione whatser-name's campaign on behalf of the house elves? To me, at least, it was rather too reminiscent of "No, no, our darkies *love* their Massa!"

That's actually a side issue, though. The core of the narrative is that the goal of the good guys, the goal that *defines* them as good guys, is to make sure that nothing changes. That becomes a source of tremendous if unintentional irony in the kind of imaginative fiction that brings imagery from mythology and legend into a contemporary setting. I'm thinking here, as one example out of many, of a series of five children's novels—*The Dark Is Rising* sequence by Susan Cooper—the first four of which were among the delights of my childhood. You have two groups of magical beings, the Light and the Dark—yes, it's pretty Manichean—who are duking it out in present-day Britain.

The Dark, as you've all probably figured out already, is trying to *change things*, and the Light is doing the plucky hero routine and trying to stop them. That's all the Light does; it doesn't, heaven help us, do anything about the many other things that a bunch of magical beings might conceivably want to fix in 1970s Britain. The Light has no agenda of its own at all; it's there to stop the Dark from *changing things*, and that's it. Mind you, the stories are packed full of splendid, magical stuff, the sort of thing that's guaranteed to win the heart and feed the imagination of any child stuck in the dark heart of American suburbia, as I was at the time.

Then came the fifth book, *Silver on the Tree*, which was published in 1977. The Light and the Dark finally had their ultimate cataclysmic showdown, the Dark is prevented from *changing things*...and once that's settled, the Light packs its bags and heads off into the sunset, leaving the protagonists sitting there in present-day Britain with all the magic gone for good. I loathed the book. So did a lot of other people—I've never yet heard it discussed without terms like "wretchedly disappointing" being bandied around—but I suspect the miserable ending was inescapable, given the frame into which the story had already been fixed. Cooper had committed herself to telling the story of The War Against Change, and it was probably impossible for her to imagine any other ending.

Now of course there's a reason why this particular narrative took on so overwhelming a role in the imaginative fiction and media of the late twentieth century, and that reason is the force of nature known as J.R.R. Tolkien. I'm by no means sure how many of my readers who weren't alive in the 1960s and 1970s have any idea how immense an impact Tolkien's sprawling trilogy *The Lord of the Rings* had on the popular imagination of that era, at a time when buttons saying Frodo Lives! and Go Go Gandalf were everywhere and every reasonably hip bookstore sold posters with the vaguely psychedelic front cover art of the first Ballantine paperback edition of *The Fellowship of the Ring*. In the formative years of the Boomer generation, Tolkien's was a name to conjure with.

What makes this really odd, all things considered, is that Tolkien himself was a political reactionary who opposed nearly everything his youthful fans supported. The Boomers who were out there trying to change the system in the Sixties were simultaneously glorifying a novel that celebrates war, monarchy, feudal hierarchy, and traditional gender roles, and includes an irritable swipe at the social welfare program of post-World War Two Britain — that's what Lotho Sackville-Baggins' government of the Shire amounts to, with its "gatherers" and "sharers." When Tolkien put together his grand epic of The War Against Change, he knew exactly what he was doing; when the youth culture of the Sixties adopted him as their patron saint — much to his horror, by the way — I'm not at all sure the same thing could be said about them.

What sets *The Lord of the Rings* apart from common or garden variety versions of The War Against Change, in fact, is precisely Tolkien's own remarkably clear understanding of what he was trying to do, and how that strategy tends to play out in the real world. *The Lord of the Rings* gets much of its power and pathos precisely because its heroes fought The War Against Change knowing that even if they won, they would lose; the best they could do is put a brake on the pace of change and keep the last dim legacies of the Elder Days for a little longer before they faded away forever. Tolkien nourished his literary sense on *Beowulf* and the Norse sagas, with their brooding sense of doom's inevitability, and on traditional Christian theology, with its promise of hope beyond the circles of the world, and managed to play these two against each other brilliantly — but then Tolkien, as a reactionary, understood what it was like to keep fighting for something even though he knew that the entire momentum of history was against him.

Does all this seem galaxies away from the crass political realities with which this week's post began? Think again, dear reader. Listen to the rhetoric of the candidates as they scramble for their party's nomination—well, except for Hillary Clinton, who's too busy declaiming "I am so ready to lead!" at the nearest available mirror—and you'll hear The War Against Change endlessly rehashed. What do the Republican candidates promise? Why, to save America from the evil Democrats, who want to *change things*. What do the Democratic candidates promise? To save America from the evil Republicans, ditto. Pick a pressure group, any pressure group, and the further in from the fringes they are, the more likely they are to frame their rhetoric in terms of The War Against Change, too.

I've noted before, for that matter, the weird divergence between the eagerness of the mainstream to talk about anthropogenic global warming and their utter unwillingness to talk about peak oil and other forms of resource depletion. There are several massive factors behind that, but I've come to think that one of the most important is that you can frame the climate change narrative in terms of The War Against Change—we must keep the evil polluters from *changing things!*—but you can't do that with peak oil. The end of the age of cheap abundant energy means that things have to change, not because the motiveless malignity of some cackling villain would have it so, but because the world no longer contains the resources that would be needed to keep things going the way they've gone so far.

That said, if it's going to be necessary to *change things*—and it is—then it's time to start thinking about options for the future that don't consist of maintaining a miserably unsatisfactory status quo or continuing along a trajectory that's clearly headed toward something even worse. The first step in making change is imagining change, and the first step in imagining change is recognizing that "more of the same" isn't going to cut it. Next week, I plan on taking some of the ideas I've floated here in recent months, and putting them together in a deliberately unconventional way.

426: THE LAST REFUGE OF THE INCOMPETENT

(Originally published 19 August 2015)

There are certain advantages to writing out the ideas central to this blog in weekly bursts. Back in the days before the internet, when a galaxy of weekly magazines provided the same free mix of ideas and opinions that fills the blogosphere today, plenty of writers kept themselves occupied turning out articles and essays for the weeklies, and the benefits weren't just financial: feedback from readers, on the one hand, and the contributions of other writers in related fields, on the other, really do make it easier to keep slogging ahead at the writer's lonely trade.

This week's essay has benefited from that latter effect, in a somewhat unexpected way. In recent weeks, here and there in the corners of the internet I frequent, there's been another round of essays and forum comments insisting that it's time for the middle-class intellectuals who frequent the environmental and climate change movements to take up violence against the industrial system. That may not seem to have much to do with the theme of the current sequence of posts—the vacuum that currently occupies the place in our collective imagination where meaningful visions of the future used to be found—but there's a connection, and following it out will help explain one of the core themes I want to discuss.

The science fiction author Isaac Asimov used to say that violence is the last refuge of the incompetent. That's a half-truth at best, for there are situations in which effective violence is the only tool that will do what needs to be done—we'll get to that in a moment. It so happens, though, that a particular kind of incompetence does indeed tend to turn to violence when every other option has fallen flat, and goes down in a final outburst of pointless bloodshed. It's unpleasantly likely at this point that the climate change movement, or some parts of it, may end up taking that route into history's dumpster; here again, we'll get to that a little further on.

It's probably necessary to say at the outset that the arguments I propose to make here have nothing to do with the ethics of violence, and everything to do with its pragmatics as a means of bringing about social change. Ethics in general are a complete quagmire in today's society. Nietzsche's sly description of moral philosophy as the art of propping up inherited prejudices with bad logic has lost none of its force since he wrote it, and since his time we've also witnessed the rise of professional ethicists, whose jobs consist of coming up with plausible excuses for whatever their corporate masters want to do this week. The ethical issues surrounding violence are at least as confused as those around any of the other messy realities of human life, and in some ways, more so than most.

Myself, I consider violence enitrely appropriate in some situations. Many of my readers may have heard, for example, of an event that took place a little while back in Kentucky, where a sex worker was attacked by a serial killer. While he was strangling her, she managed to get hold of his handgun, and proceeded to shoot him dead. To my mind, her action was morally justified. Once he attacked her, no matter what she did, somebody was going to die, and killing him not only turned the violence back on its originator, it also saved the lives of however many other women the guy might have killed before the police got to him — if they ever did; crimes against sex workers, and for that matter crimes against women, are tacitly ignored by a fairly large number of US police departments these days.

Along the same lines, a case can be made that revolutionary violence against a political and economic system is morally justified if the harm done by that system is extreme enough. That's not a debate I'm interested in exploring, though. Again, it's not ethics but pragmatics that I want to discuss, because whether or not revolutionary violence is justified in some abstract moral sense is far less important right now than whether it's an effective response to the situation we're in. That's not a question being asked, much less answered, by the people who are encouraging environmental and climate change activists to consider violence against the system.

Violence is not a panacea. It's a tool, and like any other tool, it's well suited to certain tasks and utterly useless for others. Political violence in particular is a surprisingly brittle and limited tool. Even when it has the support of a government's resource base, it routinely flops or backfires, and a group that goes in for political violence without the resources and technical assistance of some government somewhere has to play its hand exceedingly well, or it's going to fail. Furthermore, there are many cases in which violence isn't useful as a means of social change, as other tools can do the job more effectively.

Pay attention to the history of successful revolutions and it's not hard to figure out how to carry out political violence—and far more importantly, how not to do so. The most important point to learn from history is that successful violence in a political context doesn't take place in a vacuum. It's the final act of a long process, and the more thoroughly that process is carried out, the less violence is needed when crunch time comes. Let's take a few paragraphs to walk through the process and see how it's done.

The first and most essential step in the transformation of any society is the delegitimization of the existing order. That doesn't involve violence, and in fact violence at this first stage of the process is catastrophically counterproductive—a lesson, by the way, that the US military has never been able to learn, which is why its attempts to delegitimize its enemies (usually phrased in such language as "winning minds and hearts") have always been so embarrassingly inept and ineffective. The struggle to delegitimize the existing order has to be fought on cultural, intellectual, and ideological battlefields, not physical ones, and its targets are not people or institutions but the aura of legitimacy and inevitability that surrounds any established political and economic order.

Those of my readers who want to know how that's done might want to read up on the cultural and intellectual life of France in the decades before the Revolution. It's a useful example, not least because the people who wanted to bring down the French monarchy came from almost exactly the same social background as today's green radicals: disaffected middle-class intellectuals with few resources other than raw wit and erudition. That turned out to be enough, as they subjected the monarchy—and even more critically, the institutions and values that supported it—to sustained and precise attack from constantly shifting positions, engaging in savage mockery one day and earnest pleas for reform the next, exploiting every weakness and scandal for maximum effect. By the time the crisis finally arrived in 1789, the monarchy had been so completely defeated on the battlefield of public opinion that next to nobody rallied to its defense until after the Revolution was a fait accompli.

The delegitimization of the existing order is only the first step in the process. The second step is political, and consists of building a network of alliances with existing and potential power centers and pressure groups that might be willing to support revolutionary change. Every political system, whatever its official institutional form might be, consists in practice of just such a network of power centers—that is, groups of people who have significant political, economic, or social influence—and pressure groups—that is, other groups of people who lack such influence but can give or withhold their support in ways that can sometimes extract favors from the power centers.

In today's America, for example, the main power centers are found in what we may as well call the bureaucratic-industrial complex, the system of revolving-door relationships that connect big corporations, especially the major investment banks, with the major Federal bureaucracies, especially the Treasury and the Pentagon. There are other power centers as well—for example, the petroleum complex, which has its own ties to the Pentagon—which cooperate and compete by turns with the New York-DC axis of influence—and then there are pressure groups of many kinds, some more influential, some less, some reduced to the status of captive constituencies whose only role in the political process is to rally the vote every four years and have their agenda ignored by their supposed friends in office in between elections. The network of power centers, pressure groups, and captive constituencies that support the existing order of things is the real heart of political power, and it's what has to be supplanted in order to bring systemic change.

Effective revolutionaries know that in order to overthrow the existing order of society, they have to put together a comparable network that will back them against the existing order, and grow it to the point that it starts attracting key power centers away from the network of the existing order. That's a challenge, but not an impossible one. In any troubled society, there are always plenty of potential power centers that have been excluded from the existing order and its feeding trough, and are thus interested in backing a change that will give them the power they want and don't have. In France before the Revolution, for example, there were plenty of wealthy middle-class people who were shut out of the political system by the aristocracy and the royal court, and the *philosophes* went out of their way to appeal to them and get their support—an easy job, since the *philosophes* and the *nouveaux-riches* shared similar backgrounds. That paid off handsomely once the crisis came.

In any society, troubled or not, there are also always pressure groups, plenty of them, that are interested in getting more access to the various goodies that power centers can dole out, and can be drawn into alliance with a rising protorevolutionary faction. The more completely the existing order of things has been delegitimized, the easier it is to build such alliances, and the alliances can in turn be used to feed the continuing process of delegitimization. Here again, as in the first stage of the process, violence is a hindrance rather than a help, and it's best if the subject never comes up for discussion; assembling the necessary network of alliances is much easier when nobody has yet had to face up to the tremendous risks involved in revolutionary violence.

By the time the endgame arrives, therefore, you've got an existing order that no longer commands the respect and loyalty of most of the population, and a substantial network of pressure groups and potential power centers supporting a revolutionary agenda. Once the situation reaches that stage, the question of how to arrange the transfer of power from the old regime to the new one is a matter of tactics, not strategy. Violence is only one of the available options, and again, it's by no means always the most useful one. There are many ways to break the existing order's last fingernail grip on the institutions of power, once that grip has been loosened by the steps already mentioned.

What happens, on the other hand, to groups that don't do the necessary work first, and turn to violence anyway? Here again, history has plenty to say about that, and the short form is that they lose. Without the delegitimization of the existing order of society and the creation of networks of support among pressure groups and potential power centers, turning to political violence guarantees total failure.

For some reason, for most of the last century, the left has been unable or unwilling to learn that lesson. What's happened instead, over and over again, is that a movement pursuing radical change starts out convinced that the existing order of society already lacks popular legitimacy, and so fails to make a case that appeals to anybody outside its own ranks. Having failed at the first step, it tries to pressure existing power centers and pressure groups into supporting its agenda, rather than building a competing network around its own agenda, and gets nowhere. Finally, having failed at both preliminary steps, it either crumples completely or engages in pointless outbursts of violence against the system, which are promptly and brutally crushed. Any of my readers who remember the dismal history of the New Left in the US during the 1960s and early 1970s already know this story, right down to the fine details.

With this in mind, let's look at the ways in which the climate change movement has followed this same trajectory of abject failure over the last fifteen years or so.

The task of the climate change movement at the dawn of the twenty-first century was difficult but by no means impossible. Their ostensible goal was to create a consensus in the world's industrial nations that would support the abandonment of fossil fuels and a transition to the less energy-intensive ways of living that renewable resources can provide. That would have required a good many well-off people to accept a decline in their standards of living, but that's far from the insuperable obstacle so many people seem to think it must be. When Winston Churchill told the British people "I have nothing to offer but blood, toil, tears, and sweat," his listeners roared their approval. For reasons that probably reach far into our evolutionary past, a call to shared sacrifice usually gets a rousing response, so long as the people who are being asked to sacrifice have reason to believe something worthwhile will come of it.

That, however, was precisely what the climate change movement was unable to provide. It's harsh but not, I think, unfair to describe the real agenda of the movement as the attempt to create a future in which the industrial world's middle classes could keep on enjoying the benefits of their privileged lifestyle without wrecking the atmosphere in the process. Of course it's not exactly easy to convince everyone else in the world to put aside all their own aspirations for the sake of the already privileged, and so the spokespeople of the climate change movement generally didn't talk about what they hoped to achieve. Instead, they fell into the most enduring bad habit of the left, and ranted instead about how awful the future would be if the rest of the world didn't fall into line behind them.

On the off chance that any of my readers harbor revolutionary ambitions, may I offer a piece of helpful advice? If you want people to follow your lead, you have to tell them where you intend to take them. Talking exclusively about what's going to happen if they don't follow you will not cut it. Rehashing the same set of talking points about how everyone's going to die if the whole world doesn't rally around you emphatically will not cut it. The place where you're leading them can be difficult and dangerous, the way there can be full of struggle, sacrifice and suffering, and they'll still flock to your banner — in fact, young men will respond to that kind of future more enthusiastically than to any other, especially if you can lighten the journey with beer and the occasional barbecue — but you have to be willing to talk about your destination. You also have to remember that the phrase "shared sacrifice" includes the word "shared," and not expect everyone else to give up something so that you don't have to.

So the climate change movement entered the arena with one hand tied behind its back and the other hand hauling a heavy suitcase stuffed to the bursting point with middle class privilege. Its subsequent behavior did nothing to overcome that initial disadvantage. When the defenders of the existing order counterattacked, as of course they did, the climate change movement did nothing to retake the initiative and undermine its adversaries; preaching to the green choir took the place of any attempt to address the concerns of the wider public; over and over again, climate change activists allowed the other side to define the terms of the debate and then whined about the resulting defeat rather than learning anything from it. Of course the other side used every trick in the book, and then some; so? That's how the game is played. Successful movements for change realize that, and plan accordingly.

We don't even have to get into the abysmal failure of the climate change movement to seek out allies among the many pressure groups and potential power centers that might have backed it, if it had been able to win the first and most essential struggle in the arena of public opinion. The point I want to make is that at this point in the curve of failure, violence really is the last refuge of the incompetent. What, after all, would be the result if some of the middle class intellectuals who make up the core of the climate change movement were to pick up some guns, assemble the raw materials for a few bombs, and try to use violence to make their point? They might well kill some people before the FBI guns them down or hauls them off to life-plus terms in Leavenworth; they would very likely finish off climate change activism altogether, by making most Americans fear and distrust anyone who talks about it—but would their actions do the smallest thing to slow the dumping of greenhouse gases into the atmosphere and the resulting climate chaos? Of course not.

What makes the failure of the climate change movement so telling is that during the same years that it peaked and crashed, another movement has successfully conducted a prerevolutionary campaign of the classic sort here in the US. While the green Left has been spinning its wheels and setting itself up for failure, the populist Right has carried out an extremely effective program of delegitimization aimed at the federal government and, even more critically, the institutions and values that support it. Over the last fifteen years or so, very largely as a result of that program, a very large number of Americans have gone from an ordinary, healthy distrust of politicians to a complete loss of faith in the entire American project. To a remarkable extent, the sort of rock-ribbed middle Americans who used to insist that of course the American political system is the best in the world are now convinced that the American political system is their enemy, and the enemy of everything they value.

The second stage of the prerevolutionary process, the weaving of a network of alliances with pressure groups and potential power centers, is also well under way. Watch which groups are making common cause with one another on the rightward fringes of society these days and you can see a competent revolutionary strategy at work. This isn't something I find reassuring—quite the contrary, in fact; aside from my own admittedly unfashionable feelings of patriotism, one consistent feature of revolutions is that the government that comes into power after the shouting and the shooting stop is always more repressive than the one that was in power beforehand. Still, the way things are going, it seems likely to me that the US will see the collapse of its current system of government, probably accompanied with violent revolution or civil war, within a decade or two.

Meanwhile, as far as I can see, the climate change movement is effectively dead in its tracks, and we no longer have time to make something happen before the rising spiral of climate catastrophe begins — as my readers may have noticed, that's already well under way. From here on in, it's probably a safe bet that anthropogenic climate change will accelerate until it fulfills the prophecy of *The Limits to Growth* and forces the global industrial economy to its knees. Any attempt to bring human society back into some kind of balance with ecological reality will have to get going during and after that tremendous crisis. That requires playing a long game, but then that's going to be required anyway, to do the things that the climate change movement failed to do, and do them right this time.

With that in mind, I'm going to be taking this blog in a slightly different direction next week, and for at least a few weeks to come. I've talked in previous posts about intentional technological regression as an option, not just for individuals but as a matter of public policy. I've also talked at quite some length about the role that narrative plays in helping to imagine alternative futures. With that in mind, I'll be using the tools of fiction to suggest a future that zooms off at right angles to the expectations of both ends of the current political spectrum. Pack a suitcase, dear readers; your tickets will be waiting at the station. Next Wednesday evening, we'll be climbing aboard a train for Retrotopia.

427: ANOTHER WORLD IS INEVITABLE

(Originally published 16 September 2015)

I don't normally comment in these essays on the political affairs of other countries. As I've noted more than once here, the last thing the rest of the world needs is one more clueless American telling everyone else on the planet what to do. What's more, as the United States busies itself flailing blindly and ineffectually at the consequences that its own idiotically shortsighted decisions have brought down upon it, those of us who live here have our work cut out for us already.

That said, a sign I've been awaiting for quite some time has appeared on the horizon—the first rumble of a tectonic shift that will leave few things unchanged. Unsurprisingly, this didn't happen in the United States, but I was somewhat startled to see where it did happen. That would be in Britain, where Jeremy Corbyn has just been elected head of Britain's Labour Party.

Those of my readers who don't follow British politics may not know just how spectacular a change Corbyn's election marks. In the late 1990s, under the leadership of Tony Blair, the Labour Party did what erstwhile left-wing parties were doing all over the industrial world: it ditched the egalitarian commitments that had guided it in prior decades, and instead embraced a set of policies that were indistinguishable from those of its conservative opponents—the same thing, for example, that the Democratic party did here in the US. As a result, voters going to the polls found that their supposed right to shape the destiny of their nations at the voting booth had been reduced to irrelevance, since every party with a shot at power embraced the same set of political and economic policies.

That might have been bearable if the policies in question worked, but they didn't, they don't, and it's becoming increasingly clear that they never will. Proponents of the neoliberal consensus—I probably have to explain that label, don't I? It's a source of wry amusement to anybody who knows the first thing about the history of political economy that the viewpoint considered "conservative" in today's America is what used to be known as liberalism, and still has that label in economics. Unrestricted free trade, no government interference in business affairs, no government protections for the poor, and an expansionist and militaristic foreign policy: these were the trademarks of liberal political and economic thought all through the eighteenth and nineteenth centuries.

Those same policies came back into fashion as neoliberal economics, and as "conservative" politics, in the late twentieth century. Since then, proponents of neoliberalism have insisted that deregulation for industry and finance, tax cuts and government handouts for the rich, a rising spiral of punitive austerity measures for the poor, and a violent and amoral foreign policy obsessed with dominating the Middle East by force, would bring economic stability and prosperity at home and maintain peace overseas. That was the sales pitch that was used to sell these policies. I think most people have begun to notice by now, though, that the policies in question have had precisely the opposite effect, not just once but wherever and whenever they've been tried.

I encourage my readers, especially those who favor the neoliberal policies just outlined, to stop and think about that for a moment. Around the globe, where businesses have been deregulated, taxes cut for the rich and government money poured into their hands, harsh austerity measures imposed on the poor, and foreign policy turned into a set of excuses for lobbing bombs at Middle Eastern countries, stability, prosperity, and peace have not been forthcoming—in fact, quite the contrary. At best, neoliberal policies bring a brief burst of relative prosperity, followed by a long slide into increasingly intractable crisis; at worst, you go straight into the crisis phase, and then things just keep getting worse.

Logically speaking, if the policies you propose don't yield the results you expect, you change the policies. That's not what's happened in this case, though. Quite the contrary, the accelerating failures of neoliberalism have been met across the board by an increasingly angry insistence from the corridors of power that neoliberal policies are the only options there are.

What Jeremy Corbyn's election shows is that that insistence has just passed its pull date. Corbyn's an old-fashioned Labourite of the pre-Blair variety, and he's made it clear for decades that he supports the opposite of the neoliberal consensus: more regulation of finance and industry, higher tax rates and fewer handouts to the rich, more benefits for the poor, and a less aggressive foreign policy. When he entered the race to head the Labour Party after Ed Milliband's embarrassing electoral defeat earlier this year, party apparatchiks rolled their eyes and insisted that he didn't have a chance. What they hadn't noticed, and what the establishment across the industrial world has by and large never noticed either, is that the consensus is only a consensus among a privileged minority, and most people outside those rarefied and self-referential circles will vote against it if they're given half a chance.

That's what happened in the Labour Party election. When the ballots were counted, Corbyn had staged a monumental upset, winning by a landslide on the first ballot with a total three times as large as his nearest rival's. What's more, since his election, people who've stayed out of party politics in Britain have been joining the Labour Party in droves, convinced that at long last they have the chance to have their voices heard. Until and unless he loses a general election or some other Labour Party figure mounts an effective challenge against him, Corbyn's now the leader of Her Majesty's Loyal Opposition and the heir apparent to No. 10 Downing Street should Labour come out ahead in the next election.

Whether that's a desirable outcome or not is not something I propose to discuss here, as that choice is up to the people of Great Britain and nobody else. Myself, I'm not a great fan of Corbyn's variety of socialism, or for that matter most of the others; it seems to me that there are many better ways to run a society — though it's only fair to say that the neoliberal consensus is not one of these. What makes Jeremy Corbyn's meteoric rise important is that it shows just how fragile the neoliberal consensus actually is, and how readily it can be overturned by any politician who's willing to break with it and start addressing the concerns of the eighty to ninety per cent of the population who don't agree with it.

That fragility need not lead to better things. Here in the United States, Donald Trump remains sky-high in the polls for exactly the same reason Jeremy Corbyn now heads the Labour Party: he's willing to talk about things the political establishment refuses to discuss. In his case the unspeakable issue is the de facto policy, supported by both parties, of encouraging illegal immigration to the United States in order to drive down wages for the working classes and maintain a facade of prosperity for the privileged.

A great many Americans are concerned about that, and not unreasonably so. Whether allowing mass immigration to the United States is a good idea or not, it's fair to say that sharply limiting the number of legal immigrants and then turning a blind eye to illegal immigration lands us in the worst of both worlds. The only people who benefit from it are the employers who get to pay substandard wages to illegal immigrants, and the privileged classes whose lifestyles are propped up thereby. Since the voices of the privileged are the only ones that have been let into our collective conversation about politics for the last three and a half decades, the concerns of the broader public haven't been addressed; now Trump is addressing them, and he just might end up in the White House as a result.

He's not the only one who's riding that particular issue to the brink of power. Marine Le Pen, to name just one example, is more or less France's Donald Trump—though, France being France, she has better fashion sense and a less absurd hairstyle. Europe's privileged classes encourage unlimited immigration, just like their American equivalents, to force down wages and break the political power of the working classes, and Le Pen's Front National has harnessed the resentment of all those French voters who have been on the losing end of those policies for decades. Nor is France the only European nation where that's an explosive issue. The British politicians and pundits who are busy decrying Corbyn's election just now might want to temper their rage and consider the alternatives: if Corbyn falls, Nigel Farage and the UKIP party are waiting in the wings to harness the public's frustration with the abject failure of business as usual, and if Farage falls in his turn, what replaces him could be much, much worse.

The mere fact that a failed consensus is cracking at the seams, in other words, does not guarantee that what replaces it will be an improvement. All it means is that there's an opening through which a range of alternative visions can enter the political conversation of our time, and perhaps find an audience among the disenfranchised and disillusioned. That some such window of opportunity was on its way comes as no surprise; as a student of history, I've long taken comfort in the fact that even the most thoroughly entrenched political and economic orthodoxies have finite life spans, and will eventually be hauled out with the trash. Much of what I've done over the last nine years on this blog has been a matter of getting ready for the opening of that window, putting certain ideas into circulation among those few who were ready to hear them.

That's a more important step than I think many people realize. In Germany in the early 1930s, when a failed consensus finally came apart, the only alternative visions that had any significant presence were the Leninist version of Marxian socialism, on the one hand, and a bubbling cauldron of racist fantasies and radical antirationalism on the other; the latter triumphed, and no doubt most of my readers are aware of what followed. In other places and times, less psychotic options have been available, and the results have generally been much better. The Zapatista rebels in southern Mexico a while back favored the slogan "another world is possible," and of course they're quite right—but a great deal depends on what kind of other world people are prepared to imagine.

This is why, for example, the last three posts here on *The Archdruid Report* have been devoted to a narrative describing a future very different from the one that most Americans like to imagine: a future in which the United States slams facefirst into a brick wall of unintended consequences, plunges into a bloody civil war, and fragments thereafter, and in which one of the fragments pursues a set of political and economic policies that go zooming off at right angles to the conventional wisdom of our time. I expect to resume that narrative next week, and to continue it with an assortment of interruptions thereafter, precisely because a less impoverished sense of the possible futures open to us is so crucial in facing the rising spiral of crises that defines our time.

It's a source of some amusement to me that I've fielded a fair number of comments insisting that I have to reshape the narrative just mentioned to fit one or another version of the conventional wisdom. This blog's focus being what it is, most of them have fixated on one or another aspect of what might as well be called the Ecotopian model—the last really imaginative vision of the future in this country, which was midwifed by Ernest Callenbach in his brilliant 1974 utopian fiction *Ecotopia*. If you know your way around today's American Green scene, even if you haven't read a word Callenbach wrote, you know his ideas, because they still shape an enormous amount of what passes for original thought today.

That's not a model I'm interested in rehashing. Partly that's because not that many people outside the San Francisco Bay region find Callenbach's vision especially appealing; partly it's because some aspects of the model, notably the claim that solar and wind power can support something akin to modern middle class American lifestyles, haven't held up well in the light of experience; but it's also partly because other worlds are also possible. The Ecotopian conventional wisdom is not the only option. It's an option toward which I have a nostalgic fondness—I was wildly enthusiastic about Callenbach's book back in the day—but it's not the only game in town, and all things considered, it's not the option I would choose today. Thus *Retrotopia*, as the name suggests, is not going to be full of avid spandex-clad cyclists who dine on the produce of permacultured edible forests, or what have you. It's heading in directions that are far more threatening to the status quo—including, by the way, the Ecotopian status quo.

The crying need for an abundance of alternative visions of the future, apart from the conventional wisdom of our time, has also driven another core project of this blog, and with that in mind, I'm delighted to announce the winners of this year's Space Bats challenge. Those of my readers who are new to *The Archdruid Report* may not know that since 2011, this blog has hosted a series of contests in which readers have submitted short stories set in a variety of deindustrial futures—that is, futures in which industrial society as we know it is a thing of the past, our current complex technologies have faded into legend, and human beings are busy coping with the legacies of the industrial age and leading challenging, interesting, and maybe even appealing lives in that context.

The first Space Bats challenge was a shot in the dark, and to my delighted surprise, it fielded a torrent of fine short stories, which were duly published by Founders House Publishing as an anthology titled *After Oil: SF Visions of a Post-Petroleum Future*. A second contest duly followed in 2014, and produced two anthologies, *After Oil 2: The Years of Crisis* and *After Oil 3: The Years of Rebirth*. The fourth contest was launched in March of this year; as before, I was deluged with an abundance of excellent stories, and had a hard time choosing among them; I owe thanks to everyone who submitted a story and made the choice so difficult; but the following stories will be included in the next anthology, *After Oil 4: The Future's Distant Shores*:

"Sail Away Home" by Alma Arri
"Finding Flotsam" by Bill Blondeau
"Alay" by Dau Branchazel
"Crow Turns Over a Rock" by Eric Farnsworth
"Notes for a Picnic" by Phil Harris
"The Remembrancer" by Wylie Harris
"The Bald Eagle, the Lame Duck, and the Cooked Goose" by Jonah Harvey
"The Baby" by Nicky Jarman
"Northern Ghosts" by Gaianne Jenkins
"Caretaker Poinciana" by Troy Jones
"Scapegoat" by Cathy McGuire
"Flowering" by John W. Riley

I trust you'll join me in congratulating the authors and, more to the point, in reading their stories once those see print.

In its own small and idiosyncratic way, my experience with the Space Bats challenge parallels the political earthquake currently shaking the British landscape. All I did was ask readers to come up with stories that broke with the conventional wisdom concerning the future—to set aside the weary, dreary, endlessly rehashed Tomorrowland of spaceships, zap-guns, and linear technological expansion along the same lines we think we're following today, and imagine something different—and as it turned out, that's all I had to do. Given the opportunity to write about some less hackneyed future, scores of readers lunged for their keyboards and flooded each contest with quirky, thoughtful, interesting futures...you know, the kind of thing that science fiction used to feature all the time, back before it got sucked into the role of cheerleading for a suffocatingly narrow range of acceptable tomorrows.

There will be another Space Bats challenge, beginning in the spring of next year. I invite my readers to propose potential themes for that challenge — this fourth anthology consists entirely of stories set at least a thousand years in the future, and I'd like to have some equally offbeat focus or limitation on the next contest, in the hope that it will inspire an equally stellar collection of stories.

I'm also pleased to note that the *After Oil* anthologies and my post-peak novel *Star's Reach* are far from the only contributions to a growing genre. Founders House, for example, has also recently published Ralph Meima's novel *Fossil Nation*, the first volume of a trilogy, which offers its own lively and readable glimpse at a future that cuts across the conventional wisdom of our time and heads off in new directions. Other projects are in the works, at Founders House and elsewhere.

At the same time, it's worth remembering that the same process is under way on a much vaster scale, and with much more serious consequences. As the neoliberal consensus shatters and the failure of its policies becomes impossible to ignore any longer, another world is not merely possible, it's inevitable. The question is purely what ideas, visions, dreams, hopes, and shuddering terrors will shape the world that will emerge from neoliberalism's smoldering corpse — and that, dear reader, will be determined in part by what you yourself are willing to imagine, to work for, and to struggle for, during the difficult years ahead of us.

428: A LANDSCAPE OF DREAMS

(Originally published 7 October 2015)

Maybe it's just the psychology of selective attention, but tolerably often when I want to go into more detail about a point made in a previous essay here, stories relevant to that point in one way or another start popping up on the news. That's been true even during this blog's forays into narrative fiction, so it should be no surprise that it's happened again—even though, in this case, the point in question may not be obvious to most readers yet.

One of the core themes of the Retrotopia narrative I've been developing here over the last month or so is the yawning gap between the abstract notion of progress that we all have in our heads and the rather less pleasant realities to which this notion has been assigned. The imaginary Atlantic Republic, the home of the narrative's viewpoint character, is a place where progress as we know it has continued in exactly the same direction it's been going for the last half century or so. That's why it's a place where income is concentrated in ever fewer hands, leaving most of the population to struggle for survival via poorly paid part-time jobs or no jobs at all; a place where infrastructure has been allowed to fall into ruin, while investment gets focused instead on a handful of high-tech services such as the metanet (my hypothetical 2065 "improvement" of today's internet); a place where people make do with shoddy, wretchedly unpleasant consumer goods because that's what a handful of big corporations want to sell them and there are no other alternatives, and so on.

Now of course the immediate response of many people to this characterization can be summed up neatly as "but that's not progress!" Au contraire, the changes just noted, unwelcome as they are, are the necessary and inevitable consequences of exactly those technological transformations that have been lauded to the skies in recent years as evidence of just how much we've progressed. In the same way, my imaginary Lakeland Republic, with its prosperous working classes, its thriving urban centers, its comfortable clothing, and the like, has those things because it made certain collective choices that fly in the face of everything that most people these days understand as progress.

For instance, to cite a detail that sparked discussion on the comments page last week, the Lakeland Republic has abandoned computer technology — or more precisely, after the Second Civil War and the crises that followed, it rebuilt its infrastructure and economy without making computer technology part of the mix. There were a variety of reasons for that choice, but one was an issue I've raised in these essays several times already: when you have an abundance of people who want steady employment and a growing shortage of the energy and other resources needed to build and operate machines, replacing employees with machines is not necessarily a smart idea, while replacing machines with employees may just be the key to renewed prosperity and stability.

That's an issue in the story, and also in our lives today, because computers have eliminated vastly more jobs than they've created. Before computers came in, tens of millions of Americans supported themselves with steady jobs as typists, file clerks, stenographers, and so on through an entire galaxy of jobs that no longer exist due to computer technolog. The jobs that have been created by computer technology, on the other side of the balance, employ far fewer people, leaving the vast remainder to compete for the remaining bottom-level jobs, and this has driven down wages and widened the gap between the well-to-do and everyone else. That's not what progress is supposed to do, according to the conventional wisdom, but that's what it has done — and not just in this one case.

Since 1970, in point of fact, the standard of living for everyone in America outside of the wealthiest 20% or so has skidded unsteadily downward. The nation's infrastructure has been abandoned to malign neglect, and a great many amenities that used to be taken for granted either cost vastly more than they once did, even corrected for inflation, or can't be had for any price. We pretend, or at least the vast majority of us do, that these things either haven't happened or don't matter, and certainly nobody's willing to address the possibility that these things and other equally unwelcome changes have been the result of what we like to call progress — even when that's fairly obviously the case.

What's going on here, in other words, is the emergence of a widening chasm between the abstraction "progress" and the things that progress is supposed to represent, such as improved living conditions, a broader range of choices available to people, and so on. The sort of progress we've experienced over the last half century or so hasn't given us these things; quite the contrary; it's yielded degraded living conditions, a narrower range of choices, and the like. Point this out to people in so many words and the resulting cognitive dissonance tends to get some truly quirky responses; put it in the form of a narrative and — at least this is my hope — a larger fraction of readers will be able to recognize the tangled thinking at the heart of the paradox, and recognize a dysfunctional abstraction for what it is.

Dysfunctional abstractions, though, are all the rage these days. A glance through the news offers a bumper crop of examples. One that comes forcefully to mind, just at the moment, is the ongoing attempts on the part of US political and military spokescritters to find some way to talk about the US airstrike on a hospital in Kunduz, Afghanistan, without actually mentioning that the US carried out an airstrike on a hospital and killed twenty-two civilians, including three children.

It really has been a remarkable spectacle, and connoisseurs of weasel-worded evasions have had a feast spread out before them. Early on, the media in the US and its allies was full of reports that the hospital had been hit by an airstrike that somehow didn't get around to mentioning whose aircraft was involved. Then there were stalwart claims that it hadn't yet been confirmed that a US aircraft carried out the strike. Once that evasion passed its pull date — the Taliban, after all, doesn't have an air force, and the public relations flacks at the Pentagon apparently decided that it just wasn't going to work to insist that they'd somehow come up with one just for the sake of this one airstrike — the excuses began flying fast and thick. The fact that the four officially promulgated excuses I've seen so far all contradict one another doesn't exactly make any of them seem particularly convincing.

What the excuses and evasions demonstrate, rather, is that the US military and government are treating what happened entirely as a matter of abstractions, rather than dealing with the harsh but inescapable reality of twenty-two smoldering corpses in a burnt-out hospital. To the media flacks at the Pentagon, evidently, this is all merely a public relations problem, and the only response to it they can think of involves finding some set of excuses, euphemisms, and evasions that will allow them to efface the distinction between a public relations problem and a war crime.

Now of course it's not as though this sort of atrocity is unusual for the US at this point on the sorry downslope of its history. The only thing that makes the bombing of the Kunduz hospital at all unusual is that a significant fraction of the targets weren't locals—they were physicians and hospital staff from the international charity Médecins sans Frontières, who can't be ignored quite so easily. For well over a decade now, the US government has been vaporizing assorted groups of people all over the Middle East via drone strikes, and according to everybody but the paid flacks of the US government, a very large fraction of the people blown to bits in these attacks have been civilians. Here again, Washington DC treats this as a public relations problem, and simply denies that anything of the sort has happened.

The difficulty with this strategy, though, is that sooner or later you run up against an opponent that isn't stuck on the level of abstractions, isn't greatly interested in public relations, and intends to do you real, rather than abstract, harm. To some extent that's what has sown the whirlwind that the US and its allies are now reaping in the Middle East. In many of the tribal cultures of the Middle East, vengeance against the killers of one's family members is an imperative duty, and it doesn't matter how airily the flacks in Washington DC dismiss the possibility that the latest drone strike annihilated a Yemeni wedding party, or what have you. The relatives of the dead know better, and the young men among them are going to do something about it, whether that involves hiking to Afghanistan or, say, joining the current mass migration into Europe, lying low for a while, and then looking for suitable targets.

The same difficulty has shifted into overdrive over the last few weeks, though, with Russia's entry into the Syrian civil war. Russia's current leaders are realists, which is to say, they assign abstractions the limited importance they deserve. The Russian presence in Syria, accordingly, isn't a mere gesture, it's the efficient deployment of an expeditionary force that's clearly intended to wage war, and is in the early stages of turning that intention into hard reality. In an impressively short time, the Russians have built, staffed, and stocked a forward air base at Latakia, and begun systematic air strikes against rebel positions; work has gotten under way on two other bases; weapons and munitions are flooding into Syria to rearm the beleaguered Syrian army; the first detachments of Revolutionary Guard soldiers from Russia's ally Iran have arrived. Russian Spetsnaz (special forces) and airborne units are en route to Syrian soil, where they and the Iranians will doubtless have something to do besides soak up rays on Latakia's once-famous Mediterranean beaches.

Meanwhile Russia's Black Sea fleet, led by its flagship, the guided missile cruiser Moskva, has positioned itself off the Syrian coast. That in itself tells an important story. The Moskva carries long range antiship missiles and an S-300 antiaircraft system; there are reports that another S-300 system has been set up on land, and Russian electronic warfare equipment has also been reported at Latakia. Neither the Islamic State militia nor any of the other rebel forces arrayed against the Syrian government have a navy, an air force, or electronics sufficiently complex to require jamming in the event of hostilities. The only nation involved in the Syrian civil war that has all these things is the United States. Clearly, then, Russia is aware of the possibility that the US may launch an air or naval assault on the Russian expeditionary force, and has the weaponry on hand to respond in kind.

Last night, working on this post, I wrote: "The Russian airstrikes so far have concentrated on rebel forces around the edges of the territory the Syrian government still holds, with some longer-range strikes further back to take out command centers, munitions dumps, and the like. The placement of the strikes says to me that the next moves, probably within weeks, will be against the rebel enclave north of Homs and the insurgent forces in Idlib province. I expect ground assaults backed up by artillery, helicopter gunships, and close-in air support—vastly more firepower, in other words, that any side in the Syrian civil war has had at its disposal so far." This morning's news confirmed that guess, and added in another factor: Russian cruise missiles launched from the Caspian Sea fleet, most of a thousand miles from Syria. Once Idlib and the rest of western Syria is secured, I expect the Russians and their allies to march on Raqqa, the Islamic State's notional capital — and I don't expect them to waste any more time in doing so than they've wasted so far.

All this poses an immense embarrassment to the United States and its allies, which have loudly and repeatedly proclaimed the Islamic State the worst threat to world peace since the end of the Third Reich but somehow, despite a seemingly overwhelming preponderance of military force, haven't been able to do much of anything about it. Though it's hard to say for sure, given the fog of conflicting propaganda, it certainly looks as though the Russians have done considerably more damage to the Islamic State in a week than the US and its allies have accomplished in thirteen months of bombing. If that's the case, some extremely awkward questions are going to be asked. Is the US military so badly led, so heavily burdened with overpriced weapons systems that don't happen to work, or both, that it's lost the ability to inflict serious harm on an opponent? Or — let's murmur this one quietly — does the United States have some reason not to want to inflict serious harm on the Islamic State?

I suspect, though, that what's actually behind the disparity is something far simpler, if no less damaging to the prestige of the United States. I commented in an earlier post here that the US has been waging its inept campaign against Islamic State as though it's a video game — hey, we killed a commander, isn't that worth an extra 500 points? Look at that from a different perspective and it becomes another example of the disconnection of abstraction from reality.

The abstraction here is "fighting Islamic State." You'll notice that it's not "defeating Islamic State" — in the realm of dysfunctional abstractions, such differences mean a great deal. Obama has decided that under his leadership, the US is going to fight Islamic State, and that's what the Pentagon is doing. At intervals, accordingly, planes go flying over various portions of Syria and Iraq to make desultory bombing runs on places where some intelligence analyst in suburban Virginia thinks an Islamic State target might have been located at some point in the last month or so.

That's "fighting Islamic State." Nobody can point a finger at Obama and say that he's not fighting Islamic State, since the Air Force is still obligingly making those bombing runs. It doesn't matter that none of this has done anything to slow down the expansion of the Islamic State militia, or to stop its appalling human rights violations; that's in the grubby realm of realities, into which fastidious minds in Washington DC are unwilling to stoop.

Another abstraction that's getting a lot of use in the current situation is "moderate Syrian rebels." In the realm of realities, of course, those don't exist. The Pentagon's repeated attempts to find or manufacture some, to satisfy Obama's insistence that a supply of them ought to be forthcoming, have yielded one embarrassing failure after another. This is for quite a simple reason, all things considered: the word "moderate" in this context means, in effect, "willing to put the interests of the US and its European allies ahead of their country and their faith." (When American politicians use the word "moderate" about people in other countries, that's inevitably what they mean.) Nonetheless, since the abstraction is so useful, the politicians and the Pentagon keep on waving it around. You have to read carefully to find out that some groups being labeled as potential moderates, such as the al-Nusra Front, are affiliated with al-Qaeda — you know, the outfit that the Global War On Terror was supposed to fight.

Such things should probably come as no surprise during the presidency of a man who got into office via a campaign that was never anything more than a blur of feel-good abstractions: "Hope," "Change," "Yes We Can," and the like. Barack Obama will go down in history as one of the United States' least competent presidents precisely because everything he's done has been so utterly fixated on the realm of abstractions. The wretchedly misnamed "Affordable Care Act" aka Obamacare is a fine example. Its enactment has made health care more expensive and less available for most Americans; it took what was already the worst health care system in the industrial world, and accomplished the not inconsiderable feat of making it even worse.

To Obama and his dwindling crowdlet of supporters, though, that doesn't matter. What matters is that the resulting mess corresponds, to them, to the abstraction "national health care system." He promised a national health care system, we have a national health care system — and of course it's not exactly irrelevant that the privileged few who still praise that system are by and large those whose wealth shields them from having to cope with its disastrous failings.

It's only fair to note that, deeply immersed in the realm of dysfunctional abstractions as Obama is, he's got plenty of company there, and it's not limited to the faux-liberal constituencies that put him into his current address. Listen to the verbiage spewing out of the overcrowded Republican clown car and you'll get to witness any number of vague abstractions floating past, serenely disconnected from the awkward realm of facts. For that matter, take in the outpourings of the establishment's pet radicals—I'm thinking just now of Naomi Klein's embarrassingly slipshod and superficial book *This Changes Everything*, but there are plenty of other examples—and you'll find no shortage of equally detached abstractions drifting by in the breeze, distracting attention from the increasingly dismal landscape of fact down there on the ground.

What troubles me most about all this is what it says about the potential for really serious disruptions here in the US in the near future. I'm sure my readers can think of other regimes that reached the stage where moving imaginary armies across a landscape of dreams took precedence over grappling with awkward facts, and once that happened, none of those regimes were long for this world. The current US political system is so deeply entrenched in its own fantasies that a complete breakdown of that system, and its replacement by something entirely different—not necessarily better, mind you, but different—is a possibility that has to be kept in mind even in the near term.

429: THE PATIENCE OF THE SEA

(Originally published 28 October 2015)

I've noted here more than once that these essays draw their inspiration from quite a variety of sources. This week's post is no
exception to that rule. What kickstarted the train of thought that
brought it into being was a walk along the seashore last weekend
at Ocean City, Maryland, watching the waves roll in and thinking about the imminent death of a good friend.

East coast ocean resorts aren't exactly a common destination
for vacations in October, but then I wasn't there for a vacation.
I think most of my readers are aware that I'm a Freemason; it
so happens that three organizations that supervise certain of the
higher degrees of Masonry in Maryland took advantage of cheap
off-season hotel rates to hold their annual meetings in Ocean
City last weekend. Those readers who like to think of Masonry
as a vast conspiracy of devil-worshipping space lizards, or whatever the Masonophobic paranoia du jour happens to be these
days, would have been heartily disappointed by the weekend's
proceedings: a few dozen guys in off-the-rack business suits or
cheap tuxedos, most of them small businessmen, skilled trades-
men, or retirees, donning the ornate regalia of an earlier time and
discussing such exotic and conspiratorial topics as liability insurance for local lodges.

That said, a very modest sort of history was made at this year's
session of the Grand Council of Royal and Select Masters of Maryland—as the name suggests, that's the outfit that supervises the
local bodies that confer the degrees of Royal Master and Select
Master on qualified Master Masons in this state. More precisely,
it's one of two such bodies in Maryland. Back in the eighteenth
century, Masonry in the United States split into two segregated
branches, one for white and Native American Masons, the other

for African-American Masons. Late in the twentieth century, as most other segregated institutions in American life dropped the color bar, the two branches of Masonry began a rapprochement as well.

Merger was never an option, and not for the reason you're thinking. Both branches of Masonry in the US are proud organizations with their own traditions and customs, not to mention a deeply ingrained habit of prickly independence, and neither was interested in surrendering its own heritage, identity, and autonomy in a merger. Thus what happened was simply that both sides opened their doors to men of any skin color or ethnic background, formally recognized each other's validity, and worked out the details involved in welcoming each other's initiates as visiting brethren. Masonry being what it is, all this proceeded at a glacial pace, and since each state Grand Lodge makes its own rules, the glaciers moved at different speeds in different parts of the country.

A couple of years ago, the first time I was qualified to attend the state sessions of the Grand Council of Royal and Select Masters, I voted on the final stage in the movement of one particular glacierette, the establishment of full recognition and visitation between the two Maryland Grand Councils. My vote didn't greatly matter, all things considered — the resolution was approved unanimously — but I was still happy to be able to cast it. I was equally happy, at this year's grand sessions, to see the Most Illustrious Grand Master of the historically African-American Grand Council welcomed to the other Grand Council's meeting with the traditional honors, invited to the East to address the brethren, and given a standing ovation at the end of his talk. Of such small steps is history composed.

When somebody gets around to writing the definitive account of how the two branches of US Masonry healed the old division, this weekend's session will merit something between a footnote and a sentence if it gets mentioned at all. I seriously doubt the historian will even notice that one of the attendees came a day early, stayed a day late, enjoyed the quiet pleasures that an uncluttered seashore and a half-empty resort town have to offer, and figured out a detail or two about the trajectory of industrial civilization while walking along the beach on a cloudy afternoon, as a stiff breeze blew spray off the long gray rollers coming in from the North Atlantic.

All in all, it was a propitious place for such reflections. America just now, after all, has more than a little in common with an October day in Ocean City. Look around at the gaudy attractions that used to attract so much attention from adoring crowds, and you'll see many of the same things I saw along the boardwalk that day. The space program? It's boarded up for the duration like any other amusement park in the off season, though the plywood's plastered with equally garish posters announcing coming attractions off somewhere in the indefinite future. The American Dream? The lights are shining on the upper floors and big flashing neon signs say "OPEN FOR BUSINESS," but all the ground floor entrances are padlocked shut and nobody can get in.

The consumer products that fill the same pacifying function in American society as cheap trinkets for the kids at a seaside resort are still for sale here and there, though many of the shops are already closed and shuttered. The shelves of those that are still open are looking decidedly bare, and what's left has that oddly mournful quality that shoddy plastic gewgaws always get when they've been left on display too long. The one difference that stands out is that Ocean City in late October is mostly deserted, while the crowds are still here in today's America, milling around aimlessly in front of locked doors and lightless windows, while the sky darkens with oncoming weather and the sea murmurs and waits.

But that wasn't the thing that sparked this week's reflections. The thing that sparked this week's reflections was a stray question that came to mind when I abandoned the boardwalk to the handful of visitors who were strolling along it, and crossed the sand to the edge of the surf, thinking as I walked about the friend I mentioned earlier, who was lying in a hospital bed on the other side of the continent while his body slowly and implacably shut down. The boardwalk, the tourist attractions, and the hulking Babylonian glass-and-concrete masses of big hotels and condominiums stood on one side of me, while on the other, the cold gray sea surged and splashed and the terns danced past on the wind. The question in my mind was this: in a thousand years, which of these things will still be around?

That's a surprisingly edgy question these days, and to make sense of that, I'd like to jump to the seemingly unrelated subject of an article that appeared a little while ago in the glossy environmental magazine *Orion*.

The article was titled "Peak Oil Fantasy," and it was written by Charles Mann, who made a modest splash a little while back with a couple of mildly controversial popular histories of the New World before and after Europeans got there. Those of my readers who have been keeping track of the mainstream media's ongoing denunciations of peak oil will find it wearily familiar. It brandished the usual set of carefully cherrypicked predictions about the future of petroleum production that didn't happen to pan out, claimed on that basis that peak oil can't happen at all because it hasn't happened yet, leapt from there to the insistence that our very finite planet must somehow contain a limitless amount of petroleum, and wound up blustering that everybody ought to get with the program, "cast away the narrative of scarcity," and just shut up about peak oil.

Mann's article was a little more disingenuous than the run of the mill anti-peak-oil rant—it takes a certain amount of nerve to talk at length about M. King Hubbert, for example, without once mentioning the fact that he successfully predicted the peaking of US petroleum production in 1970, using the same equations that successfully predicted the peaking of world conventional petroleum production in 2005 and are being used to track the rise and fall of shale oil and other unconventional oil sources right now. Other than that, there's nothing novel about "Peak Oil Fantasy," as all but identical articles using the same talking points and rhetoric have appeared regularly for years now in *The Wall Street Journal* and other pro-industry, pave-the-planet publications. The only oddity is that a screed of this overfamiliar kind found its way into a magazine that claims to be all about environmental protection.

Even that isn't as novel as I would wish. Ever since *The Archdruid Report* began publication, just short of a decade ago, I've been fielding emails and letters, by turns spluttering, coaxing, and patronizing, urging me to stop talking about peak oil, the limits to growth, and the ongoing decline and approaching fall of industrial society, and start talking instead about climate change, overpopulation, capitalism, or what have you. No few of these have come from people who call themselves environmentalists, and tolerably often they reference this or that environmental issue in trying to make their case.

The interesting thing about this ongoing stream of commentary is that I've actually discussed climate change, overpopulation, and capitalism at some length in these essays. When I point this out, I tend to get either a great deal of hemming and hawing, or the kind of sudden silence that lets you hear the surf from miles away. Clearly what I have to say about climate change, overpopulation, and capitalism isn't what these readers are looking for, and just as clearly they're not comfortable talking about the reasons why what I have to say isn't what they're looking for.

What interests me is that in the case of climate change, at least, there are aspects of that phenomenon that get the same response. If you ever want to reduce a room full of affluent liberal climate change activists to uncomfortable silence, for example, mention that the southern half of the state of Florida is going to turn into uninhabitable salt marsh in the next few decades</a> no matter what anybody does. You can get the same response if you mention that the collapse of the West Antarctic ice sheet is so far advanced at this point that no human action can stop the drowning of every coastal city on the planet—and don't you dare mention the extensive and growing body of research that shows that the collapse of major ice sheets doesn't happen at a rate of a few inches of sea level rise per century, but includes sudden "marine transgressions" of many feet at a time instead.

This discomfort is all the more interesting because these same things were being loudly predicted not much more than a decade ago by affluent liberal climate change activists. As long as they were threats located off somewhere in the indefinite future, they were eagerly used as verbal ammunition, but each of them vanished from the rhetoric as soon as it stopped being a threat and turned into a reality. I noted in an essay some years back the way that methane boiling out of the Arctic Ocean, which was described in ghoulish detail over and over again as the climate change *über*-threat, suddenly got dropped like a anthropogenically heated rock by climate change activists the moment it began to happen.

It's still happening. As Arctic temperatures soar, rivers of meltwater are sluicing across the Greenland ice cap and cascading into the surrounding oceans, and the ice cap itself, in the words of one climate scientist cited in the article just linked, is as full of holes as Swiss cheese due to meltwater streaming through its innards. While climate change activists insist ever more loudly that we can still fix everything if only the right things happen in the next five years—okay, ten—well, make that fifteen—the cold gray seas off Greenland aren't listening. The only voices that matter to them come from the roar of waterfalls off the waning ice cap, the hiss of methane bubbles rising from the shallows, and the hushed whispers of temperature and salinity in the dark waters below.

Glaciologists and marine hydrologists know this, and so do a significant number of climate scientists. It's the would-be mass movement around climate change that has done its level best to pretend that the only irreversible tipping points are still somewhere in the future. They're not alone in that; for a good many decades now, the entire environmental movement has been stuck in a broken-record rut, saying over and over again that we still have five years to fix the biosphere. Those of my readers who doubt this might want to pick up the twenty-year and thirty-year updates to *The Limits to Growth* and compare what they have to say about how long the world has to stave off catastrophe.

That is to say, the environmental movement these days has become a prisoner of the same delusion of human omnipotence that shapes so much of contemporary culture.

That's the context in which Charles Mann's denunciation of the peak oil heresy needs to be taken. To be acceptable in today's mainstream environmental scene, a cause has to be stated in terms that feed the fantasy just named. Climate change is a perfect fit, since it starts from an affirmation of human power—"Look at us! We're so almighty that we can wreck the climate of the whole *planet!*" —and goes on to insist that all we have to do is turn our limitless might to fixing the climate instead. The campaigns to save this or that species of big cute animal draw their force from the same emotions—"We're so powerful that we can wipe out the elephants, but let's keep some around for our own greater glory!" Here again, though, once some bit of ecological damage can no longer be fixed, everyone finds something else to talk about, because that data point doesn't feed the same fantasy.

Peak oil is unacceptable to the environmental establishment, in turn, because there's no way to spin it as a story of human omnipotence. If you understand what the peak oil narrative is saying, you realize that the power we human beings currently claim to have isn't actually ours; we simply stole the carbon the planet had stashed in its underground cookie jar and used it to go on a three-century-long joyride, which is almost over. The "narrative of scarcity" Mann denounced so heatedly is, after all, the simple reality of life on a finite planet. We had the leisure to pretend otherwise for a very brief interval, and now that interval is coming to an end. There's no melodrama in that, no opportunity for striking grand poses on which our own admiring gaze can rest, just the awkward reality of coming to terms with the fact that we've made many stupid decisions and now have to deal with the consequences thereof.

This is why the one alternative to saving the world that everyone in the mainstream environmental scene is willing to talk about is the prospect of imminent universal dieoff. Near-term human extinction, the apocalypse du jour ever since December 21, 2012 passed by without incident, takes its popularity from the same fantasy of omnipotence—if we human beings are the biggest and baddest thing in the cosmos, after all, what's the ultimate display of our power? Why, destroying ourselves, of course!

There's a bubbling cauldron of unspoken motives behind the widespread popularity of this delusion of omnipotence, but I suspect that a large part of it comes from an unsuspected source. The generations that came of age after the Second World War faced, from their earliest days, a profoundly unsettling experience that very few of their elders ever had, and then usually in adulthood. In place of comfortable religious narratives that placed the origin of the universe a short time in the past, and its end an even shorter time in the future, they grew up with what paleontologist Stephen Jay Gould usefully termed "deep time"—the vision of a past and a future on time scales the human mind has never evolved the capacity to grasp, in which all of human history is less than an eyeblink, and you and I, dear reader, no matter what we do, won't even merit the smallest of footnotes in the story of life on this planet.

Growing up on the heels of the baby boom, I experienced all this myself. I read the *Life* Nature Library about as soon as I could read anything at all; by age six or so I had my favorite dinosaurs, and a little later on succumbed to the beauty of trilobites and the vast slow dances of geology. By some blend of dumb luck and happenstance, though, I missed out on the sense of entitlement so pervasive among those born when the United States was at the zenith of its prosperity and power. The gospel of "you can have whatever you desire" that Barbara Ehrenreich anatomized so pitilessly in her book *Bright-Sided* found no answering chord in my psyche, and so it never bothered me in the least to think that a hundred million years from now, some intelligent critter of a species not yet spawned might gaze in delight at my fossilized skull, and rub its mandibles together to produce some equivalent of "Ooh, look at that!"

I'm far from the only one these days who sees the unhuman vastness of nature as something to celebrate, rather than something to fear and, at least in imagination, to try to overcome through overblown fantasies of human importance. Still, it's a minority view as yet, and to judge by the points made earlier in this essay, it seems underrepresented in the mainstream of today's environmental movement. The fixation on narratives that assign the sole active role to humanity and a purely passive role to nature is, I've come to think, a reaction to the collision between two potent cultural forces in contemporary life—the widely promulgated fantasy of infinite entitlement, on the one hand, and on the other, the dawning recognition of our species' really quite modest, and very sharply limited, place in the scheme of things.

The conflict between these factors is becoming increasingly hard to avoid, and drives increasingly erratic behaviors, as the years pass. The first and largest generation to follow the Second World War in the developed world is nearing the one limit that affects each of us most personally. Thus it's probably not an accident that 2030—the currently fashionable date by which humans are all supposed to be extinct—is right around the date when the average baby boomer's statistical lifespan will run out. To my mind, the attempt to avoid that face-first encounter with limits does a lot to explain why so many boomers bailed into evangelical Protestant fundamentalism in the 1980s, with its promise that Christ would show up any day now and spare them the necessity of dying. It explains equally well why the 2012 hysteria, which made similar claims, attracted so much wasted breath in its day—and why so few people these days are able to come to terms with the reality of scarcity, of limits, and of the end of the industrial age and all its wildly overblown fantasies of self-importance.

The friend of mine who was dying as I walked the Ocean City beach last weekend was born in 1949, in the midst of the baby boom, but somehow he managed to avoid those antics and the obsessions that drove them. As a Druid among other things—he was one of the very few people I've known well who received more initiations than I have—he understood that death is not the opposite of life but the completion of it. When he collapsed at work a few weeks ago and was rushed to the hospital, his friends and fellow initiates in the Puget Sound area took up a steady vigil at his bedside, and kept those of us out of the region informed. The appropriate ceremonies prepared him for his passing, and another set of ceremonies are helping the living cope with his departure.

A thousand years from now, in all probability, nobody will remember how Corby Ingold lived and died, any more than they will remember the 2015 annual sessions of the Maryland Grand Council of Royal and Select Masters, or this blog, or its author. A thousand years from now, for that matter, fossil fuels will be a dim memory at most, and so will the Greenland ice cap, the Florida peninsula, and a great deal more. It's just possible, though very unlikely, that human beings will be among those dim memories—we rank with cockroaches and rats among Nature's supreme generalists, and like them are remarkably hard to exterminate. Whether or not human beings are there to witness it, though, waves like the ones that rolled onto the beach at Ocean City will be rolling over the sunken ruins of Ocean City hotels, just as they rolled above the mudflats where trilobites scurried six hundred million years ago, and as they will roll onto whatever shores rise up when the continents we now inhabit have long since vanished for good.

The sea is patient. It has outlived countless species and will outlive countless more, ours among them. Among the things it might be able to teach us, on the off chance that we're willing to learn, is that the life of a species, like that of an individual, is completed by death, not erased by it, and that its value is measured by the beauty and wisdom it experiences and creates, not by the crasser measurements of brute force and brute endurance.

430: THE HERESY OF TECHNOLOGICAL CHOICE

(Originally published 18 November 2015)

One of the interesting benefits of writing a blog like this, focusing as it does on the end of industrial civilization, is the opportunities it routinely affords for a glimpse at the stranger side of the collective thinking of our time. The last few weeks have been an unusually good source of that experience, as a result of one detail of the Retrotopia narrative I've been developing in the posts here.

The detail in question is the system by which residents of my fictional Lakeland Republic choose how much infrastructure they want to have and, not incidentally, to pay for via their local tax revenues. It's done on a county-by-county basis by majority vote. The more infrastructure you want, the higher your taxes are; the more infrastructure you can do without, the less of your income goes to the county to pay for it. There are five levels, called tiers, and each one has a notional date connected to it: thus tier five has the notional date of 1950, and corresponds to the infrastructure you'd expect to find in a county in the Midwestern states of the US in that year: countywide electrical, telephone, water, and sewer service; roads and related infrastructure throughout the county capable of handling heavy automobile use; and mass transit—specifically, streetcars—in the towns.

The other tiers have less infrastructure, and correspondingly lower taxes. Tier four has a notional date of 1920, tier three of 1890, tier two of 1860, and tier one of 1830. In each case, the infrastructure you'd find in such a county is roughly what you'd find in a midwestern American county in that year. With tier one, your county infrastructure consists of dirt roads and that's about it. All the other functions of county government exist in tier one, tier five, and everything in between; there are courts, police, social welfare provisions for those who are unable to take care of themselves, and so forth—all the things you would expect to find in any midwestern county in the US at any point between 1830 and 1950. That's the tier system: one small detail of the imaginary future I've been sketching here.

Before we go on, I'd like my readers to stop and notice that the only things that are subject to the tier system are the elements of local infrastructure that are paid for by local tax revenues. If you live in a county that voted to adopt a certain tier level, that tells you what kind of infrastructure will be funded by local tax revenues, and therefore what the tax bills are going to be like. That's all it tells you. In particular, the tier system doesn't apply to privately owned infrastructure—for example, railroads in the Lakeland Republic are privately owned, and so every county, whatever its tier, has train stations in any town where paying passengers and freight may be found in sufficient quantity to make it worth a railroad's while to stop there.

The tier system also, and crucially, doesn't determine what kind of technology the residents can use. If you live in a tier one county, you can use all the electrical appliances you can afford to buy, as long as you generate the electricity yourself. Some technologies that are completely dependent on public infrastructure aren't going to work in a low tier county—for example, without paved roads, gas stations, huge government subsidies for petroleum production, military bases all over the Middle East, and a great deal more, cars aren't much more than oversized paperweights—but that's built into the technology in question, not any fault of the tier system. Furthermore, the tier system doesn't determine social customs and mores. If you live in a tier four county, for example, no law requires you to dress in a zoot suit or a flapper dress, drink bootleg liquor, and say things like "Hubba hubba" and "Twenty-three skidoo!" This may seem obvious, but trust me, it's apparently far from obvious to a certain portion of my readers.

I can say this because, ever since the tier system first got mentioned in the narrative, I've fielded a steady stream of comments from people who wanted to object to the tier system because it forcibly deprives people of access to technology. I had one reader insist that the tier system would keep farmers in tier one counties from using plastic sheeting for hoop houses, for example, and another who compared the system to the arrangements in former Eastern Bloc nations, where the Communist Party imposed rigid restrictions on what technologies people could have. The mere facts that plastic sheeting for hoop houses isn't infrastructure paid for by tax revenues, and that the tier system doesn't impose rigid restrictions on anybody — on the contrary, it allows the voters in each county to choose for themselves how much infrastructure they're going to pay for — somehow never found their way into the resulting diatribes.

What made all this even more fascinating to me is that no matter how often I addressed the points in question, and pointed out that the tier system just allows local voters to choose what infrastructure gets paid for their by tax money, a certain fraction of readers just kept rabbiting on endlessly along the same lines. It wasn't that they were disagreeing with what I was saying. It's that they were acting as though I had never said anything to address the subject at all, even when I addressed it to their faces, and nothing I or anyone else could say was able to break through their conviction that in imagining the tier system, I must be talking about some way to deprive people of technology by main force.

It was after the third or fourth round of comments along these lines, I think it was, that a sudden sense of deja vu reminded me that I'd seen this same sort of curiously detached paralogic before.

Longtime readers of this blog will remember how, some years ago, I pointed out in passing that the survival of the internet in the deindustrial age didn't depend on whether there was some technically feasible way to run an internet in times of energy and resource limits, much less on how neat we think the internet is today. Rather, I suggested, its survival in the future would depend on whether it could make enough money to cover its operating and maintenance costs, and on whether it could successfully keep on outcompeting less complex and expensive ways of providing the same services to its users. That post got a flurry of responses from the geekoisie, all of whom wanted to talk exclusively about whether there was some technically feasible way to run the internet in a deindustrial world, and oh, yes, how incredibly neat the internet supposedly is.

What's more, when I pointed out that they weren't discussing the issues I had raised, they didn't argue with me or try to make an opposing case. They just kept on talking more and more loudly about the technical feasibility of various gimmicks for a deindustrial internet, and by the way, did we mention yet how unbelievably neat the internet is? It was frankly rather weird, and I don't mean that in a good way. It felt at times as though I'd somehow managed to hit the off switch on a dozen or so intellects, leaving their empty husks to lurch mindlessly through a series of animatronic talking points with all the persistence and irrelevance of broken records.

It took a while for me to realize that the people who were engaged in this bizarre sort of nonresponse understood perfectly well what I was talking about. They knew at least as well as I did that the internet is the most gargantuan technostructure in the history of our species, a vast, sprawling, unimaginably costly, and hopelessly unsustainable energy- and resource-devouring behemoth that survives only because a significant fraction of the world's total economic activity goes directly and indirectly toward its upkeep. They knew about the slave-worked open pit mines, the vast grim factories run by sweatshop labor, and the countless belching smokestacks that feed its ravenous appetite for hardware and power; they also know about the constellations of data centers scattered across the world that keep it running, each of which uses as much energy as a small city, and each of which has to have one semi-truck after another pull up to the loading dock every single day to offload pallets of brand new hard drives and other hardware, in order to replace those that will burn out the next day.

They knew all this, and they knew, or at least suspected, just how little of it will be viable in a future of harsh energy and resource constraints. They simply didn't want to think about that, much less talk about it, and so they babbled endlessly about other things in a frantic attempt to drown out a subject they couldn't bear to hear discussed openly.

I'm pretty sure that this is what's going on in the present case, too, and an interesting set of news stories from earlier this year points up the unspoken logic behind it.

Port Townsend is a pleasant little town in Washington State, perched on a bluff above the western shores of Puget Sound. Due to the vagaries of the regional economy, it basically got bypassed by the twentieth century, and much of the housing stock dates from the Victorian era. It so happens that one couple who live there find Victorian technology, clothing, and personal habits more to their taste than the current fashions in these things, and they live, as thoroughly as they can, a Victorian lifestyle. The wife of the couple, Sarah Chrisman, recently wrote a book about her experiences, and got her canonical fifteen minutes of fame on the internet and the media as a result.

You might think, dear reader, that the people of Port Townsend would treat this as merely a harmless eccentricity, or even find it pleasantly amusing to have a couple in Victorian cycling clothes riding their penny-farthing bicycles on the city streets. To some extent, you'd be right, but it's the exceptions that I want to discuss here. Ever since they adopted their Victorian lifestyle, the Chrismans have been on the receiving end of constant harassment by people who find their presence in the community intolerable. The shouted insults, the in-your-face confrontations, the death threats — they've seen it all. What's more, the appearance of Sarah Chrisman's book and various online articles related to it fielded, in response, an impressive flurry of spluttering online denunciations, which insisted among other things that the fact that she prefers to wear long skirts and corsets somehow makes her personally responsible for all the sins that have ever been imputed to the Victorian era.

Why? Why the fury, the brutality, and the frankly irrational denunciations directed at a couple whose lifestyle choices have got to count well up there among the world's most harmless hobbies?

The reason's actually very simple. Sarah Chrisman and her husband have transgressed one of the modern world's most rigidly enforced taboos. They've shown in the most irrefutable way, by personal example, that the technologies each of us use in our own lives are a matter of individual choice.

You're not supposed to say that in today's world. You're not even supposed to think it. You're allowed, at most, to talk nostalgically about how much more pleasant it must have been not to be constantly harassed and annoyed by the current round of officially prescribed technologies, and squashed into the Procrustean bed of the narrow range of acceptable lifestyles that go with them. Even that's risky in many circles these days, and risks fielding a diatribe from somebody who just has to tell you, at great length and with obvious irritation, all about the horrible things you'd supposedly suffer if you didn't have the current round of officially prescribed technologies constantly harassing and annoying you.

The nostalgia in question doesn't have to be oriented toward the past. I long ago lost track of the number of people I've heard talk nostalgically about what I tend to call the Ecotopian future, the default vision of a green tomorrow that infests most minds on the leftward end of things. Unless you've been hiding under a rock for the last forty years, you already know every detail of the Ecotopian future. It's the place where wind turbines and solar panels power everything, everyone commutes by bicycle from their earth-sheltered suburban homes to their LEED-certified urban workplaces, everything is recycled, and social problems have all been solved because everybody, without exception, has come to embrace the ideas and attitudes currently found among upper-middle-class San Francisco liberals.

It's far from rare, at sustainability-oriented events, to hear well-to-do attendees waxing rhapsodically about how great life will be when the Ecotopian future arrives. If you encounter someone engaging in that sort of nostalgic exercise, and are minded to be cruel, ask the person who's doing it whether he (it's usually a man) bicycles to work, and if not, why not. Odds are you'll get to hear any number of frantic excuses to explain why the lifestyle that everyone's going to love in the Ecotopian future is one that he can't possibly embrace today. If you want a look behind the excuses and evasions, ask him how he got to the sustainability-oriented event you're attending. Odds are that he drove his SUV, in which there were no other passengers, and if you press him about that you can expect to see the dark heart of privilege and rage that underlies his enthusiastic praise of an imaginary lifestyle that he would never, not even for a moment, dream of adopting himself.

I wish I were joking about the rage. It so happens that I don't have a car, a television, or a cell phone, and I have zero interest in ever having any of these things. My defection from the officially prescribed technologies and the lifestyles that go with them isn't as immediately obvious as Sarah Chrisman's, so I don't take as much day to day harassment as she does. Still, it happens from time to time that somebody wants to know if I've seen this or that television program, and in the conversations that unfold from such questions it sometimes comes out that I don't have a television at all.

Where I now live, in an old red brick mill town in the north central Appalachians, that revelation rarely gets a hostile response, and it's fairly common for someone else to say, "Good for you," or something like that. A lot of people here are very poor, and thus have a certain detachment from technologies and lifestyles they know perfectly well they will never be able to afford. Back when I lived in prosperous Left Coast towns, on the other hand, mentioning that I didn't own a television routinely meant that I'd get to hear a long and patronizing disquisition about how I really ought to run out and buy a TV so I could watch this or that or the other really really wonderful program, in the absence of which my life must be intolerably barren and incomplete.

Any lack of enthusiasm for that sort of disquisition very reliably brought out a variety of furiously angry responses that had precisely nothing to do with the issue at hand, which is that I simply don't enjoy the activity of watching television. Oh, and it's not the programming I find unenjoyable — it's the technology itself; I get bored very quickly with the process of watching little colored images jerking about on a glass screen, no matter what the images happen to be. That's another taboo, by the way. It's acceptable in today's America to grumble about what's on television, but the technology itself is sacrosanct; you're not allowed to criticize it, much less to talk about the biases, agendas, and simple annoyances hardwired into television as a technological system. If you try to bring any of that up, people will insist that you're criticizing the programming; if you correct them, they'll ignore the correction and keep on talking as though the programs on TV are the only thing under discussion.

A similar issue drives the bizarre paralogic surrounding the nonresponses to the tier system discussed above. The core premises behind the tier system in my narrative are, first, that people can choose the technological infrastructure they have, and have to pay for; and second, that some of them, when they consider the costs and benefits involved, might reasonably decide that an infrastructure of dirt roads and a landscape of self-sufficient farms and small towns is the best option. To a great many people today, that's heresy of the most unthinkable sort. The easiest way to deal with the heresy in question, for those who aren't interested in thinking about it, is to pretend that nothing so shocking has been suggested at all, and force the discussion into some less threatening form as quickly as possible. Redefining it in ways that erase the unbearable idea that technologies can be chosen freely, and just as freely rejected, is quite probably the easiest way to do that.

I'd encourage those of my readers who aren't blinded by the terror of intellectual heresy to think, and think hard, about the taboo against technological choice—the insistence that you cannot, may not, and must not make your own choices when it comes to whatever the latest technological fad happens to be, but must do as you're told and accept whatever technology the consumer society hands you, no matter how dysfunctional, harmful, or boring it turns out to be. That taboo is very deeply ingrained, far more potent than the handful of relatively weak taboos our society still applies to such things as sexuality, and most of the people you know obey it so unthinkingly that they never even notice how it shapes their behavior. You may not notice how it shapes your behavior, for that matter; the best way to find out is to pick a technology that annoys, harms, or bores you, but that you use anyway, and get rid of it.

Those who take that unthinkable step, and embrace the heresy of technological choice, are part of the wave of the future. In a world of declining resource availability, unraveling economic systems, and destabilizing environments, Sarah Chrisman and the many other people who make similar choices—there are quite a few of them these days, and more of them with each year that passes—are making a wise choice. By taking up technologies and lifeways from less extravagant eras, they're decreasing their environmental footprints and their vulnerability to faltering global technostructures, and they're also contributing to one of the crucial tasks of our age: the rediscovery of ways of being human that don't depend on hopelessly unsustainable levels of resource and energy consumption.

The heresy of technological choice is a door. Beyond it lies an unexplored landscape of possibilities for the future—possibilities that very few people have even begun to imagine yet. My Retrotopia narrative is meant to glance over a very small part of that landscape. If some of the terrain it's examined so far has been threatening enough to send some of its readers fleeing into a familiar sort of paralogic, then I'm confident that it's doing the job I hoped it would do.

431: THE SHADOWS IN THE CAVE

(originally published 25 November 2015)

I had intended this week's post to be the next episode in the Retrotopia narrative, chronicling Peter Carr's meeting with the irrepressible Col. Tom Pappas of the Lakeland Republic Army, and the trip out to Defiance County for the annual drone shoot, but that will have to wait another week. No, I haven't decided to comment instead on the recent spate of terror attacks in France. As people in a variety of other corners of the world have pointed out, identical outrages happen all over the Third World every few days. The only reason this latest horror has gotten so much air time is that it affected people in one of the world's privileged countries instead.

Nor am I going to be devoting this week's post to the latest, extremely troubling round of news from the climate change front—though that's going to get a post to itself down the road a bit, when I've had time to do a little more research. That's a far bigger story than the terror attacks in Paris, though of course it's not getting anything like as much attention in the media. From the beginning of serious salt water infiltration into South Florida's aquifers, through ominously bulging sediments in Arctic Ocean shallows, to an assortment of truly frightening data points from Greenland, it's clear that we've passed the threshold from "something may happen someday" to "something is happening now"—a transition that probably has quite a bit to do with the increasingly shrill tone of climate-change denialist rhetoric just now, and even more to do with the increasingly plaintive tone of those activists who still insist that everything can be fixed if we all just join hands and sing "Kum ba ya" one more time.

No, this week's post is going to explore a topic that's far less important in the overall scheme of things, though it's not without its relevance to the crisis of our age. I want to talk about the reaction I fielded in response to last week's post here on *The Archdruid Report*, which was an exploration of our culture's taboo against choosing not to use the latest technologies.

I expected that post to field its share of outraged denunciations, and it certainly did. What I didn't expect was that it would receive more comments than any other post in the history of *The Archdruid Report*, and the vast majority of those comments would agree heartily with the two points of that post. The first of these points is that there's a significant number of Americans out there who, for one good reason or another, choose not to use cell phones, televisions, automobiles, microwave ovens, and an assortment of other currently fashionable technologies. The second is that there's an even larger number of Americans out there who get really, really freaky about people who make such choices.

Some of the stories I heard from readers of my blog were absolute classics of the type. There was the couple who don't enjoy television and so don't own one, and had a relative ask them every single year, over and over again, if she could buy them a television for Christmas. They said no thank you every single year, and finally she went out and bought them a television anyway because she just couldn't stand the thought that they weren't watching one. There was the coworker who plopped a laptop playing some sitcom or other right down on the lap of one of my readers and demanded that the reader watch it, right then and there, so that they would have something to talk about. There was the person who, offended by another reader's lack of interest in television, finally shouted, "You must be living in a dream world!" Er, which of these people was spending four to six hours a day watching paid actors playing imaginary characters act out fictional events in contrived settings?

Televisions were far from the only focus of this sort of technobullying. Other readers reported getting similar reactions from other people because they didn't happen to have, and weren't interested in having, microwave ovens, smartphones, and so on down the list of currently fashionable trinkets. The stories are really quite eye-opening, and not in a good way. Forget about all the popular cant that insists that you're free in the USA to make your own choices and have whatever lifestyle you want. According to a significant fraction of Americans — and to judge from what my readers reported, that fraction isn't limited to any one class, income level, or region of the country — the only freedom you're supposed to exercise, when it comes to technology, is that of choosing which brand label will be slapped on each item in the officially approved list of devices you're expected to own.

The prevalence of technobullying and technoshaming in today's America is a fascinating point, and one we'll explore in a few moments, with the able assistance of the denunciations flung at last week's post by the minority of readers who reacted that way. What I want to consider first is the fact that so many people responded to last week's post so positively. One blog in an uncrowded corner of the internet, written by an author whose day job as an archdruid locates him squarely on the outer fringes of contemporary American life, is very nearly the opposite of a statistically valid poll. Still, the sheer volume of the response makes me suspect that something significant is going on here.

By that I don't mean that there's some sort of groundswell of renunciation, leading people to walk away from technologies in the same spirit that led medieval ascetics to don hair shirts and flog themselves for the good of their souls. That's one of the common stereotypes directed at those of us who aren't interested in the latest technotrash, and it completely misses what's actually going on. I'll use myself as an example here. I don't own a television — I haven't owned one in my adult life — and it's not because I have some moral or political objection to televisions, or because I'm into self-denial, or what have you. I don't own a television because I find watching television about as enticing as eating a bowl of warm snot.

It's not the programming, either — that's another of the standard stereotypes, that the only thing one can find objectionable about television is the programming, and it's as inaccurate as the rest. To me, quite simply, the activity of watching little colored shapes jerk around on a screen is boring and irritating, not relaxing and enjoyable, no matter what the little colored shapes are supposed to be doing. Yes, I grew up with a television in the house. I experienced plenty of it back in the day, and I have zero interest in experiencing any more, because I don't like it. It really is that simple. It's that simple for others as well: they don't find this or that technology enjoyable, useful, or relevant to their lifestyles, and so they've chosen to do something else with their money and time.

Shouldn't so simple and personal a choice be their own business, and nobody else's?

To judge by the reactions that those who make such choices routinely field, apparently not. The pushbacks discussed in the comments page last week range from the sort of in-your-face confrontations discussed above to a much-forwarded article in I forget which online rag, where somebody was airily announcing that he wasn't interested in being friends with somebody unless he could text some vacuous comment about lunch to the other person at 2:15 and get a response by 2:30. (My readers and I are good with that—somebody who insists on getting immediate feedback for their random outbursts of mental flatulence isn't somebody we want as a friend, either.) Then there were the indignant responses to last week's post, which belong in a category by themselves.

I'm sorry to say that my favorite diatribe didn't show up in the comment queue for *The Archdruid Report*. It appeared instead on one of the many other websites that carry my weekly posts, and it insisted, among several other less juicy bits, that my lack of enthusiasm for television obviously meant that I was conspiring to deprive everyone else of their teevees. You've got to admit that for sheer giddy delirium, that one's hard to beat. By the same logic, if I dislike peanuts—as in fact I do—I must be committed to some kind of anti-peanut crusade devoted to eradicating the entire species. Not so; *Arachis hypogaea* is welcome to live and thrive, for all I care, and my fellow hominids are equally welcome to eat as much of its produce as they happen to desire. In fact, they can divide my share among them. The only thing I ask in return is that nobody expect me to eat the things myself.

The same rule applies equally to television, as it does to a great many other things. Like most human beings, I enjoy some things and don't enjoy others, and in the vast majority of these cases, nobody feels particularly threatened by the fact that I don't like something they do, and avoid it for that sensible reason. For this one commenter, at least, that obviously wasn't the case, and it's worth reflecting on the vast personal insecurities that must have driven such a bizarre reaction. Still, that was one of a kind, so we'll pass on to the others.

A theme that showed up rather more often in the hate mail responding to last week's post was the insistence that if I don't have a television, a microwave, or a cell phone, I'm a hypocrite if I have an internet connection. I encourage my readers to think about that claim for a moment. I suppose a case could be made that if my lack of interest in having a television, a microwave, or a cell phone was motivated by the kind of passion for hair-shirt asceticism mentioned above, and I had an internet connection, I could be accused of the kind of slacking that used to get you thrown out of the really top-notch hermitages. From any other perspective, it's a triumph of absurdity. If people are in fact allowed to choose, from among the currently available technologies, those that make them happiest—as the cheerleaders of the consumer economy delight to insist—what could possibly be wrong with choosing some old technologies and some newer ones, if that's the mix you prefer?

Then there are the people whose response to the technology of an older time is to yammer endlessly about whatever bad things happened in those days, even when the bad things in question had nothing to do with the technology and vice versa. People like the couple I discussed in last week's post, who prefer Victorian furnishings and clothing to their modern equivalents, get this sort of bizarre non sequitur all the time, but variants of it turned up in my inbox last week as well. Here again, there's some heavy-duty illogic involved. If a technology that was invented and used in the 1850s, say, is permanently tarred with the various social evils of that era, and ought to be rejected because those evils happened, wouldn't that also mean that the internet is just as indelibly tarred with the social evils of the modern era, and ought to be discarded because bad things are happening in the world today? What's sauce for the goose, after all, is sauce for the gander...

Finally, there's the capstone of the whole edifice of unreason, the insistence that anybody who doesn't use the latest, hottest technotrash wants to go "back to the caves," or to even take all of humanity to that much-denounced destination. "The caves" have a bizarre gravitational effect on the imagination of a certain class of modern thinkers. Everything that's not part of the latest assortment of glitzy technogimmicks, in their minds, somehow morphs into the bearskin kilts and wooden clubs that so many of us still, despite well over a century of detailed archeological evidence, insist on pushing onto our prehistoric ancestors.

When people of this kind archly dismiss people like the Chrismans, the neo-Victorian couple just mentioned, as going "back to the caves," they're engaged in a very interesting kind of absurdity.

Do cavemen and Victorians belong on the same level? Sure, cavemen had flush toilets and central heating, daily newspapers and public libraries, not to mention factories, railways, global maritime trade, a telegraph network covering much of the planet's land surface, and a great deal more of the same kind! That's absurd, of course. It's even more absurd to insist that people who simply don't enjoy using this or that technology, and so don't use it, are going back to "the caves"—but I can promise you, dear reader, from my own personal experience, that if you show a lack of interest in any piece of fashionable technology, you'll have this phrase thrown at you.

That happens because "the caves" aren't real. They aren't, for example, the actual cave-shrines of the Magdalenian people who lived fifteen thousand years ago, whose lifestyles were quite similar to those of Native Americans before Columbus, and who used to go deep into the caves of Europe to paint sacred images that still stun the viewer today by their beauty and artistry. "The caves" of contemporary rhetoric, rather, are thoughtstopping abstractions, bits of verbal noise that people have been taught to use so they don't ask inconvenient questions about where this thing called "progress" is taking us and whether any sane person would actually want to go there. Flattening out the entire complex richness of the human past into a single cardboard bogeyman labeled "the caves" is one way to do that. So is papering over the distinctly ugly future we're making for ourselves with a screen shot or two from a Jetsons cartoon and a gaudy banner saying "We're headed for the stars!"

It's really rather fascinating, all things considered, that the image of the cave should have been picked up for that dubious purpose. Not that long ago, most literate people in the Western world tended to have a very different image come to mind when someone mentioned caves. That was courtesy of a man named Aristocles of Athens, who lived a little more than 2300 years ago and whose very broad shoulders got him the nickname Plato. In the longest, most influential, and most problematic of his works, usually called *The Republic*—a bad choice, as this word nowadays has connotations of rights under law that the Greek title *Politeia* lacks—he framed his discussion of the gap between perception and reality with an arresting image.

Imagine, Plato says, that we are all shackled in a cave, unable to turn our heads to either side. All we can see are dark shapes that move this way and that on the flat wall of the cave in front of us. Those dark shapes are all we know. They are our reality.

Now imagine that one of these prisoners manages to get loose from his shackles, and turns away from the cave wall and the dark shapes on it. He's in for a shock, because what he sees when he turns around is a bonfire, and people moving objects in front of the flames so that the objects cast shadows on the cave wall. Everything he thought was reality is simply a shadow cast by these moving objects.

If the prisoner who's gotten loose pays attention, furthermore, he might just notice that the cave isn't limited to the bonfire, the prisoners, the objects casting the shadows and the people who manipulate those objects. Off past the bonfire, on one side of the cave, the floor slopes upwards, and in the distance is a faint light that doesn't seem to come from the fire at all. If our escaped prisoner is brave enough, he might decide to go investigate that light. As he does so, the bonfire and the shadows slip into the darkness behind him, and the light ahead grows brighter and clearer.

Then, if he's brave enough and keeps going, he steps out of the cave and into the sunlight. That's not an easy thing, either, because the light is so much more intense than the dim red glow in the cave that for a while, he can't see a thing. He stumbles, rubs his eyes, tries to find his bearings, and discovers that the detailed knowledge he had of the way shadows moved on the cave wall won't help him at all in this new, blazingly bright realm. He has to discard everything he thinks he knows, and learn the rules of an unfamiliar world.

Bit by bit, though, he accomplishes this. His eyes adapt to the sunlight, he learns to recognize objects and to sense things—color, for example, and depth—which didn't exist in the shadow-world he thought he inhabited when he was still a prisoner in the cave. Eventually he can even see the sun, and know where the light that illumines the real world actually comes from.

Now, Plato says, imagine that he decides to go back into the cave to tell the remaining prisoners what he's seen. To begin with, it's going to be rough going, because his eyes have adapted to the brilliant daylight and so he's going to trip and stumble on the way down. Once he gets there, anything he says to the prisoners is going to be dismissed as the most consummate rubbish: what is this nonsense about color and depth, and a big bright glowing thing that crosses something called the sky? What's more, the people to whom he's addressing his words are going to misunderstand them, thinking that they're about the shadow-world in front of their eyes — after all, that's the only reality they know — and they're going to decide that he must be an idiot because nothing he says has anything to do with the shadow-world.

Plato didn't mention that the prisoners might respond by trying to drag the escapee back into line with them and bully him into putting his shackles back on, though that's generally the way such things work out in practice. Plato also never saw a television, which is unfortunate in a way — if he had, he could have skipped the complicated setup with the bonfire and the people waving around objects that cast shadows, and simply said, "Imagine that we're all watching television in a dark room."

Now of course Plato had his own reasons for using the cave metaphor, and developed it in directions that aren't relevant to this week's post. The point I want to make here is that every technology is a filter that shapes the way we experience and interact with the world. In some cases, such as television, the filtering effect is so drastic it's hard not to see — unless, that is, you don't want to see it. In other cases, it's subtle. There are valid reasons people might want to use one filter rather than another, or to set aside an assortment of filters in order to get a clearer view of some part of the world or their lives.

There are also, as already noted, matters of personal choice. Some of us prefer sun and wind and depth and color to the play of shadows on the walls of the cave. That doesn't mean that we're going to drag those who don't share that preference out into the blinding light, or that we're going to turn ourselves into the Throg the Cave Man shadow that's being waved around so enthusiastically on one corner of the cave wall. It does mean — or so the response to last week's post suggests — that a significant number of people are losing interest in the shadow-play and clambering up the awkward but rewarding journey into the sunlight and the clean cool air, and it may just mean as well that those who try to bully them into staying put and staring at shadows may have less success than they expect.

432: THE FLUTTER OF SPACE BAT WINGS

(Originally published 9 December 2015)

You don't actually know a time or a culture until you discover the thoughts that its people can't allow themselves to think. I had a reminder of that the other day, by way of my novel *Star's Reach*.

I'm pleased to say that for a novel that violates pretty much every imaginable pop-culture cliché about the future, *Star's Reach* has been selling quite well—enough so that the publisher has brought out two more SF novels set in deindustrial futures, and is looking for other manuscripts along the same lines. What's more, *Star's Reach* has also started to inspire spinoffs and adaptations: a graphic novel is in the works, so is a roleplaying game, and so is an anthology of short stories by other authors set in the world sketched out in my novel. All of this came as a welcome surprise to me; far more surprising, though ultimately rather less welcome, was an ebullient email I received asking whether Star's Reach was available to be optioned for a television miniseries.

For a variety of reasons, some of which will become clear as we proceed, I'll call the person who got in touch with me Buck Rogers. He praised *Star's Reach* to the skies, and went on at length about wanting to do something that was utterly faithful to the book. As I think most of my readers know by now, I haven't owned a television in my adult life and have zero interest in changing that, even to see one of my own stories on the screen. I could readily see that people who like television might find a video adaptation entertaining, though, and no doubt it would make a welcome change from the endless rehash of overfamiliar tropes about the future that fills so much of science fiction these days.

Ah, but then came the inevitable email explaining exactly what kind of adaptation Buck Rogers had in mind. It was going to be more than just a miniseries, he explained. It was going to be a regular series, the events of my novel were going to provide the plot for the first year, and after that—why, after that, he was promptly going to drag in one of the currently popular bits of hypertechnological handwaving so the characters in my story could go zooming off to the stars. Whee!

Those of my readers who haven't turned the pages of *Star's Reach* may welcome a bit of explanation here. The core theme of *Star's Reach*—the mainspring that powers the plot—is precisely that humanity isn't going to the stars; the contrast between the grandiose gizmocentric fantasies of today's industrial world and the grubby realities of life in 25th-century Meriga frames and guides the entire novel. An adaptation of *Star's Reach* that removes that little detail and replaces it with yet another rehash of the interstellar-travel trope is thus a bit like an adaptation of Tolkien's *The Lord of the Rings* in which the hobbits enthusiastically sell out to the powers of evil and Sauron wins.

I communicated this to Buck Rogers, and got back a lengthy response of the take-my-ball-and-go-home variety, saying in a hurt tone that I was wrong and just didn't understand how his proposal fit perfectly with my story. I sent him a polite note wishing him luck in his future projects, and that was that. All in all, I think the situation turned out for the best. I'm not particularly desperate for money—certainly not desperate enough to be willing to see one of my favorite books gutted, stuffed, and mounted on the nose cone of an imaginary starship—and this way I still have the movie and TV rights, on the off chance that somebody ever wants to film the story I wrote, rather than a parody of it.

It was only after I'd clicked the "send" button on the short polite note just mentioned that I realized that there was something really quite strange about Buck Rogers' final email. He had taken issue at rather some length with almost everything I'd said while trying to explain to him why his proposal wasn't one I could accept, with one exception. It wasn't a small exception, either. It was the core issue I'd raised at quite some length: that he'd taken a story about what happens when humanity can't go to the stars, and tried to turn it into a story about humanity going to the stars.

I don't think that absence was any kind of accident, either. You don't actually know a time or a culture until you discover the thoughts that its people can't allow themselves to think.

This wasn't the only time *Star's Reach* had attracted that same sort of doublethink, for that matter. Back when it was being written and posted online an episode at a time, I could count nearly every month on hearing from people who enthused about how wonderful the story was, and in the next breath tried to push me into inserting some pop-culture cliché about what the future is supposed to look like. Far more often than not, the point of the insertion was to show that "progress" was still on track and would eventually lead to a more "advanced" society—that is, a society like ours. When I explained that the story is about what happens when "progress," in the sense that word has today, is over forever, and our kind of society is a fading memory of the troubled past, they simply insisted all the louder that the changes they wanted me to make were perfectly consistent with my story.

Regular readers may also recall the discussion a few weeks back of the way so many people's brains seem to freeze up when faced with the idea that others might choose not to use the latest technology, and might instead keep using older technologies they like better. Further back in this blog's trajectory, three or four other topics—most notably the prospects for the survival of the internet in a deindustrializing world—reliably triggered the same odd behavior pattern, an obsessive evasion of the point accompanied by the weirdly stereotyped repetition of some set of canned talking points.

It's fascinating, at least to me, that so many topics relevant to this blog seem to function as a kind of elephant's graveyard of the mind, a place where thinking goes to die. That said, among all the things that trigger a mental Blue Screen of Death in a portion of my readers, challenging the frankly rather bizarre notion that humanity's destiny centers on interstellar travel stands at least a little apart, in the sheer intensity of the emotional reactions it rouses. If I try to call attention to the other evasions on the list, I get a blank look or, at most, an irritated one, followed by an instant return to the evasions. On the subject of interstellar travel, by contrast, I get instant pushback: "No, no, no, there's got to be some grandiose technofetishistic *deus ex machina* that will let us go to the STARZ!!!"

The question in my mind is why this particular bit of overly rehashed science fiction has gotten so tight a hold on the collective imagination of our age.

I suppose a case can be made that its ascendancy in science

fiction was inevitable. SF in its pulp days found its main audience among teenage boys, after all, and thus it makes sense that the genre would fixate on the imagery of climbing aboard a giant metal penis to be squirted into the gaping void of space. Even so, plenty of other images that were just as appealing to the adolescent male imagination, and just as popular in the early days of the genre, somehow got recognized as hackneyed tropes along the route that led from the pulp magazines of the 1920s and 1930s to the paperback SF novels of today, while interstellar travel has so far evaded that fate.

By the time I first started writing science fiction, for example, everyone had more or less noticed that traveling to an exotic future by way of suspended animation, or the couple of other standard gimmicks, had been done to death decades before, and deserved a rest. Somehow, though, very few people noticed that traveling to an exotic planet by way of one of the three or four standard gimmicks for interstellar travel had been overused just as thoroughly by that time, if not more so, and deserved at least as much of a break—and of course it's gotten even more of a workout since then.

It's reached the point, in fact, that you basically have your choice between two and only two futures in much of today's science fiction: you can have interplanetary travel or apocalyptic collapse, take your pick. No other futures need apply—and of course the same thing is true to an embarrassing extent even when people think they're talking about the actual future. So taut a fixation clearly has something to communicate. I think I've figured out part of what it's trying to say, with the help of one of the authors who helped make science fiction what it was in the days before the Space Patrol took over exclusive management of the genre. Yes, that would be the inimitable H.P. Lovecraft.

Few people nowadays think of Lovecraft as a science fiction writer at all. This strikes me as a major lapse, and not just because the man wrote some classic gizmocentric stories and made the theme of alien contact a major concern of his fiction. He was unique among the authors of imaginative fiction in his generation in tackling the most challenging of all the discoveries of twentieth century science—the sheer scale, in space and time, of the universe in which human beings find themselves.

Paleontologist Stephen Jay Gould coined the term "deep time" for the immensities of past and future that reduce our familiar human timescales to pipsqueak proportions. It's a useful coinage, and might well be paired with the phrase "deep space," meaning the spatial vastness that does the same trick to our human sense of distance. Lovecraft understood deep time and deep space to an extent few of his contemporaries shared—an extent that allowed him to take firm grasp of the yawning chasm between our species' sense of self-importance and its actual place in the cosmos.

If the view of the universe revealed to us by modern science is even approximately accurate—and, like Lovecraft, I personally have no doubt of this—then the entire history of our species, from its emergence sometime in the Pleistocene to its extinction at some as yet undetermined point in the future, is a brief incident on the wet film that covers the surface of a small planet circling an undistinguished star over to one side of an ordinary galaxy. Is it important, that brief incident? To us, surely—but only to us. In Lovecraft's words, we are "faced by the black, unfathomable gulph of the Outside, with its forever-unexplorable orbs & its virtually certain sprinkling of utterly unknowable life-forms." Notice the adjectives here: unfathomable, unexplorable, unknowable. What he's saying here, and throughout his fiction as well, is plain: the cosmos is not there for our benefit.

That's precisely the realization that so much of today's science fiction is frantically trying not to get. The same sort of thinking that led ancient cultures to see bears, queens, and hunting dogs in the inkblot patterns of the skies has been put to hard work in the attempt to reimagine the cosmos as "New Worlds For Man," a bona fide wonderland of real estate just waiting for our starships to show up and claim it. It's not just ordinary acquisitiveness that drives this, though no doubt that plays a part; the core of it is the desperate desire to reduce the cosmos, even in imagination, to a human scale.

The same kind of logic drives the fatuous claims that humanity will be around to watch the sun die, or what have you. We won't. If we get lucky, not to mention a good deal smarter than we've shown any sign of being so far, we might make it a few tens of millions of years (that is, five or ten thousand times the length of all recorded history) before our own mistakes or the ordinary crises of planetary history push us through extinction's one-way turnstile. For all we know, other intelligent species may arise on this planet long after we're gone, and pore over our fossilized bones, before they depart in turn. "Nor is it to be thought" — this is Lovecraft again, quoting his fictional *Necronomicon* — "that man is either the oldest or the last of earth's masters." Spooky, isn't it? Now ask yourself this: why is it spooky?

The modern attempt to impose a human scale on the utterly un-human vastness of the cosmos is actually something of an anoma-ly in terms of human cultures. If the ancient Greeks, for example, had gotten to telescopes and stratigraphy first, and figured out the actual immensity of space and time, that discovery wouldn't have bothered them at all. Ancient Greek religion takes it as given that human beings simply aren't that important in the scheme of things; turn the pages of Hesiod, to drop only one famous name, and you'll find a clear sense of the sharply limited place humanity has in the cosmos, and a calm acceptance of the eventual certainty of human extinction.

It's one of history's most savage ironies that the scientific dis-coveries that revealed the insignificance of humanity were made by societies whose religious ideas are all but unique in assigning tremendous cosmic importance to our species. Most versions of traditional Christian teaching place humanity at the center of the cosmic story: the world was made for our benefit, God himself became a human being and died to save us, and as soon as the drama of human salvation is over, the world will end. Of all the world's religions, Christianity has historically been the most re-lentlessly anthropocentric — it can be understood in less obsessive-ly human-centered terms, but by and large, it hasn't been — and it was societies steeped in Christian ideas that first found themselves staring in horror at a cosmos in which anthropocentric ideas are all too clearly the last word in absurdity.

I've discussed at some length in my recent book *After Progress* how belief in progress was turned into a surrogate religion by peo-ple who found that they could no longer believe in Christian doc-trines but still had the emotional needs that had once been met by Christian faith. The inability to tolerate doubts concerning "Man's Destiny In The Stars" unfolds from the same conflict. Raised in a culture that's still profoundly shaped by Christian attitudes, taught to think of the cosmos in anthropocentric terms, people in the United States today crash facefirst into the universe revealed by science, and cognitive dissonance is the inevitable result. No wonder so many of us are basically gaga these days.

Such reflections lead out toward any number of big questions. Just at the moment, though, I want to focus on something on a slightly less cosmic scale. Regular readers will remember a while back, at the conclusion of the last Space Bats challenge, that I wished aloud that someone would launch a quarterly magazine to publish the torrent of good stories set in deindustrial futures that people were clearly eager to write. I'm pleased to say that the publication fairy was apparently listening, and I'm therefore delighted to announce the launch of a new quarterly magazine of deindustrial science fiction, *Into The Ruins*, which is now accepting submissions for its inaugural issue. Given the frankly astonishing quality of the stories submitted to the three Space Bats challenges we've had so far, I suspect that *Into The Ruins* is going to become one of those "must read" magazines that, like *Weird Tales* in the 1920s and 1930s, defines a genre and launches the careers of any number of major writers. This is a paying market, folks; let your writer friends know.

With that in place, we can start pushing the boundaries even further.

One criticism that's been directed at past Space Bats challenges, and at the three published *After Oil* anthologies that have come out of them so far (the fourth will be published early in the new year), is that collapse has become a cliché in contemporary science fiction and culture. Mind you, a lot of those who make this criticism are in the unenviable position of the pot discussing the color of the kettle—I'm thinking here especially of SF writer and prolific blogger David Brin, whose novels fixate on the even more spectacularly overworked trope of salvation through technological progress, with space travel playing its usual hackneyed part—but there's a point to the critique.

Mind you, I still think that the decline and fall of industrial civilization and the coming of a deindustrial dark age is far and away the most likely future we face. Day after day, year after year, decade after decade, the opportunities that might have gotten us out of that unwelcome future have slipped past, and the same mistakes that have been made by every other civilization on its way down have been made by ours. What's more, there are still plenty of good stories waiting to be written about how industrial society ran itself into the ground and what happened then—it's the apocalyptic end of the spectrum of possibilities that's been written into the ground at this point, while the kind of ragged decline that usually happens in real history has barely been tapped as a source of stories. That said, since we're talking about imaginative fiction, maybe it's worth, for once, stepping entirely outside the binary of progress versus collapse, and seeing what the landscape looks like from a third option.

Yes, the sound that you're hearing is the flutter of space bat wings. It's time for a new challenge, and this one is going to take a leap into the unthinkable.

The mechanics are the same as in previous challenges. Write your story and post it to the internet—if you don't have a blog, you can get one for free from Blogspot or Wordpress. Post a link to it in the comments section of this blog, preferably in the comments to whatever the latest post is, so everyone sees it. Stories are due by the last day of June, 2016—fans of Al Stewart are welcome to insert the appropriate joke here.

The rules of the contest are almost the same as before:

Stories should be between 2500 and 8500 words in length;

They should be entirely the work of their author or authors, and should not borrow characters or setting from someone else's work;

They should be in English, with correct spelling, grammar and punctuation;

They should be stories—narratives with a plot and characters—and not simply a guided tour of some corner of the future as the author imagines it;

They should be set in our future, not in an alternate history or on some other planet;

They should be works of realistic fiction or science fiction, not magical or supernatural fantasy—that is, the setting and story should follow the laws of nature as those are presently understood;

They should take into account the reality of limits to growth, finite supplies of nonrenewable resources, and the other hard realities of our species' current predicament;

They should not include space travel—again, that's been rehashed enough by now;

They should not rely on "alien space bats" to solve humanity's problems—miraculous technological discoveries, the timely arrival of advanced alien civilizations, sudden lurches in consciousness that make everyone in the world start acting like characters in a bad utopian novel, or what have you;

And they must be set in futures in which neither continued technological progress nor the collapse of civilization take place.

I probably need to explain this last point in more detail. Through most of human history, progress was a very occasional thing, and most people could expect to use the same tools, do the same work, and live in the same conditions as their great-grandparents. The last three centuries changed that for a while, but that change was a temporary condition driven by the reckless exploitation of a half billion years of fossil sunlight. Now that the earth's cookie jar of carbon is running short, to say nothing of all the other essential resources that are rapidly depleting, the conditions that made that burst of progress possible are ending, and it's reasonable to assume that progress as we know it will end as well.

Does that mean that nothing new will ever be invented again? Of course not. It does mean the end of the relentless drive toward ever more extravagant uses of energy and resources that characterizes our current notions of progress. Future inventions will by and large use fewer resources and less energy than the things they replace, as was generally the case in the preindustrial past, and the pace of invention and technological obsolescence will decline very sharply from its present level. Authors who want to put interesting technologies into their stories are entirely welcome to do so—but don't make the story about the onward march of gizmocentricity, please. That's been done to death, and it's boring.

In the same way, history is full of crises. Major wars come every few generations, nations collapse from time to time, whole civilizations decline and fall when they've exhausted their resource bases. All these things will happen in the future as they happened in the past, and it's perfectly okay to put crises large or small into your stories. What I'm asking is that this time, your stories should not center on the process of collapse. Mind you, quite a few of the stories in the first three anthologies didn't have that focus, and the fourth anthology—consisting of stories set at least a thousand years in the future—is entirely about other themes, so I don't think this one will be too difficult.

Neither progress nor collapse. That opens up a very wide and almost unexplored territory. What does the future look like if those overfamiliar options are removed from the equation? Give it a try.

433: TOO LITTLE, TOO LATE

(Originally published 23 December 2015)

Last week, after a great deal of debate, the passengers aboard the *Titanic* voted to impose modest limits sometime soon on the rate at which water is pouring into the doomed ship's hull. Despite the torrents of self-congratulatory rhetoric currently flooding into the media from the White House and an assortment of groups on the domesticated end of the environmental movement, that's the sum of what happened at the COP-21 conference in Paris. It's a spectacle worth observing, and not only for those of us who are connoisseurs of irony; the factors that drove COP-21 to the latest round of nonsolutions are among the most potent forces shoving industrial civilization on its one-way trip to history's compost bin.

The core issues up for debate at the Paris meeting were the same that have been rehashed endlessly at previous climate conferences. The consequences of continuing to treat the atmosphere as a gaseous sewer for humanity's pollutants are becoming increasingly hard to ignore, but nearly everything that defines a modern industrial economy as "modern" and "industrial" produces greenhouse gases, and the continued growth of the world's modern industrial economies remains the keystone of economic policy around the world. The goal pursued by negotiators at this and previous climate conferences, then, is to find some way to do something about anthropogenic global warming that won't place any kind of restrictions on economic growth.

What that means in practice is that the world's nations have more or less committed themselves to limit the rate at which the dumping of greenhouse gases will increase over the next fifteen years. I'd encourage those of my readers who think anything important was accomplished at the Paris conference to read that sentence again, and think about what it implies. The agreement that came out of COP-21 doesn't commit anybody to stop dumping carbon dioxide and other greenhouse gases into the atmosphere, now or at any point in the future. It doesn't even commit anybody to set a fixed annual output that will not be exceeded. It simply commits the world's nations to slow down the rate at which they're increasing their dumping of greenhouse gases. If this doesn't sound to you like a recipe for saving the world, let's just say you're not alone.

It wasn't exactly encouraging that the immediate aftermath of the COP-21 agreement was a feeding frenzy among those industries most likely to profit from modest cuts in greenhouse gas consumption—yes, those would be the renewable-energy and nuclear industries, with some efforts to get scraps from the table by proponents of "clean coal," geoengineering, fusion-power research, and a few other subsidy dumpsters of the same sort. Naomi Oreskes, a writer for whom I used to have a certain degree of respect, published a crassly manipulative screed insisting that anybody who questioned the claim that renewable-energy technologies could keep industrial society powered forever was engaged in, ahem, "a new form of climate denialism." She was more than matched, to be fair, by a chorus of meretricious shills for the nuclear industry, who were just as quick to insist that renewables couldn't be scaled up fast enough and nuclear power was the only alternative.

The shills in question are quite correct, as it happens, that renewable energy can't be scaled up fast enough to replace fossil fuels; they could have said with equal truth that renewable energy can't be scaled up far enough to accomplish that daunting task. The little detail they're evading is that nuclear power can't be scaled up far enough or fast enough, either. What's more, however great they look on paper or PowerPoint, neither nuclear power nor grid-scale renewable power are economically viable in the real world. The evidence for this is as simple as it is conclusive: no nation anywhere on the planet has managed either one without vast and continuing government subsidies. Lacking those, neither one makes enough economic sense to be worth building, because neither one can provide the kind of cheap abundant electrical power that makes a modern industrial society possible.

Say this in the kind of company that takes global climate

change seriously, of course, and if you aren't simply shouted down by those present—and of course this is the most common response—you can expect to hear someone say, "Well, *something* has to do it." Right there you can see the lethal blindness that pervades nearly all contemporary debates about the future, because it's simply not true that something has to do it. No divine providence nor any law of nature guarantees that human beings must have access to as much cheap abundant electricity as they happen to want.

Stated thus baldly, that may seem like common sense, but that sort of sense is far from common these days, even—or especially—among those people who think they're grappling with the hard realities of the future. Here's a useful example. One of this blog's readers—tip of the archdruidical hat to Antroposcen—made an elegant short film that was shown at a climate-themed film festival in Paris while the COP-21 meeting was slouching toward its pointless end. The film is titled "A Message from the Past," and as the title suggests, it portrays an incident from a future on the far side of global climate change. I encourage my readers to click through and watch it; it's only a few minutes long, and its point will be perfectly clear to any regular reader of this blog.

The audience at the film festival, though, found it incomprehensible. The nearest they came to making sense of it was to guess that, despite the title, it was about a message from our time that had somehow found its way to the distant past. The thought that the future on the far side of global climate change might have some resemblance to the preindustrial past—that people in that future, in the wake of the immense collective catastrophes our actions are busy creating for them, might wear handmade clothing of primitive cut and find surviving scraps of our technologies baffling relics of a bygone time—seems to have been wholly beyond the grasp of their imaginations.

Two factors make this blindness to an entire spectrum of probable futures astonishing. The first is that not that long ago, plenty of people in the climate change activism scene were talking openly about the possibility that uncontrolled climate change could stomp industrial society with the inevitability of a boot descending on an eggshell. I'm thinking here, among other examples, of the much-repeated claim by James Lovelock a few years back that the likely outcome of global climate change, if nothing was done, was heat so severe that the only human survivors a few centuries from now would be "a few hundred breeding pairs" huddled around the shores of the Arctic Ocean.

It used to be all the rage in climate change literature to go on at length about the ghastly future that would be ours if global temperatures warmed far enough to trigger serious methane releases from northern permafrost, tip one or more of the planet's remaining ice sheets into rapid collapse, and send sea water rising to drown low-lying regions. Lurid scenarios of civilizational collapse and mass dieoff appeared in book after lavishly marketed book. Of late, though, that entire theme seems to have dropped out of the collective imagination of the activist community, to be replaced by strident claims that everything will be just fine if we ignore the hard lessons of the last thirty years of attempted renewable-energy buildouts and fling every available dollar, euro, yuan, etc. into subsidies for an even more grandiose wave of uneconomical renewable-energy powerplants.

The second factor is even more remarkable, and it's the existence of that first factor that makes it so. Those methane releases, rising seas, and collapsing ice sheets? They're no longer confined to the pages of remaindered global warming books. They're happening in the real world, right now.

Methane releases? Check out the massive craters blown out of Siberian permafrost in the last few years by huge methane burps, or the way the Arctic Ocean fizzes every summer like a freshly poured soda as underwater methane deposits get destabilized by rising temperatures. Methane isn't the world-wrecking ultrapollutant that a certain class of apocalyptic fantasy likes to imagine, mostly because it doesn't last long in the atmosphere — the average lifespan of a methane molecule once it seeps out of the permafrost is about ten years — but while it's there, it traps heat much more effectively than carbon dioxide. The Arctic is already warming far more drastically than any other region of the planet, and the nice thick blanket of methane with which it's wrapped itself is an important part of the reason why.

Those methane releases make a great example of the sudden stop that overtook discussions of the harsh future ahead of us, once that future started to arrive. Before they began to occur, methane releases played a huge role in climate change literature — Mark Lynas' colorful and heavily marketed book *Six Degrees* is only one of many examples. Once the methane releases actually got under way, as I noted in a post here some years ago, most activists abruptly stopped talking about it, and references to methane on the doomward end of the blogosphere started fielding dismissive comments by climate-change mavens insisting that methane doesn't matter and carbon dioxide is the thing to watch.

Rising seas? You can watch that in action in low-lying coastal regions anywhere in the world, but for a convenient close-up, pay a visit to Miami Beach, Florida. You'll want to do that quickly, though, while it's still there. Sea levels off Florida have been rising about an inch a year, and southern Florida, Miami Beach included, is built on porous limestone. These days, as a result, whenever an unusually high tide combines with a strong onshore wind, salt water comes bubbling up from the storm sewers and seeping right out of the ground, and the streets of Miami Beach end up hubcap-deep in it. Further inland, seawater is infiltrating the aquifer from which southern Florida gets drinking water, and killing plants in low-lying areas near the coast.

The situation in southern Florida gets some press, but I suspect this is because Florida is a red state and the state government's frantic denial that global warming is happening makes an easy target for humor. The same phenomenon is happening at varying paces elsewhere in the world, as a combination of thermal expansion of warming seawater, runoff from melting glaciers, and a grab-bag of local and regional oceanographic phenomena boosts sea level well above its historic place. Nothing significant is being done about it—to be fair, it's unlikely that anything significant can be done about it at this point, short of a total moratorium on greenhouse gas generation, and the COP-21 talks made it painfully clear that that's not going to happen.

Instead, southern Florida faces a fate that's going to be all too familiar to many millions of people elsewhere in the world over the years ahead. As fresh water runs short and farm and orchard crops die from salt poisoning, mass migration will be the order of the day. Over the short term, southern Florida will gradually turn into salt marsh; look further into the future, and you can see Florida's ultimate destiny, as a region of shoals, reefs, and islets extending well out into the Gulf of Mexico, with the corroded ruins of skyscrapers rising from the sea here and there as a reminder of the fading past.

Does this sound like science fiction? It's the inescapable consequence of changes that are already under way. Even if COP-21 had produced an agreement that mattered—say, a binding commitment on the part of all the world's nations to cut greenhouse gas emissions immediately and lower them to zero by 2030— southern Florida would still be doomed. The processes that are driving sea levels up can't turn on a dime; just as it took more than a century of unrestricted atmospheric pollution to begin the flooding of southern Florida, it would take a long time and a great deal of hard work to reverse that, even if the political will was available. As it is, the agreement signed in Paris simply means that the flooding will continue unchecked.

A far more dramatic series of events, meanwhile, is getting under way far north of Florida. Yes, that's the breakup of the Greenland ice sheet. During the last few summers, as unprecedented warmth gripped the Arctic, rivers of meltwater have begun flowing across Greenland's glacial surface, plunging into a growing network of chasms and tunnels that riddle the ice sheet like the holes in Swiss cheese. This is new; discussions of Greenland's ice sheet from as little as five years ago didn't mention the meltwater rivers at all, much less the hollowing out of the ice. Equally new is the fact that the vast majority of that meltwater isn't flowing into the ocean—scientists have checked that, using every tool at their disposal up to and including legions of yellow rubber ducks tossed into meltwater streams.

What all this means is that in the decades immediately ahead of us, in all likelihood, we'll get to see a spectacle no human being has seen since the end of the last ice age: the catastrophic breakup of a major ice sheet. If you got taught in school, as so many American schoolchildren were, that the great glacial sheets of the ice age melted at an imperceptible pace, think again; glaciologists disproved that decades ago. What happens, instead, is a series of sudden collapses that kick the pace of melting into overdrive at unpredictable intervals. What paleoclimatologists call global meltwater pulses—sudden surges of ice and water from collapsing ice sheets—send sea levels soaring by several meters, drowning large tracts of land in an impressively short time.

Ice sheet collapses happen in a variety of ways, and Greenland is very well positioned to enact one of the better documented processes. The vast weight of all that ice pressing down on the crust through the millennia has turned the land beneath the ice into a shallow bowl surrounded by mountains—and that shallow bowl is where all the meltwater is going. Eventually the water will rise high enough to find an outlet to the sea, and when it does, it will begin to flow out—and it will take much of the ice with it.

As that happens, seismographs across the North Atlantic basin will go crazy as Greenland's ice sheet, tormented beyond endurance by the conflict between gravity and buoyancy, begins to break apart. A first great meltwater surged will vomit anything up to thousands of cubic miles of ice into the ocean. Huge icebergs will drift east and then south on the currents, and release more water as they melt. After that, summer after summer, the process will repeat itself, until some fraction of Greenland's total ice sheet has been dumped into the ocean. How large a fraction? That's impossible to know in advance, but all other things being equal, the more greenhouse gases get dumped into the atmosphere, the faster and more complete Greenland's breakup will be.

Oh, and did I mention that the West Antarctic ice sheet is beginning to break up as well ?

The thing to keep in mind here is that the coming global meltwater pulse will have consequences all over the world. Once it happens—and again, the processes that will lead to that event are already well under way, and nothing the world's industrial nations are willing to do can stop it—it will simply be a matter of time before the statistically inevitable combination of high tides and stormwinds sends sea water flooding into New York City's subway system and the vast network of underground tunnels that houses much of the city's infrastructure. Every other coastal city in the world will wait for its own number to come up. No doubt we'll hear plenty of talk about building vast new flood defenses to keep back the rising waters, but let us please be real; any such project would require years of lead time and almost unimaginable amounts of money, and no nation anywhere in the world is showing the least interest in doing the thing now, when it might still be an option.

There's a profound irony, in other words, in all the rhetoric from Paris about balancing concerns about the climate with the supposed need for perpetual economic growth. Imagine for a moment just how the coming global meltwater pulse will impact the world economy. Countless trillions of dollars in coastal infrastructure around the world will become "sunk costs" in more than a metaphorical sense; millions of people in low-lying areas such as southern Florida will have to relocate as their homes become uninhabitable, and trillions of dollars of real estate will have its value drop to zero. A galaxy of costs for which nobody is planning will have to be met out of government and business revenue streams that have been hammered by the direct and indirect effects of worldwide coastal flooding.

What's more, it won't be a single event, over and done with in a few weeks or months or years. Every year for decades or centuries to come, more ice and meltwater will go sluicing into the oceans, more coastal cities and regions will face that one seawater surge too many, more costs will have to be met out of what's left of a global economy that's running out of functioning deepwater ports among many other things. The result, as I've noted in previous posts here, will be the disintegration of everything that counts as business as usual, and the opening phases of the bleak new reality that Frank Landis has sketched out in his harrowing new book *Hot Earth Dreams* — the best currently available book on what the world will look like in the wake of severe climate change, and thus inevitably ignored by everyone in the current environmental mainstream.

By the time COP-21's attendees convened in Paris, it was probably already too late to keep global climate change from spinning completely out of control. The embarrassingly feeble agreement that came out of that event, though, has guaranteed that nothing significant will be done. The hard political and economic realities that made any actual cut in greenhouse gas emissions all but unthinkable are just layers of icing on the cake, part of the predicament of our time — a predicament that defines the words "too little, too late" as our basic approach to the future looming up ahead of us.

ABOUT THE AUTHOR

Born in the gritty Navy town of Bremerton, Washington, and raised in the wastelands of mid-twentieth century suburbia, John Michael Greer has been writing since about ten minutes after he figured out how to hold a pencil. He is the author of more than fifty books on a range of subjects from the future of industrial society to Druid nature spirituality, and currently blogs at www. ecosophia.com. He lives in Rhode Island with his wife Sara.

Made in the USA
Columbia, SC
15 June 2018